Interprofessional Education and Medical Libraries

Medical Library Association Books

The Medical Library Association (MLA) features books that showcase the expertise of health sciences librarians for other librarians and professionals.

MLA Books are excellent resources for librarians in hospitals, medical research practice, and other settings. These volumes will provide health care professionals and patients with accurate information that can improve outcomes and save lives.

Each book in the series has been overseen editorially since conception by the Medical Library Association Books Panel, composed of MLA members with expertise spanning the breadth of health sciences librarianship.

Medical Library Association Books Panel

About the Medical Library Association

Founded in 1898, MLA is a 501(c)(3) nonprofit, educational organization of 3,500 individual and institutional members in the health sciences information field that provides lifelong educational opportunities, supports a knowledgebase of health information research, and works with a global network of partners to promote the importance of quality information for improved health to the health care community and the public.

Books in the Series

The Medical Library Association Guide to Providing Consumer and Patient Health Information edited by Michele Spatz
Health Sciences Librarianship edited by M. Sandra Wood
Curriculum-Based Library Instruction: From Cultivating Faculty Relationships to Assessment edited by Amy Blevins and Megan Inman

Mobile Technologies for Every Library by Ann Whitney Gleason
Marketing for Special and Academic Libraries: A Planning and Best Practices 6. Sourcebook Patricia Higginbottom and Valerie Gordon
Translating Expertise: The Librarian's Role in Translational Research edited by Marisa L. Conte
Expert Searching in the Google Age by Terry Ann Jankowski
Digital Rights Management: The Librarian's Guide edited by Catherine A. Lemmer and Carla P. Wale
Interprofessional Education and Medical Libraries: Partnering for Success edited by Mary Edwards

Interprofessional Education and Medical Libraries

Partnering for Success

Edited by Mary E. Edwards

ROWMAN & LITTLEFIELD
Lanham • Boulder • New York • London

Published by Rowman & Littlefield
A wholly owned subsidiary of The Rowman & Littlefield Publishing Group, Inc.
4501 Forbes Boulevard, Suite 200, Lanham, Maryland 20706
www.rowman.com

Unit A, Whitacre Mews, 26-34 Stannary Street, London SE11 4AB

British Library Cataloguing in Publication Information Available

Library of Congress Cataloging-in-Publication Data

Names: Edwards, Mary (Mary Elizabeth), 1979- , editor. | Medical Library Association.
Title: Interprofessional education and medical libraries : partnering for success / edited by Mary Edwards.
Other titles: Medical Library Association books.
Description: Lanham, Maryland : Rowman &Littlefield, [2016] | Series: Medical Library Association books
Identifiers: LCCN 2016012312 (print) | LCCN 2016014793 (ebook) | ISBN 9781442263895 (cloth : alk. paper) | ISBN 9781442263901 (electronic)
Subjects: | MESH: Health Occupations–education | Education, Professional–methods | Interdisciplinary Communication | Interprofessional Relations | Libraries, Medical
Classification: LCC R834 (print) | LCC R834 (ebook) | NLM W 18 | DDC 610.71–dc23
LC record available at http://lccn.loc.gov/2016012312

∞ ™ The paper used in this publication meets the minimum requirements of American National Standard for Information Sciences Permanence of Paper for Printed Library Materials, ANSI/NISO Z39.48-1992.

Printed in the United States of America

Contents

Figures

Tables

Preface

Mary E. Edwards, Nina Stoyan-Rosenzweig, and Paulette Hahn

Interprofessional education (IPE) is described as education about teamwork provided to groups composed of practitioners or students of diverse healthcare professions. IPE focuses on the roles of various health professionals (physicians, nurses, pharmacists, social workers, mental health practitioners, etc.) on patient care teams, the importance of teamwork, strategies for creating effective teams, the role of teamwork in patient safety, and other areas related to an interprofessional approach to healthcare. To prepare future healthcare professionals for work in a clinical setting that increasingly features interprofessional care (IPC) and to fulfill accreditation requirements, medical and health colleges across the nation have created IPE programs. The purposes of this book are to describe the variety of interprofessional education programs in both didactic and clinical settings, discuss how libraries are partnering to further the success of these programs, and expand the notion of "interprofessional" beyond the typical health professions. It was designed with a variety of audiences in mind: medical educators new to interprofessional education, experienced IPE practitioners, and medical librarians who want to learn more about IPE and the ways in which libraries can support interprofessional initiatives on their campuses. This book illustrates both a theoretical and practical approach to interprofessional education. Chapter topics range from foundational information such as the history of IPE, theoretical underpinnings, and pedagogical perspectives to more practical information regarding program implementation, accreditation, service learning, interprofessional care and patient safety, best practices for medical libraries, and assessing IPE programs. The book can be read in its entirety, or each chapter can be consulted as needed, and while there is some overlap, each chapter provides a unique discussion of relevant IPE topics.

The preface both introduces the chapters contained within the book and expands upon the classical definition of interprofessional education by discussing how medical humanities and other disciplines are important considerations for a truly holistic view of IPE.

HOW THE BOOK IS ORGANIZED

Chapter 1, "The History of Interprofessional Education," authored by Robyn Dickie, of Mater Health Services in Australia, provides an overview of the historical background of IPE and introduces the current state of IPE programs across several countries including Australia, the United Kingdom, Japan, and the United States. The past informs the future; this knowledge helps illustrate how interprofessional programs developed from early forays into interdisciplinary teams to the robust educational programs of today in order to see what the future may hold.

The foundation for interprofessional education draws from various disciplines and professions including anthropology, sociology, psychology, and education. Chapter 2, "Theories Underlying Interprofessional Education: A Pragmatic Approach," by James Ballard at the University of Illinois (recently at the University of Kentucky), thoroughly introduces the relevant theories and describes how theoretical insights from these fields influence interprofessional education.

With the recent trends in education including an emphasis on active learning and teamwork, massively open online courses (MOOCs), and flipped classrooms, it is important to have an understanding of the underlying pedagogical principles involved with successful interprofessional education programs in order to efficaciously implement these methods. Andrea Pfeifle (University of South Carolina) and Amy V. Blue (University of Florida) authored chapter 3, "Pedagogical Perspectives on Interprofessional Education," which provides a discussion of the instructional theories and practices associated with demonstrated student success and satisfaction in interprofessional education programs.

As interprofessional education programs continue to expand, the goals of such programs are linked to accreditation standards and learning outcomes for a variety of healthcare professions. Chapter 4, "Interprofessional Education as Organizational Change," authored by Alan Dow, Colleen Lynch, John Cyrus, and Tanya Huff introduces theories of organizational change and describes their influence on the planning and implementation of IPE programs. Case studies embedded within the theoretical discussions illustrate how the theories translate to practice. This chapter also includes a discussion of how accreditation standards throughout the health sciences can be used to leverage organizational change in support of interprofessional education.

In chapter 5, "Designing an Interprofessional Education Program from Planning to Implementation," Jean Shipman (director of the Spencer S. Eccles Health Sciences Library) and a team from the University of Utah provide recommendations on how to design, plan, and implement an IPE program. Included in this chapter are descriptions of how other professions, that is medical librarians, education specialists, and instructional designers, can add support and value to the process. While many schools have rigorous interprofessional education programs and seek to expand or revise their programs, others are still in the nascent stages of development, and this chapter has information relevant to anyone interested in planning and implementation, including librarians and medical educators.

Service learning is not new to medical education, but has not routinely been a part of interprofessional education experiences in the past. In chapter 6, "Engaging Service Learning in Interprofessional Education: The University of Florida Experience," Erik Black, Nichole Stetten, and Amy V. Blue describe a unique IPE course (Putting Families First [PFF], formerly known as Interdisciplinary Family Health [IFH]) that focuses on interprofessional groups of first-year students from all six of the health science colleges working with families in the community. Figures and tables are used to illustrate relationships and the composition of the complex, but effective PFF course. This long-standing, service-based IPE course can serve as a model for institutions wanting to implement service components into their IPE program or design a program from scratch.

Evidence has shown that communication failures in healthcare can result in medical errors and negative patient outcomes. One of the goals of interprofessional education is to break down communication barriers among the various professions in the healthcare team and improve patient safety. In chapter 7, "Interprofessional Education and Patient Care: Supporting Patient Safety," Karen McDonough and Brenda Zierler of the University of Washington review the literature on IPE and patient safety to qualitatively describe various programs and evaluate the data resulting from evaluation of those programs for the purpose of connecting patient safety with interprofessional practice and education.

Chapter 8, "Medical Libraries Supporting Interprofessional Education," authored by Lauren M. Young, a team of librarians from the University of Mississippi Medical Center's Rowland Medical Library, and the Executive Director for Academic Effectiveness, describes the ways in which librarians are supporting IPE and includes vignettes as "sidebars" highlighting activities from several institutions. From liaison programs to embedded librarians, medical libraries have supported the educational activities of the healthcare professions in their schools and programs through instruction, outreach, and providing access to resources. As interprofessional education programs become incorporated into the institutions in which we work, there is a need to support them as well as we have supported other disciplines and activities.

Chapter 9, "Clinical Medical Librarians and Interprofessional Practice," written by Lisa Travis (Emory University) and Skye Bickett (Philadelphia College of Osteopathic Medicine–Georgia Campus), provides an overview of clinical medical librarianship, introduces results from their survey of Clinical Medical Librarians, and presents examples where librarians are included as one of the professions in IPE or are otherwise integrated into the interprofessional patient care team in didactic or clinical instruction. Clinical librarians are increasingly participating in rounds and clinical care as part of the interdisciplinary patient team. The evidence suggests that this is a valuable service and, as such, interprofessional education content should expand to include the librarian's role on the healthcare team.

As interprofessional education continues to develop and be incorporated into the accreditation requirements for healthcare professions, the need for rigorous assessment of these programs is paramount. The final chapter, "Assessing Interprofessonal Education," authored by Erin Blakeney and Brenda Zierler at the University of Washington, focuses on successful assessment strategies and programs.

While the previously described chapters include various components and aspects of interprofessional education, an exploration of how other disciplines, including the humanities, can contribute to the interprofessional experience, support interprofessional care, and impact patient outcomes is a part of the "big picture" of IPE. The following section is a departure from the typical IPE content, with the hopes that more IPE work will include the humanities and other disciplines in the future.

EXPANDING INTERPROFESSIONAL EDUCATION: MEDICAL HUMANITIES AND BEYOND

Much of the book focuses on the traditional healthcare disciplines as components of interprofessional education, but expanding beyond those professions and disciplines provides a more complex, holistic view of IPE and IPC. This section will first explore the emerging area of medical humanities and then branch out into additional disciplines of relevant interest.

Recently, the value of humanities—first in medical education and then in the practice of all health professions—has come to be more clearly recognized, studied, and appreciated. The term medical humanities is commonly used; however the longer phrase "humanities in health and illness" is more accurate and encompasses other related subjects including social sciences, humanities, and arts. Studying the health humanities, indeed incorporating them into practice, offers a number of benefits for healthcare practitioners, including the development of reflective practice and broadening understanding of the experience of illness and the role of healthcare systems in larger societies. These insights can improve clinical skills and empathy, help avoid caregiver burnout, and thus potentially reduce medical errors and lead to greater patient satisfaction. In particular, the humanities offer great opportunities in interprofessional education, providing models for teamwork, as well as additional communication skills and greater understanding of the role each profession plays in healthcare.

The humanities are a valuable tool because, first and foremost, the humanities study humanity and the forms of expression that are most basic to the function of human beings and their societies. Research shows that material is most easily learned through telling, interpreting, and understanding stories. Thus, when their work includes the study and understanding of stories, learning formal narrative analysis, and engaging in narrative study, student learning and practice are inevitably enhanced (Cron 2012; de la Mothe and Foray 2012; Haven 2007; Prusak 2001; Roche and Sandowsky 2003).

Additionally, and by their very nature, the humanities attempt to understand and depict human experience. They are used to depict suffering, triumph, fear, helplessness, and joy, among other emotions. People try to explain the great questions through art and thus to make sense of their experiences through music, dance, writing, visual arts, and theater (Dewey 2005). The humanities essentially explore those aspects of life that define the human condition and thus are, at some level, universal. They help to articulate emotional and intellectual responses to these experiences and by so doing help to expand understanding and foster empathy (Curtis 2009).

And, of course, humanities offer opportunities to foster creativity. In fact, arts and humanities can arguably profoundly facilitate communication, according to neuroscientist Daniel Levitin, who argues that the universality of music shaped culture even as humans created music that made possible intergenerational memory, work synchronization, and the creation of civilizations (Levitin 2009). In addition, participating in the humanities can offer profound opportunities to reflect on self and others, and engagement in the creative process can help to alter mood and reduce stress (Pennebaker, Kiecolt-Glaser, and Glaser 1988; Davidson and Goldberg 2004).

The value of the humanities for explicating human experience and thus enhancing and fostering reflection, creativity, empathy, and understanding has been well-recognized in the practice of medicine, medical education, and in the practice of nursing and in nursing education (Meites, Bein, and Shafer 2003). In general, medical humanities have the capacity to enhance medical practice and outcomes in a number of ways, but most can relate to the power of storytelling and narrative and how the humanities impact creativity, human emotion, and empathy. This same ability to provide a universal message also makes humanities ideal for interprofessional education. Teaching through the use of stories, or with a focus on the narrative helps all students retain information and ultimately a greater sense of empathy (Dellasega et al. 2007; Paliadelis et al. 2014; Paliadelis et al. 2015). The use of humanities also helps to provide metaphors, means, and models for interprofessional collaboration (Dellasega et al. 2007; Rogers and Chesters 2014).

The essence of interprofessional education and practice has the patient at the center of the healthcare team. The humanities provide a universal language in interprofessional education by strengthening the collaborative approach to patient-centered care and linking the professions together in a neutral educational experience. This allows individuals from each profession to understand the expertise and role of other professions in the care of patients. Through the universal educational experience in the humanities, the professions develop communication not only with patients, but also between professions, enhancing leadership and the ability to resolve conflict heightens collaborative practice.

Universal interprofessional education has been accomplished through mutual educational experiences in ethics, narrative stories, and art exposure, enhancing observation skills, reasoning, visual thinking, and an understanding of the integration of the humanities in the direct care of patients. Literature, music, art, dance, and writing have become part of the patient experience as well as the experience of healthcare professionals in healing and health (Brajtman, Hall, and Barnes 2009; Charon 2001a; 2001b; Charon 2006; Klugman, Peel, and Beckmann-Mendez 2011; Reilly, Ring, and Duke 2005).

The stressors of complex healthcare systems and emotions related to the care of patients may erode the self-care of professionals leading to burnout, ultimately compromising quality and safe patient care. Reflection within each profession and also between professions helps to restore an understanding of experiences. When professionals reflect together they see the "sameness" between their experiences, leading to less fragmentation between professions, better teamwork, and respect and understanding of the values and uniqueness of other professions. This helps sustain compassion and humanism in the care of patients, the care of each other, and the care of self. The humanities, through "health humanities," ultimately bring together science, art, and humanism (Moyle, Barnard, and Turner 1995; Wershof Schwartz et al. 2009).

Including medical humanities into the scope of interprofessional education can help expand upon traditional definitions that focus on the typical health professions, and there is growing evidence that doing so can impact patient care and, potentially, health outcomes. It is also important to consider social science disciplines and how they can contribute to interprofessionality, both in terms of education and clinical practice. Specifically, the fields of library and information science, psychology, social work, and education can provide support for and further insight into IPE and help develop health professionals who are equipped to work in a dynamic interprofessional team environment and think creatively when it comes to patient care and research. In fact, many of the underlying theories that contribute to interprofessional education are drawn from a wide variety of disciplines in the social sciences and chapter 2 provides a thorough examination of the theories and how they impact IPE.

As illustrated in several of the chapters in this book (chapters 5 and 8 specifically), libraries and librarians are providing support for IPE activities in terms of space, infrastructure, services, and personnel. Clinical librarians present another, potentially high impact, type of library integration into interprofessional care. Chapter 9 provides a detailed examination of clinical librarians and the ways in which they have been integrated into patient care teams. While it is clear from the discussion in chapter 9 that librarians are functioning as part of interdisciplinary patient care teams, this addition to the team is not widely communicated to IPE faculty, who could incorporate that knowledge into curricula and educate future healthcare providers about the benefits of having librarians as active members of interprofessional care teams. Integrating medical humanities, various social science disciplines, and clinical librarians into interprofessional education and care helps push the boundaries of interprofessional education and practice to form a more inclusive, expansive definition of what it means to be interprofessional.

CONCLUSIONS AND IMPLICATIONS

This book provides a unique perspective of interprofessional education by first describing the foundations upon which it is built and then transitioning to a more pragmatic discussion of significant issues including accreditation, implementation, collaboration with libraries and librarians, and practical recommendations and best practice. The authors include health science educators and librarians with years of experience working with interprofessional education. It is clear from the chapters contained in this book and the discussion of medical or "health humanities" that interprofessional education is a significant and evolving area with opportunities for educational and clinical research.

REFERENCES

Brajtman S., P. Hall, and P. Barnes. 2009. "Enhancing Interprofessional Education in End-of-Life Care: An Interdisciplinary Exploration of Death and Dying in Literature." *Journal of Palliative Care* 25, no. 2: 125–31.

Charon, R. 2001a. "Narrative Medicine: a Model for Empathy, Reflection, Profession, and Trust." *Journal of the American Medical Association* 286, no. 15: 1897–902.

———. 2001b. “Narrative Medicine: form, Function, and Ethics.” *Annals of Internal Medicine* 134, no. 1: 83–87.

———. 2008. *Narrative Medicine: Honoring the Stories of Illness*. New York: Oxford University Press.

Cron, L. 2012. *Wired for Story: The Writer’s Guide to Using Brain Science to Hook Readers from the Very First Sentence*. Danvers, MA: Ten Speed Press.

Curtis, D. 2009. “Creating Inspiration: The Role of the Arts in Creating Empathy for Ecological Restoration.” *Ecological Management and Restoration* 10, no. 3: 174–84.

Davidson, C. N., and D. T. Goldberg. 2004. “A Manifesto for the Humanities in a Technological Age.” *Chronicle Review* (February 13).http://chronicle.com/weekly/v50/i23/23b00701.htm.

de la Mothe, J., and D. Foray. 2012. *Knowledge Management in the Innovation Process*. New York: Springer Science + Business Media, LLC.

Dellasega, C., P. Milone-Nuzzo, K. M. Curci, J. O. Ballard, and D. G. Kirch. 2007. “The Humanities Interface of Nursing and Medicine.” *Journal of Professional Nursing* 23, no. 3: 174–79.

Dewey, J. 2005. *Art as Experience*. New York: Penguin Books.

Dolev, J. C., L. K. Friedlaender, and I. M. Braverman. 2001. “Use of Fine Art to Enhance Diagnostic Skills.” *Journal of the American Medical Association* 286: 1020–21.

Haven, K. 2007. *Story Proof: The Science behind the Startling Power of Story*. Santa Barbara, CA: Libraries Unlimited.

Hunter, K. M., R. Charon, and J. L. Coulehan. 1995. “The Study of Literature in Medical Education.” *Academic Medicine* 70, no. 9 (September): 787–94.

Klugman, C. M., J. M. Peel, and D. Beckmann-Mendez. 2011. “Art Rounds: Teaching Interprofessional Students Visual Thinking Strategies at one School.” *Academic Medicine* 86, no. 10: 1266–71.

Levitin, D. 2009. *The World in Six Songs: How the Musical Brain Created Human Nature*. London: Aurum Press Ltd.

Meites, E., S. Bein, and A. Shafer. 2003. “Researching Medicine in Context: the Arts and Humanities Medical Scholars Program.” *Medical Humanities* 29: 104–8.

Moyle, W., A. Barnard, and C. Turner. 1995. “The Humanities and Nursing: Using Popular Literature as a Means of Understanding Human Experience.” *Journal of Advanced Nursing* 21, no. 5: 960–64.

Novack D. H., R. M. Epstein, and R. H. Paulsen. 1999. “Toward Creating Physician-Healers: Fostering Medical Students’ Self-Awareness, Personal Growth, and Well-Being.” *Academic Medicine* 74, no. 5 (May): 516–20.

Paliadelis, P., I. Stupans, V. Parker, H. M. Jarrott, A. Fagan, P. Gillan, D. Piper, R. Wilson, J. Lea, and J. Hudson. 2014. “The Development and Evaluation of Online Stories to Enhance Clinical Learning Experiences Across Health Professions in Rural Australia.” *Collegian*. Online DOI: http://dx.doi.org/10.1016/j.colegn.2014.08.003.

Paliadelis, P., P. Wood, C. Mesagno, W. Penney, and J. Porter. 2015. “Learning from Final Year Nursing Students’ Stories of Rural Practice.” *13th National Rural Health Conference*. http://www.ruralhealth.org.au/13nrhc/images/paper_Paliadelis,%20Penny.pdf.

Pennebaker, J. W. 1997. *Opening Up: The Healing Power of Expressing Emotion*. New York: Guilford Press.

———. 2004. *Writing to Heal: A Guided Journal for Recovering from Trauma and Emotional Upheaval*. Denver, CO: Center for Journal Therapy.

Pennebaker, J. W., and J. F. Evans. 2014. *Expressive Writing: Words that Heal*. Enumclaw, WA: Idyll Arbor.

Pennebaker, J. W., J. Kiecolt-Glaser, and R. Glaser. 1988. “Disclosure of Traumas and Immune Function: Health Implications for Psychotherapy.” *Journal of Consulting and Clinical Psychology* 56: 239–45.

Prusak, L. 2001. “Practice and Knowledge Management.” *Economics of Science, Technology and Innovation* 24: 153–58.

Reilly, J., J. Ring, and L. Duke. 2005. “Visual Thinking Strategies: a New Role for Art in Medical Education.” *Family Medicine* 37, no. 4: 250–52.

Roche, L., and J. Sadowsky. 2003. " The Power Of Stories (I): a Discussion of Why Stories are Powerful." *International Journal of Information Technology and Management* 2, no. 4: 377–88.

Rogers, G., and J. Chesters. 2014. "An Orchestral Metaphor for Interprofessional Collaborative Practice?" *The Clinical Teacher* 11: 317–18.

Wershof Schwartz, A. J., S. Abramson, I. Wojnowich, R. Accordino, E. J. Ronan, and M. R. Rifkin. 2009. "Evaluating the Impact of the Humanities in Medical Education." *Mt. Sinai Journal of Medicine* 76, no. 4: 372–80.

Acknowledgments

The editor gratefully acknowledges the contributions of all the chapter authors, all experienced medical educators or librarians, who provided their best work for this book. Additionally, the editor would like to acknowledge the faculty in her department, especially Michele Tennant, for their understanding and support during the process of compiling this book.

Chapter One

The History of Interprofessional Education

Robyn Dickie

Interprofessional education (IPE) and its subsequent learning and practice are not new. Like most educational phenomena, it was not constructed by an individual or a team overnight, but like Rome, its foundations have been built over the last forty years due to a number of political, academic, economic, and population-based reasons.

The most commonly used definitions for interprofessional education and learning arise from the Centre for the Advancement of Interprofessional Education (CAIPE), a global collaborative established in 1987 to support and promote interprofessional education and practice. IPE "occurs when two or more professions learn with, from, and about each other to improve collaboration and the quality of care" (CAIPE 2002). Interprofessional Learning (IPL) encompasses a larger sphere and may "arise [from] interaction between members (or students) of two or more professions. This may be a product of interprofessional education or happen spontaneously in the workplace or in education settings" (Freeth et al. 2005).

CAIPE's contribution in encouraging and supporting academics and clinicians in seeking to implement IPE initiatives, particularly in the United Kingdom, has enabled a common language to promote the interprofessional cause. CAIPE's establishment in the United Kingdom coincided with the publication of two World Health Organization (WHO) reports in 1988, *Continuing Education for Physicians* and *Learning Together to Work Together for Health*. These reports highlighted the importance of training health professionals together to enable patients to receive coordinated, collaborative, and safer team-based care.

While these reports provided an impetus for change in the 1990s, from the published literature it appears that initiatives were either implemented in local areas on a small scale or were not reported or widely disseminated through conventional academic channels. Early IPE has a somewhat unchartered history. By undertaking a quick database search using the search term "interprofessional education" and the publication date limiter to the year 2000, a researcher is likely to find a less than one hundred publications.

IPE's early story is not illuminated from the pages of peer-reviewed journals or carefully crafted texts. Its story was initially disseminated through what one might describe as "urban legends." These legends belonged to small groups of highly motivated individuals seeking global health professional education reform. Baldwin in the United States, McCreary and Szasz in Canada, Areskog in Sweden, and Pietroni in the United Kingdom pioneered various IPE initiatives and are widely regarded as the early leaders of global IPE with their seminal work still influencing IPE policy and strategic direction today.

IPE together with IPL and interprofessional practice (IPP) has gained global momentum, assisted with the introduction of interprofessional-specific journals, such as the *Journal of Interprofessional Care* and the *Journal of Research in Interprofessional Education.* Such publications have improved the quality of the published IPE studies, with greater emphasis placed on rigorous methods and evaluation of initiatives in the past decade. Fast forward to 2015 and the same rudimentary search yields over three thousand publications. Numerous literature reviews and synthesis of the published IPE literature have been conducted in the last eight years offering universities and healthcare settings a comprehensive overview of past and present IPE initiatives, evaluation methods, and outcomes (Brandt 2014).

This exponential increase in IPE literature can be attributed to a variety of factors. The number of IPE initiatives occurring globally has increased, particularly since the release of the Institute of Medicine (IOM) report *To Err Is Human* along with the *Bristol Royal Infirmary Report* from 2001 and most recently the *Mid-Staffordshire Report*. The reports highlighted specific deficiencies in the healthcare system, particularly in relation to effective leadership, teamwork, and communication. While these reports generally attribute failure to implement interprofessional practice within a health service, interprofessional education at both prelicensure and post-licensure healthcare professionals levels appears to be the "magic bullet" to address to shortcomings in our healthcare system.

Today's healthcare consumer is not willing to accept failings in our healthcare system as, perhaps, our forefathers did. The majority of healthcare consumers are astute; and while during their episode are vulnerable, have high expectations that they are being cared for by a highly trained and integrative team. Brandt, Lutifyya, King, and Chioreso (2014) describe the

"Triple Aim"; a concept initially put forward by Berwick, Nolan, and Whittington (2008) to improve the quality of patient care, patient experiences within the healthcare system, to reduce cost, and to improve overall population health.

Together with consumer demand for cohesive, team-based, patient centered-care, there is an increased demand to include interprofessional education within a health-professional student curriculum. This is to ensure that professional competencies and capabilities, together with regulatory requirements, are met. Globally, four competency and capability frameworks have been developed and published to improve interprofessional education outcomes for students. These are: Interprofessional Capability Framework (Sheffield Hallam University, Combined Universities Interprofessional Learning Unit, United Kingdom, 2010); National Interprofessional Competency Framework (Canadian Interprofessional Health Collaborative Working Group, 2010); Core Competencies for Interprofessional Collaborative Practice (Interprofessional Education Collaborative Expert Panel, United States of America, 2011); and Interprofessional Capability Framework (Curtin University, Australia, 2011).

The development of interprofessional competencies and capability frameworks offers a guide to those educators seeking to implement an IPE "endpoint" for their education. These endpoints enable us to determine whether a student or participant undertaking education has become "competent" or "achieved competency." Thistlethwaite and colleagues (2014), however, suggest that by ensuring that students are "competent" in interprofessional education and practice, the creation of meaningful learning objectives and outcomes, the true interprofessional learning that may not be inherent within the curriculum design, along with the formative learning with, from, and about each other could be lost.

In reality, most healthcare education continues to occur in discipline-specific silos, despite the best efforts of interprofessional educators to dismantle them. When reviewing discipline-specific accreditation and licensure requirements in Australia (Australian Health Professional Regulatory Authority [AHPRA], 2015), twelve of the fourteen registered health practitioners have multidisciplinary or interprofessional teamwork standards as part of their core behavioral and professional standards. While the need for interprofessional capabilities is evident, further emphasis must be placed on individual professional groups to enable health professionals to adequately fulfil their mandatory licensure requirements. However, we should not throw the "IPE baby out with the bath water"; on the contrary; we need to be mindful when and to whom these capability frameworks and competency standards are applied when designing, implementing, and, particularly, evaluating interprofessional education success.

Along with IPE competency and capability frameworks, the WHO provides the following guidelines for Interprofessional Education (as cited in Rodger et al. 2010).

1. IPE should be a mandatory component of every health professional's education.
2. IPE should be offered based on explicit learning outcomes that are made clear to both staff and students.
3. IPE should be assessed with respect to what students were intended to learn.
4. IPE should be offered by trained facilitators who have received staff development in this area.
5. IPE should be evaluated for both process and outcomes.

A review of the collected WHO data undertaken by Rodger et al. (2010) found that only 38 percent of higher education institutions reported that IPE was mandatory for all their students, with some differing requirements for specific health disciplines. Objectives and outcomes were poorly understood with only 37 percent of respondents stating that IPE learning objectives were assessed. Faculty training was also limited; however, this is understandable given the global current state of IPE. While IPE is evaluated, the current plethora of tools or instruments are often specific to domains of interprofessional learning such as teamwork, and are often specific to the context of the activity, such as emergency care. Brandt and colleagues (2014) share Rodgers's and colleagues (2010) concerns in relation to evaluation of IPE, stating that while individual (student or staff) impacts and reactions following the activity is common, very little literature focuses on population or patient health outcomes or reduction of cost in healthcare by implementing interprofessional education. When examining longitudinal educational outcomes, there are often numerous confounding factors, which cannot be controlled. Therefore, it is difficult to know the true impact and effectiveness of IPE on patient and population health outcomes; however, it is a question that needs to be answered.

LOOKING BACK, LOOKING AROUND, AND LOOKING FORWARD: A REVIEW OF KEY IPE INITIATIVES ACROSS THE GLOBE

There are many quality IPE activities occurring globally, many remaining unpublished for a variety of reasons. IPE activities come in different shapes and sizes; influenced by the type of health professional students involved, faculty commitment, logistical and geographical barriers, financial considerations, and involvement of the local health delivery service. The snapshot of both historical and current interprofessional activities below highlights a variety of IPE activities across the globe.

United States of America: A New Beginning

Interprofessional education is not a new phenomenon for the United States, where initiatives date back to the early 1960s. The likes of Baldwin, Brandt, and Schmitt have lead IPE initiatives across the country, with seminal works providing global IPE foundations. Early IPE activities in the United States concentrated on primary care, and were often unfunded, and relied heavily on the goodwill of interprofessional faculty (Blue, Brandt, and Schmitt 2010). Like most countries attempting to implement a coordinated, centralized IPE curriculum across numerous health services without sustained financial support, the United States has yet to achieve the WHO guidelines for interprofessional education.

However, there are a number of notable projects across the country particularly at a prelicensure level. Within the United States, IPE has a number of "productive" pockets, each with their unique approach to interprofessional education and practice.

University of Nevada

The University of Nevada, Reno implemented an interprofessional curriculum in the late 1970s, which required students to undertake a number of scaffolded IPE activities as part of their health professional studies. A core "Introduction to Health Sciences" course was used to promote the use of common healthcare language, an understanding of the healthcare system that students would be graduating into, and finally the introduction of teamwork using group projects (Baldwin and Baldwin 2007). The university used a facilitation model, using vignettes or role plays to illustrate key learnings. This curriculum was finally cemented with a clinical program "Team Approach to Healthcare," a student-led patient clinic supervised by university faculty.

Tucson, Arizona

There are many factors that influence the implementation of IPE. Technology has increased its role over the past ten years, with many universities implementing online or e-learning IPE environments in which their students interact. These online forums and activities offer opportunities for students early in their health professional studies to learn about the roles and responsibilities of other health professional students to take care of a "virtual patient." These activities are often supplemented using simulation-based IPE training.

Simulation-Based IPE

Simulation-based IPE has offered new avenues for universities to provide team-based training that minimizes harm to patients, maximizes interprofessional learning opportunities to achieve desired learning outcomes, and can be tailored to meet the needs of the universities and healthcare facilities. Palaganas, Epps, and Raemer (2012) state that simulation offers authentic experiential learning opportunities within an environment that represents a real clinical environment; allows participants to practice technical and non-technical skills (communication and teamwork) in an environment that eliminates risks to patients; and provides opportunities for faculty to observe teamwork in action in a controlled environment.

Simulation may hold the key to dismantling what Baldwin (2007) describes as academic or professional "silos" that contribute to the poor uptake to interprofessional education, along with the healthcare settings, which promote hierarchical and authoritarian systems in which students undertake their clinical practice. Simulation-based healthcare training is strongly aligned with patient safety, which often provides an impetus to implement interprofessional education and practice changes within a healthcare facility. Simulation training compliments IPE as both emphasize the patient being at the "center" of the activity. See chapter 5 for more information about simulation in IPE including a discussion of how the University of Utah uses simulation in IPE training experiences.

Canada: The Pioneers of British Columbia

As previously mentioned, Szasz was one of the founders of IPE in Canada, with a paper published in 1969 entitled "Interprofessional Education in the Health Sciences: A Project Conducted at the University of British Columbia." Szasz (1969) highlighted issues that still exist today: poor utilization of minimal human resources, poor teamwork, and poor communication—all contributing to fragmented patient care. Like many developed countries, it wasn't until the early 2000s that this vision in Canada was realized. Following a review of publically funded Canadian health services in 2001, a report entitled *Building on Values: The Future of Health Care in Canada* (Romanow 2002) was released, highlighting the need to train healthcare professionals together to improve and create an efficient and high-reliability health system. This recommendation, together with other key points, led to the creation and implementation of the Interprofessional Education for Collaborative Patient-centred Practice (IECPCP) across all areas of health. A National Expert Committee (NEC) oversaw the implementation of the IECPCP strategy, with IPE initiatives subsequently funded by Health Canada. It must be noted that any funded initiative had to be linked to clinical practice, rather than a stand-alone university IPE project. It is this criterion that may be the key to Canada's success; ensuring that IPE leadership was not restricted to the university, but a collaborative between health services, universities, and most importantly patients.

The University of British Colombia has implemented (and continues to implement) an integrated IPE program, offering students a number of IPE interactions throughout their studies. IPE activities are underpinned by educational theory; appropriately timed to ensure junior students are exposed to health professionals other than their own in activities that promote active reflection. Activities such as Health Care Team Challenge and immersion in interprofessional placements such as the Interprofessional Rural Program for British Columbia allows students to enhance collaborative, communication, and care coordination skills, with interprofessional mastery occurring as a qualified health professional undertaking further study and collaborative clinical practice (Charles, Bainbridge, and Gilbert 2010).

While Canada is seen as a global leader of IPE and interprofessional care (IPC), Gilbert (2014) highlights that there are numerous barriers that prevent the successful implementation of IPE. Institutional structures both in academic and health delivery sectors such as timetabling, lack of staff, and poorly trained faculty are often barriers to the successful introduction of IPE and Gilbert (2014) suggests that that evidence-informed leadership is the key for success.

Sweden—Linkoping University: The Birthplace of IPE Training Wards

In 1986, Linkoping University in Sweden established what the world now refers to the "Linkoping IPE model." While many universities and healthcare facilities cite logistical and geographical barriers to implement IPE initiatives, in the late 1980s Linkoping University was able to embed IPE within programs as many "hospital-trained" healthcare professionals transitioned to "academic programs." The influx of new health professionals offered the faculty a unique opportunity to design a program that would meet Sweden's future healthcare and educational policy and address the changes in public healthcare and new models of healthcare delivery. Curriculum development was led by Professor Areskog, with a scaffolded, experiential learning experience the result. Students undertake a problem-based learning introductory module, followed by a clinical team training experience within orthopaedic and geriatric wards and Linkoping University Hospital. Evaluation of the program was initially conducted for internal curriculum review with little evaluation data published until the early 1990s (Bredange 1991). Program evaluation results indicate that IPE prepares students for professions where understanding each other's roles and responsibilities to the patient allows for improved delegation, differentiation, and discussion (Fallsberg and Hammer 2000). Similar to the majority of IPE literature, Wilhelmsson and colleagues (2009) report that engagement, faculty ownership, and curriculum renewal are important to the success of IPE initiatives. Wilhelmsson and colleagues (2009) note the importance of student and alumni involvement, not only as participants but as curriculum reviewers, for it is these people who will potentially have the greatest ability to improve student engagement and ultimately interprofessional practice.

United Kingdom Experience: Sheffield

IPE in the United Kingdom has been integrated and prioritized into prelicensure education since 1997, with partnerships between education institutions and local health authorities enabling this to occur. Creating an "authentic" learning environment was a key driver when Sheffield Hallam and Sheffield Universities created the Combined Universities Interprofessional Learning Unit (Gordon et al. 2006). Too often IPE activities force interaction between health professional students that are not usually found within the healthcare system, creating a "poorly simulated" environment. The Learning Unit created a flexible interprofessional curriculum offering students face-to-face, e-learning, problem-based learning, and mentoring to achieve knowledge in practice, ethical practice, reflection in learning, and interprofessional working capabilities according to the Framework for Interprofessional Capability.

The Japanese Experience

Tamura and colleagues (2005) used metaphors to enable first-year students to understand the key concepts related to interprofessional education and practice. Students were asked to create a visual "menu," which included sushi rolls and curry to illustrate how health professionals can work in harmony to achieve success. Each ingredient, such as nori sheets or curry spices represented how an individual profession could influence or create cohesion within the team. This novel exercise engages students in their first interprofessional education encounter. More recently, the focus of Japanese IPE faculty has been to validate instruments to the Japanese context to improve the rigour of their quantitative IPE evaluations (Tamura et al. 2012).

Australia: The Resurgence of IPE

Following a hiatus, Australia is currently seeing a revival of IPE activities following the *Curriculum Renewal for Interprofessional Education in Health* commissioned by the Office of Learning and Teaching (Dunston et al. 2014).

The report highlights the pockets of quality IPE activities occurring across both metropolitan and regional areas. The Australian government has provided additional funding through Health Workforce Australia, prioritizing interprofessional education, particularly utilizing simulation as a key initiative to improve patient safety and address workforce shortages.

Curtin University located in Perth, Western Australia, is one pocket that continues to provide IPE leadership within both acute and primary healthcare settings. Curtin University, along with medical students from University of Western Australia, partnered with Royal Perth Hospital to establish a student training ward, similar to those found in Sweden. Students from medicine, nursing, social work, physiotherapy, occupational therapy, and pharmacy undertook a two- to three-week clinical placement in a medical ward, which aimed to improve collaborative practice, provide client-centered care, and improve safety outcomes for patients. Student capabilities were measured against the Interprofessional Capability Assessment Tool (Brewer and Jones 2013) and the Interprofessional Socialisation and Valuing Scale (King et al. 2010). Overall, students reported an increased awareness and respect of each other's roles within the interprofessional team, with the training ward providing them an opportunity to practice autonomously, and improve their confidence within their own professional role.

Like most countries, Australia's healthcare delivery system is a complex web, with funding arising from federal- and state-based sources. Local health districts or areas liaise with universities and other higher education intuitions across the country to enable student clinical placements to occur. Student clinical placements, like the ones utilized by Curtin University, are ideal to implement IPE initiatives as health services can tailor a student's clinical experience in include IPE exposure. Of course, this relies on health services utilizing an interprofessional practice model; a model that is desired, but for the most part, not yet achieved.

CONCLUSION

Historically, interprofessional education has occurred in isolated pockets across the globe, with little published literature available to faculty wishing to implement similar activities. The increased evaluation and subsequent reporting has resulted in an exponential rise in the number of peer-reviewed articles and textbooks examining interprofessional education, learning, and practice. As highlighted above, many countries are implementing activities in attempt to meet WHO guidelines for IPE. Rigorous evaluation of longitudinal outcomes appear to be difficult to establish due to a number of confounders. This, along with traditional barriers to IPE implementation and evaluation are key priorities for our IPE leaders globally.

REFERENCES

Australian Health Professional Regulatory Authority [AHPRA]. 2015. https://www.ahpra.gov.au. Accessed June 2015.

Baldwin, D. C., Jr. 2007. "Some Historical Notes on Interdisciplinary and Interprofessional Education and Practice in Health Care in the USA." *Journal of Interprofessional Care* 21: 23–37.

Baldwin, D. W. C., and M. A. Baldwin. 2007. "Interdisciplinary Education and Health Team Training: A Model for Learning and Service." *Journal of Interprofessional Care* 21, Supp. 1: 52–69.

Berwick, D. M., T. W. Nolan, and J. Whittington. 2008. "The Triple Aim: Care, Health, and Cost." *Health Affairs* 27: 759–69.

Blue, A., B. F. Brandt, and M. H. Schmitt. 2010. "American Interprofessional Health Collaborative: Historical Roots and Organizational Beginnings." *Journal of Allied Health* 39, Supp. 1: 204–9.

Brandt, B. F. 2014. "Update on the US National Center for Interprofessional Practice and Education." *Journal of Interprofessional Care* 28, no. 1: 15–17.

Brandt, B. F., M. N. Lutifyya, J. King, and C. Chioreso. 2014. "A Scoping Review of Interprofessional Collaborative Practice and Education Using the Lens of the Triple Aim." *Journal of Interprofessional Care* 28, no. 5: 393–99.

Bredange, G. 1991. *Faculty of Health Sciences from the Nursing Perspective. Final report of an Evaluation of the shorter health education courses at the Faculty of Health and Sciences*, Faculty of Health Sciences, Linkoping University: Sweden.

Brewer, M. L., and S. Jones. 2013. "An Interprofessional Practice Capability Framework Focusing on Safe, High-Quality, Client-Centred Health Service." *Journal of Allied Health* 42, no. 2: e45–e49.

Bristol Royal Infirmary Inquiry Chairman: Professor Ian Kennedy. 2001. *The Report of the Public Inquiry into Children's Heart Surgery at the Bristol Royal Infirmary 1984-1995: Learning from Bristol.* http://webarchive.nationalarchives.gov.uk/+/www.dh.gov.uk/en/Publicationsandstatistics/Publications/PublicationsPolicyAndGuidance/DH_4005620. Accessed June 15, 2015.

Canadian Interprofessional Health Collaborative Working Group. 2010. *A National Interprofessional Competency Framework.* http://www.cihc.ca/files/CIHC_IPCompetencies_Feb_2012.pdf. Accessed June 2015.

Centre for the Advancement of Interprofessional Education. 2002. *Interprofessional Education: A Definition.* http://www.caipe.org.uk/about-us/defining-ipe. Accessed June 15, 2015.

Charles, G., L. Bainbridge, and J. H. V. Gilbert. 2010. "The University of British Columbia Model of Interprofessional Education." *Journal of Interprofessional Care* 24, no. 1: 9–18.

Curtin University. 2011. *Curtin Interprofessional Capability Framework.* http://healthsciences.curtin.edu.au/local/docs/IP_Capability_Framework_booklet.pdf. Accessed June 2015.

Dunston, R., D. Forman, J. Hager, M. Manidis, G. Rogers, C. Rossiter, J. Thistlethwaite, and T. Yassine. 2014. *Curriculum Renewal for Interprofessional Education in Health, Final Report for Office for Learning and Teaching*, Commonwealth of Australia: Sydney.

Fallsberg, M., and M. Hammer. 2000. "Strategies and Focus at an Integrated, Interprofessional Training Ward." *Journal of Interprofessional Care* 14: 337–50.

Freeth, D., M. Hammick, S. Reeves, I. Koppel, and H. Barr. 2005. *Effective Interprofessional Education: Development, Delivery and Evaluation.* Oxford: Blackwell.

Gilbert, J. H. V. 2014. "Interprofessional Education in Canada: Initiatives 2003–11." In *Leadership Development for Interprofessional Education and Collaborative Practice*, edited by D. Forman, M. Jones, and J. Thistlethwaite. Basingstoke, United Kingdom: Palgrave Macmillan.

Gordon, F., C. Walsh, M. Marshall, F. Wilson, and T. Hunt. 2005. *The Combined Universities Interprofessional Learning Unit: Final Report.* Sheffield Hallam University and University of Sheffield.

Interprofessional Education Collaborative Expert Panel. 2011. *Core Competencies for Interprofessional Collaborative Practice: Report of an Expert Panel*, Washington, DC.

King, G., L. Shaw, C. A. Orchard, and S. Miller. 2010. "The Interprofessional Socialization and Valuing Scale: A Tool for Evaluating The Shift Toward Collaborative Care Approaches in Health Care Settings." *Work* 35: 77–85.

Kohn, L. T., M. Coorigan, and S. Donaldson (eds.). 1999. *To Err Is Human: Building a Safer Health System*. Insitute of Medicine. Washington, DC: National Academies Press.

Mid Staffordshire NHS Foundation Trust Public Inquiry Chairman Robert Francis. 2013. *Report of the Mid Staffordshire NHS Foundation Trust Public Inquiry: Executive summary.* https://www.gov.uk/government/uploads/system/uploads/attachment_data/file/279124/0947.pdf. Accessed September 20, 2015.

Palaganas, J. C., C. Epps, and D. B. Raemer. 2014. "A History of Simulation-Enhanced Interprofessional Education." *Journal of Interprofessional Care* 28, no. 2: 110–15.

Rodger, S., S. J. Hoffman, and the World Health Organization Study Group on Interprofessional Education and Collaborative Practice. 2010. "Where in the World is Interprofessional Education? A Global Environmental Scan." *Journal of Interprofessional Care* 24, no. 5: 479–91.

Romanow, R. J. 2002. *Building on Values: The Future of Health Care in Canada. Final Report*, November. Ottawa, Canada: Comission on the Future of Health Care in Canada.

Sheffield Hallam University. 2010. *Interprofessional Capability Framework 2010 Mini-Guide*. London: Higher Education Academy Subject Centre for Health Sciences and Practice. http://www.health.heacademy.ac.uk/doc/resources/icf2010.pdf/at_download/file.pdf. Accessed June 2015.

Szasz, G. 1969. "Interprofessional Eductional in The Health Sciences: a Project Conducted at the University of British Columbia." *Milbank Quarterly* 4, no.4: 449–75.

Tamura, Y., P. Bontje, Y. Nakata, Y. Ishikawa, and N. Tsuda. 2005. "Can One Eat Collaboration? Menus as Metaphors of Interprofessional Collaboration." *Journal of Interprofessional Care* 19, no. 3: 215–22.

Tamura, Y., K. Seki, M. Usami, S. Taku, P. Bontje, H. Ando, C. Taru, Y. Ishikawa, et al. 2012. "Cultural Adaptation and Validating a Japanese Version of the Readiness for Interprofessional Learning Scale RIPLS." *Journal of Interprofessional Care* 26, no. 1: 56–63.

Thistlethwaite, J. D., L. Forman, G. Matthews, G. Rogers, C. Steketee, and T. Yassine. 2014. "Competencies and Frameworkds in Interprofessional Education: A Comparative Analysis." *Academic Medicine* 89, not. 6: 869–75.

Wilhelmsson, M., S. Pelling, J. Ludvigsson, and M. Hammer. 2009. "Twenty Years Experiences of Interprofessional Education in Linkoping—Ground-Breaking and Sustainable." *Journal of Interprofessional Care* 23, no. 2: 121–33.

World Health Organization. 1988. *Continuing Education for Physicians*. Geneva: World Health Organization.

———. 1988. *Learning Together to Work Together for Health. Report of a WHO Study Group on Multiprofessional Education for Health Personnel: The Team Approach.* Technical Report Series 769: 1–72. Geneva: World Health Organization.

Chapter Two

Theories Underlying Interprofessional Education

James Ballard

This is not a definitive survey of all of the potential theories that might impact development of interprofessional curricula. Work toward this end has been done in earnest and can be reviewed elsewhere (Adams et al. 2006; Colyer, Helme, and Jones 2012; Hean, Craddock, and Hammick 2012; Reeves et al. 2007). Rather, it is a selection of theories and related models, from a pragmatic orientation, that educators who embark on the murky journey of interprofessional education might consider as they design, implement, and evaluate interprofessional curricula.

According to Clark (2006), one application of theory in interprofessional education (IPE) is to guide instructional practice. The other is to inform research and, although, this is important, this chapter will focus on the implication of theory for instructional practice and curricula design. This includes components such as, (a) determining major concepts to guide the structures and process of educational experiences, (b) determining appropriate learning objectives and the strategies to achieve them, (c) understanding and defining effective roles for faculty and students in the educational process, and (d) measuring programmatic impacts and outcomes. These components should not be surprising to educators; yet, the early days of interprofessional curriculum design have been criticized for a lack of theoretical grounding (Freeth et al. 2002). Recently, however, this landscape has changed dramatically as more and more educators are, indeed, designing and describing curricula that is developed upon a sound theoretical footing. That is the good news. The bad news is, as Hean, Craddock, and O'Halloran (2009) well describe "this plethora of theories has become a confusing, and un-navigable quagmire" (251). Further, there is no, and perhaps cannot be, an overarching and consolidated theory that encompasses interprofessional education. Nonetheless, as more and more institutions and professions struggle to make sense of this literature in order to develop sound curricula and evaluations of that curricula, the need for a digestible account of relevant theory is apparent. That is what has been attempted in this chapter. From this perspective a selection of relevant theories from education, social psychology, and organizational psychology will be put forth. All have been selected because of their pragmatic utility in developing IPE curricula within authentic, purposeful, and contextually appropriate environments. Subsequently, a brief discussion of the developmental nature of learning in tandem with its implications for interprofessional education will be offered.

EDUCATIONAL THEORIES

Adult Learning

It seems reasonable that one cannot approach a discourse on educational theories that are appropriate for learning among the population of health professions students without a discussion of adult learning. Yet, there is no single theory of learning that is appropriately applicable to all adults. Nevertheless, the literature has described a number of constructs that can be subsumed under the heading of adult learning. All attempt to describe the distinctions between learning as adults and as children. Three prominent theories of adult learning include adult learning theory, self-directed learning, and transformative learning theory.

Adult Learning Theory

Knowles (1980) proposed a set of assumptions about adult learners that, perhaps, are unique to adults, and implications for educational practice that follow from these assumptions. Accordingly, he assumed that (a) as learners mature, they move from a dependence on others toward a self-directed mode of learning; (b) adult learners draw on past experiences gained through formal and informal life experiences to aid learning; (c) adults are motivated to learn when they assume new life or professional roles; (d) adults are motivated to focus on problems and prefer immediate application of learning toward solving problems; and (e) adults are internally, as opposed to externally, motivated to learn.

Implications for educators follow from these assumptions and suggest that learning should be situated within an appropriate climate, and should focus on addressing the learner's specific interests and needs at the appropriate skill level. Additionally, Knowles proposed that the adult learner needs to be actively involved in planning the instruction and that learning based on experiences, both positive and negative, is important. The notion of experiential learning is also important within Knowles's framework and has been expanded by Kolb (1984), who describes learning as an interactive process among members of a community of learners who collectively explore the meaning of problems. This requires learners to reflect on their experiences from multiple perspectives and to create an integrated understanding that includes logical theories that are used to make decisions and solve problems.

The construct of self-directed learning in adulthood is another central theme of Knowles's conception of adult learning. Specifically, it is described as a process of taking the initiative for planning, implementing, and evaluating one's own learning experiences based on one's own perceived needs and goals (Knowles 1975). Knowles argues that this leads to better learning in terms of both the quantity of information learned and the quality, or effectiveness, of how it is learned. Hiemstra (1994) cautions that self-directed learning is not, in and of itself, a theory; yet, given its seeming persistence in adulthood, and an acknowledgment of the socially constructed nature of knowledge, it is worth mentioning in the context of completing the paradigm of adult learning. It is important to note that self-directed learning does not necessarily take place in the academic environment; yet, it may, as is the case when learners become empowered to take responsibility for their own learning efforts.

From the perspective of interprofessional education, Barr (2013) reminds that adult learning principles are relevant to, yet distinct from, interprofessional learning. Whereas adult learning principles place the responsibility of learning on the individual, in interprofessional education this responsibility is shared among all individuals within the group as they jointly attempt to learn with, from, and about each other. Likewise Clark (2006) argues for the relevance of adult learning principles in IPE in that they accentuate cooperation and collaboration in addition to emphasizing the importance of socially constructed knowledge. This emphasis on the cognitive construction of knowledge is the focus of many educational theories that have roots in the social cognitive perspective to be described later.

Transformative Learning Theory

Transformative Learning Theory has been described by Mezirow (1997) as a process of causing change within one's frame of reference. These frames develop as a result of life experiences and include concepts, values, feelings, and associations that create assumptions through which future experiences are understood. They shape expectations, perceptions, thoughts, and feelings in subsequent interactions with the environment. Once these frames are established, there is a tendency to reject ideas that run counter to these preconceived "habits of mind" described as "broad, abstract, orienting, habitual ways of thinking, feeling, and acting, influenced by assumptions that constitute a set of codes" (Mezirow 1997, 5). Within the context of interprofessionalism, an example of a habit of mind can be found in the construct described by Pecukonis, Doyle, and Bliss (2008) as profession-centrism representing a predisposition to potentially see others outside one's own profession as inferior. Clearly this is not an optimal perception to be held by learners yet it is an understandable outcome of silo-based care that, hopefully, can be transformed through experiences received within IPE. Frames of reference can be transformed through critical reflection on the assumptions that undergird interpretations of the world. Educators can transform habits of mind by helping learners uncover and critically reflect on their own frames of reference in order to see things from different perspectives.

Educational Learning Theories from Cognitive and Social Cognitive Perspectives

Educational learning theories are vast as are specific definitions of learning. Together Illeris (2004) and Ormrod (1995) offer a view of learning that seems especially pertinent to educators in interprofessional education. Accordingly, they describe learning as a confluence of cognitive, emotional, and environmental factors that allow the learner to gain or enhance understanding in order to make changes to one's own skills, values, or worldview. The importance of this definition is the recognition that learning must be viewed as a continual process as opposed to the end-product of what has been learned. From this perspective, learning can be described through a number of theories, all focusing on particular components of the process, be they the behaviors elicited among learners, their cognitions, or the contextual environmental influences impacting the learning process. Given the number of potential directions involved with describing educational theories relevant to IPE, this section will concentrate on what generally are described as cognitivist, social cognitivist, and constructivist perspectives of learning as these have significant relevance for affecting the learning processes of health professions students who are learning with, about, and from each other.

According to Merriam, Caffarella, and Baumgartner (2007) the behaviorist perspective on learning, with its focus on stimulus and response reinforces in the learning context, that became prominent in the early to mid-1900s was challenged in 1929 by those within the Gestalt psychology camp for being overly particularistic and dependent upon overt behaviors to explain learning. This criticism continued and blossomed throughout the mid-twentieth century in concert with the cognitive revolution during which there was a redefinition among the fields of psychology, anthropology, and linguistics in addition to the genesis of fields such as computer sciences and neurosciences. During this time scholars such as B. F. Skinner, Noam Chomsky, and

Jerome Bruner argued for the need to include internal (not obviously observable) processes involved in learning rather than adhering to the strict assumptions of the behaviorists (Miller 2003).

The cognitivist perspective of learning is based on two primary assumptions (Merriam, Caffarella, and Baumgartner 2007): (1) the memory system is involved in storing and processing information to be learned, and (2) new knowledge is built upon prior knowledge. From this perspective memory is perceived through the sensory system and is interpreted and given meaning. Here we see a shift in locus from the environment (as in behaviorism) to the individual's mental processes. Emerging in the 1970s its proponents rejected the idea that learners are passive recipients of information. Rather, they argued that learners actively engage with their environment in a developmental process of cognitive reorganization to construct meaning. A leader within this perspective, John Piaget, was instrumental in calling attention to the relationship between maturation (development) and learning. In particular he proposed that cognitive structures change as a result of both the maturation process and the individual's interaction with the environment. This in turn affects what can be learned, how it is learned, and when it can be learned (Duckworth 1964).

Building on the cognitivist perspective, the *social cognitivists* shared the focus on internal processes and combined some of the views of the behaviorists, namely reinforcement contingencies. The social cognitive perspective of learning grew out of the work of Bandura (1986). It focuses on learning that occurs in the social context. Specifically, this perspective posits that learning occurs in a social context and that people can learn by observing others (Merriam, Caffarella, and Baumgartner 2007). From this perspective, learning can be vicarious (learned through the observation of others) and does not require imitation of behaviors as posited by the behaviorists. Similar to the cognitivists, the learning process is based loosely on the metaphor of the computer (sometimes referred to as the information-processing model) and involves four processes including: attention, retention (memory), rehearsal, and motivation (Cowen 1988). For example, actions of others are observed and attended to. This information is retained and processed in memory until the individual is motivated to act on it.

According to social cognitive theory, learning is predicated on a number of assumptions about learning and behavior. This includes that personal (cognitive), behavioral, and contextual (environmental) factors interact in a reciprocal method to produce learning. As such learning is affected by the reinforcements occurring in the learning environment in addition to the learners own beliefs about themselves and their interpretation of the learning environment. Additionally, social cognitive theory assumes that learners influence their own learning through purposeful, goal-directed methods. Finally, the theory posits that a distinction be made between learning and behavior. That is, that learning may occur, but may or may not be demonstrated through behavior until the learner is motivated to do so (Bandura 1986).

Constructivist and Social Constructivist Perspectives of Learning

The central premise of constructivism is that learning involves the process of meaning-making. However, constructivist perspectives differ among several lines including, and importantly for IPE, the distinction between whether this meaning-making is fundamentally an individual or social function (Steffe and Gale 1995). In regard to the former, Piaget described learning as an internal cognitive activity of an individual's adapting cognitive schema in response to the changing physical environment. Learning operates as an equilibration model. New knowledge encountered by the learner is assimilated into existing knowledge structures. However, when this new information does not fit within an existing schema, cognitive disequilibrium occurs, and the learner is forced to reconcile the fit of the new information to old by accommodating the existing schema to master the new challenge. As the learner encounters experiences that are counter to a current understanding, cognitive conflict occurs. By working through this conflict the learner acquires new schema that leads to new ways of understanding.

Alternatively, whereas the constructivist perspective of learning posits that learning is constructed through interaction with one's environment (Merriam, Caffarella, and Baumgartner 2007), the social constructivist perspective posits that learning is not constructed in isolation from the social context. Rather, it is mediated by the social environment with emphasis directed toward how social encounters influence learners' understanding and meaning-making within a collaborative circumstance, especially with a facilitator or some other external other (Davis 1994). The social constructivist view postulates that meaning–making is a dialogic process through which knowledge is constructed within a social context through communication or shared problem solving. Driver, Asoko, Leach, Mortimer, and Scott (1994), drawing from Vygotsky (1978) describe this process as one in which learners build an understanding of the culturally shared worldview of others. Recalling the learning with, from, and about description of IPE (Barr 2002), this perspective is vital for understanding interprofessional education (Hean, Craddock, and O'Halloran 2009).

Although not a theory itself, a related construct that should be considered, especially as it relates to social constructivism in developing IPE, is the "hidden curriculum." Philip Jackson (1968) first introduced the concept of the hidden curriculum in the context of general education. Specifically, he observed children in primary education and identified values, dispositions, and behavioral expectations that were rewarded in school. Although these components were not tied explicitly to educational goals and objectives, they were critical for success in school. In the 1960s Fredric Hafferty first introduced the concept of the hidden curriculum to educators in medical education (Hafferty 1998). Recently, this construct was operationalized for the medical education community by Gaufberg, Badalden, Sands, and Bell (2010) as learning that occurs through informal interactions among students, faculty, and others or learning through organizational, structural, and cultural influences intrinsic to training institutions. Others, such as Gofton and Regehr (2006), describe the hidden curriculum as a function of implicit values held by the institution, the education, and the professionals who work in the trainees learning environment who impact students' behaviors and attitudes. Likewise, Haidet and Stein (2005) argue that the student–teacher relationship that emerges within the medical education context is an important mediating factor that influences how the culture of medicine, in its broadest sense, is learned, both positively and negatively. Importantly, within the discussion of social cognitive learning, the hidden curriculum is an important feature of the learning context that must be considered if educators are to be successful in developing and fomenting a positive interprofessional worldview among learners. According to Gaufberg, Badalden, Sands, and Bell (2010), medical educators who, themselves, were socialized by the hidden curriculum during training, may not recognize the messages they send to their own trainees, thus proliferating the attitudes toward collaboration, positively or negatively, that they hold themselves. As such it is important for educators to remain mindful of their own values and cognitions when interacting with learners.

THEORIES FROM SOCIAL PSYCHOLOGY

Thus far learning has been described as occurring at an internal level, influenced by the environment. Within IPE, the context of learning should be as authentic as possible. This often involves a learning environment in which groups of learners from multiple professions are interacting. Social psychology reminds us of the potential dangers that may lurk below the surface of learning when multiple groups of learners, or professionals, interact. Research from this paradigm has provided a rich landscape of useful theories for understanding how groups can coexist effectively and why bias between and among groups can form. Much of this work has focused generally on understanding and mitigating intergroup bias. Intergroup bias is best understood as a tendency to systematically view members of one's own group (in-group) more positively that nonmembers (out-group). This bias can be manifested in multiple forms across behavioral (discrimination), attitudinal (prejudice), and cognitive (stereotyping) domains (Mackie and Smith 1998; Wilder and Simon 2001). As such, this literature is relevant to IPE in so much as it both describes the circumstances in which bias between and among professional groups can occur and strategies for mitigating this bias. We begin first with some of the primary theories that have been developed to understand how intergroup bias occurs. In turn, a description of mitigating strategies is discussed.

Self-Categorization Theory

Self-Categorization Theory describes the circumstances under which individuals from one group assimilate the self into an in-group prototype, or category (Turner and Reynolds 2001). This is a cognitive model whereby individuals reduce the organization of the social world into social categories in an effort to reduce the complexity of information occurring within a social context. This abridged information is used to more efficiently, but not necessarily more accurately, predict and guide behaviors. One example of the outcome of relaying on these simplistic inferences is stereotyping, a process in which individuals ignore individual characteristics of group members and concentrate on a more generalized understanding that may occur as a function of highly observable (i.e., gender, race, profession) features, ascribing a limited set of attributes to most members of that group. As a result, members of the out-group are seen as more homogeneous while members of the in-group continue to perceive themselves to be part of a more diverse group.

Members of the in-group tend to extend trust, positive regard, mutual cooperation, and empathy toward fellow in-group members, excluding those in the out-group (Brewer 1999). This in-group favoritism has been demonstrated to arise automatically without the individual's awareness (Otten and Wentura 1999). It is generally associated more strongly with an increased regard for one's own group as opposed to strongly negative attitudes toward the out-group (Dovidio and Gaertner 2000), although out-group derogation can occur in circumstances in which strong emotional reactions may lift the normally occurring constraints that typically lead to in-group favoritism (Brewer 2001).

Social Identity Theory

Social Identity Theory (Tajfel and Turner 1979) posits a self-esteem hypothesis that leads to intergroup bias. Accordingly, successful intergroup bias functions to enhance or create high in-group status that offers a positive social identity for members of the in-group, thus satisfying a need for positive self-esteem. In general, the theory concludes that one's identity as an individual is derived from the social group to which one belongs. Groups provide a sense of social identity or belonging. Given the tendency to prefer seeing oneself in a positive light the in-group, of which one is a member, is seen more positively than the out-group. In other words, individuals tend to increase their own self-image by enhancing the status of the group in which they belong. The corollary to this is that the image of the in-group, and by extension, one's own self-image can be increased by denigrating members of the out-group.

According to Tajfel and Turner (1979) three variables contribute to the tendency toward in-group favoritism. First, favoritism is dependent upon the level of identification with an in-group. Greater identification leads to an internalization of group membership as an aspect of one's self-concept. The second involves the extent to which the context provides opportunity for comparison between groups. Finally, the perception of relevance of the comparison group to one's own can influence in-group favoritism. Generally, individuals are likely to display favoritism when self-definition is highly related to identification with an in-group and when a comparison between groups is meaningful (i.e., in the case of power differentiation).

Optimal Distinctiveness Theory

Optimal Distinctiveness Theory (Brewer 1991) is related to Social Identity Theory and postulates that the opposing needs of assimilation and differentiation must be cognitively reconciled. That is, individuals are motivated to identify with groups that provide a balance between these dichotomous needs. If, for example, individuals feel too similar to others in their in-group they will seek ways to be different. Likewise, if they perceive themselves to be too different than others in the in-group, they are motivated to become more similar.

According to this theory individuals are more likely to identify with groups that can resolve the conflict between these two needs. A good example of this is found in a study by Lau (1989) that demonstrated the group identity of African Americans was strongest when individuals lived in communities that were more integrated rather than being predominantly black or white. It was hypothesized that African Americans in this context were able to identify themselves as somewhat similar to other African Americans, but somewhat different as when they compared themselves to whites, thus reconciling the balance between their assimilation and differentiation needs.

Social Dominance Theory

Social Dominance Theory (Sidanius and Pratto 1999) posits that intergroup hierarchies are either promoted or attenuated by ideologies supported by society. Individuals in groups that have greater access to power or privilege possess an amplified social dominance orientation and, as such, have a stronger desire to endorse intergroup hierarchies. Within these hierarchies their own in-group maintains superiority over out-group members in terms of status and power. Examples of groups that maintain a higher social dominance orientation in our society traditionally have included men in comparison to women. This also has been examined within the context of whites and blacks in South Africa (Sidanius and Pratto 1999). One could hypothesize that within the current hierarchically based healthcare system that power differentials may be important to consider in the development of IPE experiences.

Given the implications of these various theories discussed above that all describe nuances about why individuals tend to cluster into and identify with subgroups, it is important to moderate the effects of group identification when planning and implementing IPE curricula. Two strategies in particular, decategorization and recategorization, have been well-documented in the literature. Both focus specifically on mitigating the tendency of individuals to isolate people into discreet categories by designing contextual features of experiences in order to decategorize or recategorize group boundaries, thus reducing intergroup bias (Wilder 1986).

Decategorization

Decategorization is accomplished through a process of individuation through which one is drawn to attend to individual differences of individuals, as opposed to undifferentiated cognitive representations of the group to which they belong, in essence counteracting the cognitive efficiency of developing strict categorical separations. Accordingly, as a result, repeated personal exposures with members from other groups in which members of opposing groups become acquainted, the strength of out-group categories diminishes and intergroup bias is reduced (Miller, Brewer, and Edwards 1985). Miller and Brewer (1984) describe this process as occurring when members of groups attend to information that is relevant to the self as an individual as opposed to the self as a member of a group. That is, category identity as a source of classification is replaced with individualized information. In practical terms this suggests that interprofessional education groups should be organized in such a way as to reduce categorical distinctions by allowing for the development of personal connections between and among group members. This might be done formally by devising experiences in which learners are scaffolded to focus on the personal and individual characteristics of each other; or, perhaps, it can be accomplished informally by providing learners the opportunity to socialize in a "neutral" or non-academic context.

Recategorization and the Common In-Group Identity Model

Recategorization is similar to decategorization in that it functions to reduce the salience of distinctions between in- and out-groups. However, rather than focusing on reducing or eliminating categorizations, the emphasis is on restructuring group categorizations at a higher level of inclusiveness. This can be accomplished by strategies designed to create a common in-group identity whereby members' perceptions of group boundaries change from a perspective of *us* and *them* as individuals to *we* as members of unique yet complementary groups consisting of members functioning together at a superordinate level of identity (Gaertner et al. 1993). This does not mean, however, that this process requires an abandonment of one's own group identity. Rather it is a process more akin to members holding a dual identity in which they become members of subgroups consumed within one cooperative larger group (Brewer and Schneider 1990; Hewstone and Brown 1986).

Within the context of interprofessional education recategorization suggests that the role of curricula is not to circumvent students' development of a professional identity, but rather, to help learners develop a complementary interprofessional identity as members of an interprofessional team. Here each profession maintains its own group identity, yet by refocusing efforts on a superordinate goal (i.e., patient care) they transform their strictly individual identities into one as members of an interprofessional team focusing of patients.

Intergroup Contact Theory

Intergroup Contact Theory is drawn from the work of Gordon Allport (1954), and was developed to explain how tensions between divergent groups, mostly based on racial and ethnic boundaries at the time, could be reduced. Accordingly the theory proposes that these tensions can be mitigated by bringing together members of each group to interact under four necessary conditions. Group members must have equal status, work toward a common goal, cooperate with other, and must have the institutionalized support (i.e., laws or customs). Expanding on this, Hewstone and Brown (1986) added that groups must engage in positive contact, hold positive expectations for the outcome of shared tasks, and have success in achieving these tasks, and must intentionally focus on understanding each other's similarities and differences. It is suggested that bias is reduced through intergroup contact through the process of decategorization. As members of in-groups and out-groups cooperate interdependently, individuated perceptions of each other are formed and less attention to expectancy consistent information is attended to (Miller and Brewer 1984; Erber and Fiske 1984; Neuberg and Fiske 1987).

Intergroup Contact Theory has led to a significant amount of research, expanding beyond its original focus on ethnic and racial groups to include target groups such as the elderly, physically disabled, and mentally ill (Pettigrew and Tropp 2006). Likewise it has been applied to numerous social issues such as racial desegregation (Pettigrew 1971), and mainstreaming of children with mental and physical disabilities within the educational system (Harper and Wacker 1985; Naor and Milgram 1980). Recently Pettigrew and Trapp (2006) conducted a meta-analysis with samples from 515 studies and concluded that the theory holds up in reducing intergroup conflict across a wide range of groups and contexts.

The importance of this work for informing IPE cannot be understated. The four theories discussed above (social categorization, social identity, optimal distinctiveness, and social dominance) describe the tendency of humans to naturally refocus the social world into smaller groups within which they identify as individuals and how this can result in intergroup bias and reduced cooperation. As described by Leape and Berwick (2005) entrenched hierarchy and professional conflict result in faculty decision making and reduced safety and quality of care. Social identity theory in addition to the related constructs of decategorization and recategorization processes provide guidance for how this progression toward bias, and potential conflict, might be mitigated. The salience of group distinction among health professionals is enhanced by the current, but evolving, uniprofessional structure of health professions training. It is hoped that by bringing students together to learn cooperatively, using methods informed by social identity theory and the processes of decategorization and recategorization, that the potential bias existing among and between professions can be reduced. This may pave the way toward developing fully functional teams, unencumbered by intergroup or interprofessions biases.

ORGANIZATIONAL PSYCHOLOGY

In this section, research from the field of organizational psychology will be introduced as it relates to teams. This is included because it is important not only to understand variables associated with group functioning, typically the purview of the social psychological theories, but also the effectiveness of interprofessional collaborative teams. Too often, these components are approached in isolation, rather than together. The ultimate goal of interprofessional collaborative practice is to provide the best possible care for patients. This can only be accomplished if the healthcare team is effective in its functioning. Although the focus of this chapter is on theories that can inform education, not practice, the field of organizational psychology is ripe with models that may inform our understanding of team effectiveness and, in turn, guide interprofessional curriculum development.

According to Jex and Britt (2008), research in organizational psychology goes beyond the study of team dynamics, the foci of social psychology, to concentrate on team effectiveness. Toward this end, the literature informs that team effectiveness cannot be assessed in isolation of the context in which it occurs. That is, before one can determine the effectiveness of a team, one must understand what kind of team is being observed, if a team at all, and in what context the team is functioning. In relationship to IPE, this indicates that context is important and the components of the team in which students learn are dynamic and important considerations.

The construct of team is more complex than it appears at face value. The literature is ripe with information about teams, but teams are multifaceted and the structural dimensions of teams must be considered as variables that affect their effectiveness. Hollenbeck, Beersma, and Shouten (2012), offer a typology of team that can inform educators about developing appropriate curricular experiences that authentically represent the team environment. According to their model, teams differ along three underlying structural dimensions. The first of these, *Skill Differentiation* describes the degree of differentiation among members' skills and knowledge. At its most basic level, uniprofessional teams are composed of individuals from the same profession who hold a similar professional identity in addition to similar skills and knowledge. As the complexity of care, or the task demands of the interprofessional learning team, increases the need for additional team members from multiple professions, with additional skills and knowledge are required. With this comes the additional complexity of how decisions are made and who makes them within the team. This leads to the second dimension, *Authority Differentiation*, described by Hollenbeck, Beersma, and Shouten (2012), and refers to the extent to which the entire team is involved in decision making. It can range from some members, those of whom have higher levels of authority based on professional role or status within the team, making all or most of the decisions to a true collaborative team decision-making process. The final dimension is *Temporal Stability*. This term refers to the extent to which teams are composed of the same members over time or are thrown together, ad hoc, to deal with a particular problem. All of these three dimensions must be considered in an evaluation of team effectiveness and in the development of educational interventions.

In addition to the structural features of team, the team itself can affect functioning. According to West and Lyubovnikova (2012), "real teams" can be distinguished from "pseudo teams." Accordingly, these authors describe real teams as those characterized by (1) working together with clear and shared objectives, (2) working interdependently, and (3) purposely reflecting on team effectiveness. Alternatively, although members of pseudo teams may believe they are working together as a team, they tend to function independently with little communication, unknown or disparate objectives, and with little or no reflection on the team's performance. According to West and Lyubovnikova, most medical errors occur among groups characterized as pseudo teams. As such, it is important to distinguish the extent to which groups of individuals are functioning as real teams if one attempts to study the effectiveness of healthcare teams. Likewise if we wish to develop team skills among learners it is important to situate learners within a context in which "real" teams can develop.

Input-Process-Output Framework

West and Lyubovnikova (2014), propose the input-process-output (IPO) framework developed by Cohen and Bailey (1997) as the most widely accepted framework for understanding teams. Beginning with the end in mind, the output of the model (hopefully) results in high-quality care, high levels of patient satisfaction, and high levels of team member well-being.

Within this framework, the *inputs* include the elements of the teams' task and composition in addition to organizational support. Each affects the output of the team. Taken sequentially, the team's *task* determines whether the demands of the task warrant a team approach. If the task is relatively simple, preferable outcomes may be achieved without a team. However, within the context of healthcare and interprofessional education, teams should be utilized when dealing with complex tasks that require task interdependence in which members of the team must rely on the knowledge and skills of others to effectively complete the task. Salas, Dickinson, Converse, and Tannenbaum (1992) consider interdependence in it broadest sense (related to tasks, goals, feedback, and reward) as the hallmark characteristic of teams. Of course, even given task demands that optimally call for a collaborative team approach, members within the team must cognitively decide that they should work together as a team. As such, individual characteristics such as preference for teamwork (Campion, Papper, and Medsker 1996) play a critical role in groups coming together as teams.

A second input variable is *team composition.* According to this framework, members within team must possess the appropriate knowledge and skills to complete the complex task at hand. Recalling the important role of attitudes for impacting behaviors suggests that attitudes are as important as skills and knowledge. The Theory of Planned Behavior demonstrates that behavioral achievement is dependent on intention or motivation to engage in a behavior in addition to having the individual control to perform a behavior. That is, one's behavioral performance is dependent upon an intention to perform and the ability to perform (Ajzen 1985). According to Ajzen (1991), this perceived behavioral control combined with behavioral intention can predict behavioral achievement.

Finally, the model recognizes the importance of organizational *support.* The organization within which team function is important, not just to provide required resources for the tasks (i.e., equipment, tools), but also to ensure that contingencies are in place to recognize and value collaboration over individual efforts. This should include reward systems that encourage collaboration and recognize the task interdependence of the work. Within the context of education, the reward system is most akin to the evaluation methodologies utilized. Therefore, it is important to avoid the assumption that evaluation is impact neutral in IPE. One must consider the potential impact of evaluating the individual rather than the team within IPE.

The second component of the IPO Frames work involves team *processes* that affect team effectiveness. Within this sphere, three subcomponents are important and include: (1) team objectives, (2) leadership, and (3) reflexivity. Each will be discussed below, beginning with the third component, reserving team objectives and leadership for the end. Of the three, *reflexivity* is most basic. It simply refers to the team's ability to reflect on its performance and to build team awareness that allows the team to critically evaluate its performance and identify areas for improvement.

According to Poulton and West (1999), shared *team objectives* are essential for motivating and guiding team behavior. However, the construct of team objectives is more complex, especially when considered within the context of teams with members who may differ in terms of varying levels of hierarchical authority. Here it is important to look additionally at the goals of the team. Social Categorization Theory informs this process well. Recall that this theory describes factors that help individuals within separate groups come together as a unified group, and includes retaining one's own identity as a member of a profession, while all members of the team focus on the superordinate goal of treating the patients (Haslam 1997). This theory has been an important approach to issues of social influence, group cohesion, group polarization, and collective action in addition to topics of leadership development (Turner et al. 1987). Implied in all of these are issues of in-group/out-group homogeneity, and power (Turner 2001). Also, implicit in the issue of goal orientation and team objectives is leadership. Teams cannot function effectively in a state of anomie. Someone must provide leadership.

Leadership is the third process component included in the IPO framework that impacts the output of team effectiveness. However, leadership within an interprofessional healthcare team is more complex when the team's structure is composed of a diverse combination of professions. Specifically, interprofessional practice calls for answers to the questions: Who is the leader? Are multiple leaders possible and appropriate? And, what new leadership skills will become paramount under this new model of practice. Recently Hall (2005) argued that if physicians are to provide effective leadership to interprofessional teams they must have specific leadership skills. These skills include: (a) identifying problems of group dynamics, and (b) being able to blend the multiple professional cultures within the clinical team. This seems clear enough yet the underlying, and debatable, assumption is that the physician must be, and is always, the leader of the team.

According to Dow, DiazGranados, Mazmanian, and Retchin (2013), leadership in dynamic environments such as the healthcare team is coproduced rather than fixed. It involves the cooperation of leaders and followers to achieve patient outcomes. Depending on the situation, all members of the team may be called on to lead or follow at times, yet all must enhance and influence the collaborative process. Leaders in this context must be able to involve team members who may be separated by hierarchical barriers, yet recognize instances when one member is better equipped to lead the team. For this to occur, all members of the team must have information about the range of professionals on the team, their scope of practice, and the resources each needs to accomplish its work (Carsten and Uhl-Bien 2013). In cases where leadership is ineffective in pulling together the multiple professionals cultures, obstacles can ensue in the form of conflict that negatively affects team process and outcomes (West et al. 2003). This may occur for many reasons, one of which is profession-centrism through which status hierarchies and profession-specific values bias members of the team to consider one's own profession as most important and, therefore, rightfully in control (Pecukonis, Doyle, and Bliss 2008).

COGNITIVE DEVELOPMENT AND PERSONAL EPISTEMOLOGY

The connection between human development and learning is, at first glance, obvious; yet, there is a rich history of varying conceptions of the relationship between these separate yet interrelated constructs (Hatch 2010). Notable exemplars of this controversy can be seen by the discrepant notions of the learning-development relationship characterized by Piaget and Vygotsky. Piaget argued that learning is dependent upon development—that underlying cognitive structures must be in place before learning can occur. In other words cognitive development leads learning (Duckworth 1964). Alternatively, Vygotsky argued that learning is a primary mechanism through which development occurs (Harland 2003). From this perspective learning leads development. Regardless of where one falls on this continuum it is apparent that the two must be considered as they each frame learning and development in a different light and influence how learning is defined and how the process is described.

Learning as a function of development was initially envisioned via the rise of behaviorism in the early twentieth century when learning was seen as an observable change in behavior as a function of one's interaction with the environment (Merriam, Caffarella, and Baumgartner 2007). Although the definition of the term learning has changed as a result of varying perspectives of learning, the idea of change remains a key feature of most definitions. According to Merriam and colleagues, an appropriate working definition that encompasses most theoretical frameworks is that "learning is a process that brings together cognitive, emotional, and environment influences and experiences for acquiring, enhancing, or making changes in one's knowledge, skills, values, and world views" (2007, 277).

From the perspective of cognitive or intellectual development the study of personal epistemology is an important concept. According to Clark (2006) each profession defines and defends its own type of complex knowledge and, often, does not see the whole due to a concentration on the parts. Personal epistemology is described by Hofer (2001) as the process through which one develops a conception of knowledge and how an individual uses that knowledge to understand the world. The seminal work of Perry in 1970 laid the foundation for this work. Perry developed a scheme of epistemological development by analyzing how students described their experiences and transformations with ways of thinking as they journeyed from their first to last years as undergraduates at Harvard University. Perry (1970) describes their "pilgrimage" as beginning from a conception that the world consists of absolute truths toward a recognition of the importance of context and finally toward commitment, where one recognizes the need to make a stand toward one way of thinking.

Perry (1970) describes movement through nine positions, or stages, which can be grouped into four major categories that describe one's epistemological stance. Perry describes individuals at the beginning of the spectrum as *dualists* (positions 1 and 2). At this stage, truth is experienced as absolute and unquestioned. To the dualist, the world is entirely black and white or right and wrong. There is an unquestioned identification with authority figures (i.e., parents or teachers) from whom all knowledge is garnered. At the next level, *multiplicity*, the individual begins to acknowledge uncertainty. As such a third conceptualization of knowledge develops and is included with the two opposing camps of right or wrong. Now the category of the "not yet known" is added. However, even though an individual recognizes that some things are not yet known, she or he still believes that they are indeed knowable, given more or better information. The transition to level three, *contextual relativism*, is seen as the most significant. At this level, the individual views the world as highly relativistic and context dependent. Most importantly, at this stage the individual begins to understanding that people are active meaning-makers. In both academic and personal contexts the individual must actively construct their own meaning rather than depend on authority figures to accomplish this for them. The final stage of Perry's scheme is *commitment with relativism*. At this point, knowledge is understood as a clarification of one's own understanding of the world. This continual clarification and refinement of one's way of knowing is accomplished through a continual process of reflection and reassessment.

Hofer (2004) argued that epistemic thought is theory-like and within the metacognitive processing domain. That is, epistemic beliefs are constructs, organized as theories that are activated during learning situations by the individual. According to this view, learning and knowledge building are influenced by "metacognitive monitoring of epistemological beliefs, resources and theories" (Hofer 2004, 46) and this metacognitive process that can be altered by context (e.g., teachers, task, learning environment). From this perspective, like Perry's conceptualization, epistemic cognition includes beliefs about the *nature of knowledge* (what one believes knowledge is). This includes beliefs about the *certainty of knowledge* (the degree that knowledge is perceived as fixed or modifiable) and *simplicity of knowledge* (the continuum of knowledge as discrete facts or as an interrelated whole, the components of which are relative, contingent, and contextual). Additionally, epistemic cognition involves the *nature of knowing* (how one comes to know) and includes beliefs about the *source of knowledge* (from outside, transmitted by authority or actively constructed by the self) and *justification of knowing* (knowledge claims are justified either through a reliance on authority or self-evaluative methods). From this perspective epistemic metacognition views epistemology as a set of beliefs that are organized into theories that operate at the metacognitive level that impact learning. These theories are engaged when one encounters new knowledge, attempts to solve an ill-structured problem or when one must construct knowledge in ill-defined contexts (having contradictory interpretations or claims).

According to Clark (2006), this sequential development of personal epistemology suggests that interprofessional education may help students transcend the dualistic nature of thinking, with a singular focus on their own profession's worldview, toward a stance of commitment with relativism with the acceptance that multiple professions are needed to adequately promote patient care. Likewise, when juxtaposed with social categorizations theory it may be that interprofessional experiences that promote epistemic growth will reduce intergroup bias. The construct of decentering, originally posed by Piaget (Piaget and Inhelder 1969), is particularly relevant here. Decentering occurs as a process of interacting with one's environment and results in an individual having the ability to attend to multiple attributes of a situation rather than just one. This foundational work was expanded to demonstrate its importance in cognitively structuring the social environment in order to develop successful interprofessional relationship (Feffer and Jahelka 1968; Feffer and Suchotliff 1966). As one becomes better able to understand the multiple perspectives of others, positive interpersonal relationship are more likely to be forged and maintained.

However, one question that remains is how one designs interprofessional curricula to propel students toward higher levels of epistemic cognition and an increased recognition of the complexity and multiplicity of care that can be achieved through interprofessional collaboration. One useful strategy has been proposed by Hofer (2001), who suggests that students must be challenged, by faculty or the experience itself, to foster epistemic doubt in order to lead to change. Clark (2006) posits that learning is a developmental process that requires time and effort. He suggests that the concept of scaffolded instruction (e.g., Vygotsky 1978) is important for supporting emerging interprofessional skills. Multiple and varied opportunities for practicing interprofessional skills can be used beginning with highly structured activities moving toward less structure as learners become more competent.

CONCLUSION

Clearly, theory is important for designing any educational intervention, yet given the additional confounders that may transpire when learning occurs within a social context among a diverse group of learners, no single theory, or constellation of theories from a specific paradigm can accommodate interprofessional learning. Rather, a number of diverse yet complimentary theories must be considered. Theories of learning provide a rich landscape describing how individuals learn alone, and with others in the social context. Theories from social psychology provide a view of how the context of learning within diverse groups can impact one's identity as a professional and how the learning environment can be articulated to reduce interprofessional bias and increase the likelihood of interprofessional identity development. Likewise, theories from organizational psychology further illuminate ways in which the structure of the learning environment can be authentically fashioned to promote a sense of team. Finally, as in all educational contexts, designers of IPE must consider the implications of cognitive and intellectual development for both learners and for curricular development.

REFERENCES

Adams, A., H. Barr, J. Carpenter, D. Cleverly, D. Colyer, C. Dickenson, D. Forman, J. Gilbert, M. Helme, L. Jones, and S. Lindqvist. 2006. *The Theory-Practice Relationship in Interprofessional Education*. London: The Higher Education Academy: Health Sciences and Practice. http://www.health.heacademy.ac.uk.

Ajzen I. 1985. "From Intentions to Actions: A Theory of Planned Behavior." In: *Action-control: From cognition to behavior*, edited by J. Kuhl and J.Beckmann, 11–39. Heidelberg, Germany: Springer.

———. 1991. "The Theory of Planned Behavior." *Organizational Behavior and Human Decision Processes* 50: 179–211.

Allport, G. W. 1954. *The Nature of Prejudice*. Cambridge, MA: Perseus Books.

Bandura, A. 1977. *Social Learning Theory*. Englewood Cliffs, NJ: Prentice Hall.

———. 1986. *Social Foundations of Thought and Action: A Social-cognitive Theory*. Englewood Cliffs, NJ: Prentice Hall.

Barr, H. 2002. *Interprofessional Education: Today, Yesterday and Tomorrow*. Occasional paper No. 5. London: Center for the Advancement of Interprofessional Education.

———. 2013. "Toward a Theoretical Framework for Interprofessional Education." *Journal of Interprofessional Care* 271, 4–9.

Brewer, M. B. 1991. "The Social Self: On Being the Same and Different at the Same Time." *Personality and Social Psychology Bulletin* 17: 475–82.

———. 1999. "The Psychology of Prejudice: Ingroup Love and Outgroup Hate?" *Journal of Social Issues* 55: 429–44.

Brewer, M. B., and N. Miller. 1988. "Contact and Co-Operation: When do they Work?" In *Eliminating Racism: Roles in Controversy*, edited by P. Katz and D. Taylor, 315–26. New York: Plenum Press.

Brewer, M. B., and S. Schneider. 1990. *Social Identity and Social Dilemmas: A Double-Edged Sword*. In *Social Identity Theory: Constructive and Critical Advances*, edited by D. Abrams and M. Hogg, 169–84. London: Harvester-Wheatsheaf.

Campion, M. A., E. M. Papper, and G. J. Medsker. 1996. "Relations between Work Team Characteristics and Effectiveness: A Replication and Extension." *Personnel Psychology* 49, no. 2: 429–52.

Carsten M. K., and M. Uhl-Bien. 2013. "Ethical Followership: An Examination of Followership Beliefs and Crimes of Obedience." *Journal of Leadership and Organizational Studies* 20: 49–61.

Clark, P. G. 2006. "What Would a Theory of Interprofessional Education Look Like? Some Suggestions for Developing a Theoretical Framework for Teamwork Training." *Journal of Interprofessional Care* 206: 577–89.

Cohen, S. G., and D. E. Bailey. 1997. "What Makes Teams Work: Group Effectiveness Research from the Shop Floor to the Executive Suite." *Journal of Management* 233: 239–90.

Colyer, H., M. Helme, and I. Jones. 2005. "The Theory-Practice Relationship in Interprofessional Education." Paper 7. London: The Higher Education Academy: Health Sciences and Practice. http://www.health.heacademy.ac.uk.

Cowen, N. 1988. "Evolving Conceptions of Memory Storage, Selective Attention, and Their Mutual Constraints Within the Human Information-Processing System." *Psychological Bulletin* 1042: 163–91.

Davis, L. L. 1994. "Looking Through the Constructivist Lens: The Art of Creating Nursing Work Groups." *Journal of Professional Nursing* 101: 38–46.

Dovidio, J. F., and S. L. Gaertner. 2000. "Aversive Racism and Selection Decisions: 1989 and 1999." *Psychological Science* 11: 1319–23.

Dow, A. W., D. DiazGranados, P. E. Mazmanian, and S. M. Retchin. 2013. "Applying Organizational Science to Health Care: A Framework for Collaborative Practice." *Academic Medicine* 887: 953–57.

Driver, R., H. Asoko, J. Leach, E. Mortimer, and P. Scott. 1994. "Constructing Scientific Knowledge in the Classroom." *Educational Researcher* 237: 5–12.

Duckworth, E. 1964. "Piaget Rediscovered." *Journal of Research in Science Teaching* 2: 172–75.

Erber, R., and S. T. Fiske. 1984. "Outcome Dependency and Attention to Inconsistent Information." *Journal of Personality and Social Psychology* 47: 709–26.

Feffer, M. H., and M. Jahelka. 1968. "Implications of the Decentering Concept for the Structuring of Projective Content." *Journal of Consulting and Clinical Psychology* 32: 434–41.

Feffer, M., and L. Suchotliff. 1966. "Decentering Implications of Social Interactions." *Journal of Personality and Social Psychology* 4: 415–22.

Freeth, D., M. Hammick, S. Reeves., I. Koppel, and H. Bar. 2005. *Effective Interprofessional Education: Development, Delivery and Evaluation.* Oxford: Blackwell Publishing.

Gaertner, S. L., J. F. Dovidio, P. A. Anastasio, B. A. Bachman, and M. C. Rust. 1993. "The Common Ingroup Identity Model: Recategorization and the Reduction of Intergroup Bias." In *European Review of Social Psychology*, edited by W. Stroebe and M. Hewsto, vol. 4, 1–26. New York: John Wiley.

Gaufberg, E. H., M. Badalden, R. Sands, and S. K. Bell. 2010. "The Hidden Curriculum: What Can We Learn from Third-Year Medical Student Narrative Reflections?" *Academic Medicine* 85, 11: 1709–16.

Gofton, W. and G. Regehr. 2006. "What we Don't Know we Are Teaching: Unveiling the Hidden Curriculum." *Clinical Orthopedics and Related Research* 449: 20–27.

Haidet, P., and H. F. Stein. 2005. "The Role of the Student–Teacher Relationship in the Formation of Physicians: The Hidden Curriculum as Process." *Journal of General Internal Medicine* 211, Suppl: 16–20.

Hafferty, F. W. 1998. "Beyond Curriculum Reform: Confronting Medicine's Hidden Curriculum." *Academic Medicine* 73: 403–7.

Hall, P. 2005. "Interprofessional Teamwork: Professional Cultures as Barriers." *Journal of Interprofessional Care* 191: 188–96.

Harland, T. 2003. "Vygotsky's Zone Of Proximal Development and Problem-Based Learning: Linking a Theoretical Concept with Practice through Action Research." *Teaching in Higher Education* 82: 263–72.

Harper, D. C., and D. P. Wacker. 1985. "Children's Attitudes toward Disabled Peers and the Effects of Mainstreaming." *Academic Psychology Bulletin* 7: 87–98.

Haslam, S. A. 1997. "Stereotyping and Social Influence: Foundations of Stereotype Consensus." In *The Social Psychology of Stereotyping and Group Life*, edited by R. Spears, P. J. Oakes, and N. Ellemers, 119–43. Oxford: Blackwell.

Hatch, J. A. 2010. "Rethinking the Relationship between Learning and Development: Teaching for Learning in Early Childhood Classrooms." *Educational Forum* 74, no. 3: 258–68

Hean, S., D. Craddock, and M. Hammick. 2012. "Theoretical Insights into Interprofessional Education: AMEE Guide No. 62." *Medical Teacher* 342: e78–e101.

Hean, S., D. Craddock, and C. O'Halloran. 2009. "Learning Theories and Interprofessional Education: A User's Guide." *Learning in Health Care and Social Care* 84: 250–62.

Hewstone, M., and R. J. Brown. 1986. "Contact is Not Enough: An Intergroup Perspective on the Contact Hypothesis." In *Contact and Conflict in Intergroup Encounters*, edited by M. Hewstone and R. J. Brown, 1–44. Oxford: Blackwell.

Hiemstra, R. 1994. "Self-Directed Learning." In *The International Encyclopedia of Education*, edited by T. Husen and T. N. Postlethwaite, second edition, 5394–99. Oxford: Pergamon Press.

Hofer, B. K. 2001. "Personal Epistemology Research: Implications for Learning and Teaching." *Journal of Educational Psychology Review* 134: 353–83.

———. 2004: "Epistemological Understanding as a Metacognitive Process: Thinking Aloud During Online Searching." *Educational Psychologist* 39, no. 1: 43–55.

Hollenbeck, J. R., B. Beersma, and M. E. Shouten. 2012. "Beyond Team Types and Taxonomies: A Dimensional Scaling Conceptualization for Team Description." *Academy of Management Review* 37: 82–106.

Illeris, K. 2004. *Adult Education and Adult Learning*. Malabar, FL: Krieger.

Jackson, P. 1968. *Life in Classrooms*. New York: Rinehart and Winston.

Jex, S. M., and T. W. Britt. 2008. *Organizational Psychology: A Scientist-Practitioner Approach*. Hoboken, NJ: Wiley.

Knowles, M. S. 1975. *Self-Directed Learning*. New York: Association Press.

———. 1980. *The Modern Practice of Adult Education: From Pedagogy to Andragogy*, second edition. New York: Cambridge Books.

Kolb, D. A. 1984. *Experiential Learning: Experience as the Source of Learning and Development*. Englewood Cliffs, NJ: Prentice Hall.

Lau, R. R. 1989. "Individual and Contextual Influences on Group Identification." *Social Psychology Quarterly* 52: 220–31.

Leape, L. L., and D. M. Berwick. 2005. "Five Years after to Err Is Human: What Have We Learned?" *Journal of the American Medical Association* 29319: 2384–90.

Mackie, D. M., and E. R. Smith. 1998. "Intergroup Relations: Insights form a Theoretical Integrative Approach." *Psychological Review* 105, 499–529.

Merriam, S. B., R. S. Caffarella, and L. M. Baumgartner. 2007. *Learning in Adulthood: A Comprehensive Guide*, third edition. San Francisco: Jossey Bass.

Mezirow, J. 1997. "Transformative Learning: Theory to Practice." In *New Directions for Adult and Continuing Education*, no. 74, edited by S. Imel, J. Ross-Grodon, and J. E. Coryell, 5–12. San Francisco: Jossey Bass.

Miller, G. 2003. "The Cognitive Revolution: A Historical Perspective." *Trends in Cognitive Science* 73: 141–44.

Miller N., and M. B. Brewer, eds. 1984. *Groups in Contact: The Psychology of Desegregation.* Orlando, FL: Academic.

Miller, N., M. B. Brewer, and K. Edwards. 1985. "Co-operative Interaction in Desegregated Settings: A Laboratory Analogue." *Journal of Social Issues* 41: 63–79.

Naor, M., and R. M. Milgram.1980. "Two Preservice Strategies for Preparing Regular Class Teachers for Mainstreaming." *Exceptional Children* 47: 126–29.

Neuberg, S. L., and S. T. Fiske. 1987. "Motivational Influences on Impressions Formation: Outcome Dependency, Accuracy-Driven Attention, and Individuating Processes." *Journal of Personality and Social Psychology* 53: 431–44.

Ormrod, J. E. 1995. *Human Learning*, second edition. Englewood Cliffs, NJ: Merrill.

Otten, S., and D. Wentura. 1999. "About the Impact of Automaticity and the Minimal Group Paradigm: Evidence form the Affective Priming Tasks." *European Journal of Social Psychology* 29: 1049–71.

Pecukonis, E., O. Doyle, and D. L. Bliss. 2008. "Reducing Barriers to Interprofessional Training: Promoting Interprofessional Cultural Competence." *Journal of Interprofessional Care* 224: 417–28.

Perry, W. G. 1970. *Forms of Intellectual and Ethical Development in the College Years: A Scheme.* New York: Holt, Rinehart, and Winston.

Pettigrew, T. F. 1971. *Racially Separate or Together?* New York: McGraw-Hill.

Pettigrew, T. F., and L. R. Tropp. 2006. "A Meta-Analytic Test of Intergroup Contact Theory." *Journal of Personality and Social Psychology* 905: 751–83.

Piaget, J., and B. Inhelder. 1969. *The Psychology of the Child.* Translated by H. Weaver. New York: Basic Books.

Poulton, B. C., and M. A. West. 1999. "The Determinants of Effectiveness in Primary Health Care Teams." *Journal of Interprofessional Care* 13, no. 1: 7–18.

Rankin, J. L., and J. L. Allen. 1991. "Investigating the Relationship between Cognition and Social Thinking in Adulthood: Stereotyping and Attributional Process." In *Bridging Paradigms: Positive Development in Adulthood and Cognitive Aging*, edited by J. D. Sinnott and J. C. Cavanaugh, 131–52. New York: Praeger.

Reeves, S., E. Suter, J. Goldman, T. Martimianakis, C. Chatalalsingh, and D. Dematteo. 2007. "A Scoping Review to Identify Organizational and Education Theories Relevant for Interprofessional Practice and Education Final Report to Health Canada. Toronto, Canada." University of Toronto, Li Ka Shing Knowledge Institute of St. Michael's Hospital.

Salas, E., T. L. Dickinson, S. A. Converse, and S. I. Tannenbaum. 1992. "Toward an Understanding of Team Performance and Training." In *Teams: Their Training and Performance*, R. W. Swezy and E. Salas, 3–29. Norwood, NJ: Ablex.

Sidanius, J., and F. Pratto. 1999. *Social Dominance: an Intergroup Theory of Social Hierarchy and Oppression*. Cambridge, UK: Cambridge University Press.

Steffe, L. P., and J. Gale, eds. 1995. *Constructivism in Education.* Hillsdale, NJ: Erlbaum.

Tajfel, H., and J. C. Turner. 1979. "An Integrative Theory of Intergroup Conflict." In *The Social Psychology of Intergroup Relations*, edited by W. G. Austin and S. Worchel, 33–47. Monterey, CA: Brooks/Cole.

Turner, J. C., M. A. Hogg, P. J. Oakes, S. D. Reicher, and M. S. Wetherell. 1987. *Rediscovering the Social Group: A Self-Categorization Theory*. Oxford: Blackwell.

Turner, J. C., and K. J. Reynolds. 2001. "The Social Identity Perspective in Intergroup Relations: Theories, Themes, and Controversies." In *Blackwell Handbook of Social Psychology: Intergroup Processes*, edited by R. Brown and S. L. Gaertner, 133–52. Malden, MA: Blackwell.

Vygotsky, L. S. 1978. *Mind in Society: The Development of Higher Psychological Processes.* Cambridge, MA: Harvard University Press.

West, M. A., C. S. Borrill, J. F. Dawson, F. Brodbeck, D. A. Shapiro, and B. Haward. 2003. "Leadership Clarity and Team Innovation in Health Care." *Leadership Quarterly* 144/5: 393–410.

West, M. A., and J. Lyubovnikova. 2012. “Real Teams or Pseudo Teams? The Changing Landscape Needs a Better Map.” *Industrial and Organizational Psychology* 51: 25–28.

———. 2014. “Illusions of Team Working in Health Care.” *Journal of Health Organization and Management* 27, no. 1: 134–42.

Wilder, D. A. 1986. “Social Categorization: Implications for Creation and Reduction of Intergroup Bias.” In *Advances in Experimental Social Psychology, 19*, edited by L. Berkowitz, 291–355. San Diego, CA: Academic Press.

Wilder, D., and A. F. Simon. 2001. “Affect as a Cause of Intergroup Bias.” In *Blackwell Handbook of Social Psychology: Intergroup Processes*, edited by R. Brown and S. L. Gaertner, 153–72. Malden, MA: Blackwell.

Chapter Three

Pedagogical Perspectives on Interprofessional Education

Andrea Pfeifle and Amy V. Blue

Educational theory includes the purpose, application, and interpretation of education and learning. As such, it can guide educational practice (Craddock 2006). Interprofessional education (IPE) is an educational practice wherein students from two or more professions learn about, from, and with each other to enable effective collaboration and improve health outcomes (World Health Organization 2010). As the term implies, IPE is a specific pedagogical approach that has an agreed-upon and overt purpose, for example, education across professions expressly directed to change health outcomes. This definition suggests that IPE includes two components: Attention to process, or the interaction that occurs between learners and attention to content that provides the context wherein IPE occurs. For educators who have been traditionally educated and trained in a particular area of expertise, such as medicine, nursing, psychology, and such, this emphasis on content and process presents a challenge, even for the most talented teachers. IPE can be difficult for a number of reasons: perhaps, because educators are unfamiliar with the term or the concept; or are uncomfortable working with learners from multiple professions; or because IPE superimposes nonconventional teaching of learners from different professions in a conventional uniprofessional environment; or because they are uncomfortable with learning formats other than the traditional lecture.

ADULT LEARNING THEORY

Viewed simplistically, IPE is inherently a student-centric approach, grounded in adult learning theory. The application of adult learning theory, developed by Knowles (1984; 1990) is frequently associated with IPE (Barr 2002, 23). Briefly, the assumptions of adult learning theory are as follows:

1. Adults need to know the relevance of what they are to learn.
2. Adults are task- and problem-oriented and prefer to learn when a task or problem is presented.
3. Adults bring life experience and existing knowledge to their learning.
4. Adults are self-directed in their learning.
5. Adult learners want to be treated with respect.
6. Adults are ready to learn things when they need to know them.

Other educational theories that can inform best practices in IPE and that have been discussed in the literature are experiential theory, social learning theory, constructivist theory, and transformative learning theory.

EXPERIENTIAL AND SOCIAL LEARNING THEORIES

The fundamental premise for IPE is the transference of knowledge and skills that students learn "about, from, and with" each other into intentional practice that ultimately benefits individual and population health. Preparing students for interprofessional practice through IPE requires a theoretical foundation that supports their evolution as effective team members within the context of interprofessional collaborative practice and research. This requires students to work together in interdependent work groups periodically over the course of their educational programs wherein they progressively apply newly acquired competencies in real-world experiential settings (IPE Collaborative 2011). Not surprisingly then, much of the literature describing a conceptual framework to support IPE is grounded in experiential and social learning theories.

Experiential learning theory (ELT) draws on the work of several well-known twentieth-century scholars such as William James, John Dewey, Kurt Lewin, Jean Piaget, Carl Jung, and others who made experience central to their theories of human development and learning (Kolb 1984). ELT defines learning as "the process whereby knowledge is created through the transformation of experience. Knowledge results from the combination of grasping and transforming experience" (Kolb 1984, 41). Learning is thus conceived as a continuous cycle (Kolb 1984), wherein immediate concrete experience forms the basis for observation and reflection on this experience is assimilated and generalized into the learner's "theory," from which new implications or hypotheses for action can be deduced. These hypotheses subsequently serve as guides from which the learner creates additional, new experiences that can be tested in other situations (Kolb 1984, 21–22). Accordingly, experience plays a central part in the learning process that builds upon the intimate relationships between learning, work, and other life activities. The benefits of interprofessional learning within an experiential context can facilitate students' socialization into the culture of interprofessional collaborative care (Kettenbach et al. 2011; Ker, Mole, and Bradley, 2014).

Social learning theory (SLT) recognizes learning as a cognitive process that takes place within a social context (Bandura 1963). Ball State University illustrated the overlapping constructs in ELT and SLT by applying these concepts in a service-learning curriculum for interdisciplinary student teams participating in "immersive learning" experience and producing a tangible outcome or product at the end of the experience (Gora 2007a; 2007b; Sanyal 2012).

Building on the integration of experiential and social learning theories, Clark (2006) suggested three underpinnings for IPE: epistemology and ontology of interdisciplinary inquiry, attention to cognitive and ethical student development, and attention to the development of learners as reflective practitioners.

Epistemology is the philosophical study of the origin, nature, limits, methods, and justification of knowledge (Piaget 1972). Many health professions education programs have evolved based on students' mastery of and the ability to generate and use specific types of complex knowledge and skills. This set of knowledge and skills in turn forms a cognitive framework or map for the profession's basic concepts, modes of inquiry, problem definitions, observational categories, representational techniques, standards of proof, types of explanation, and general ideas of what represents a discipline (Kuhn 1970). In addition to these cognitive maps, each profession has normative maps that include basic values, modes of moral reasoning, and methods of resolving ethical dilemmas (Drinka and Clark 2000). According to Clark (2006, 582),

> The acquisition of cognitive and normative maps is driven by the process of professional socialization. Becoming a health care professional means acquiring the particular traditions, customs, and practices; knowledge, beliefs, morals, and rules of conduct; and linguistic and symbolic forms of communication and the meanings they share that are associated with the practice of that particular profession. (citing Becher 1989)

The implications of these epistemological and ontological concepts for the development of a theoretical framework to undergird IPE have significant implications when teaching emerging members of the health professions. Clark (2006) further suggests that developmental theory is important when designing IPE. Blue and colleagues (2010) have similarly described IPE as a transformative process and integrated Mezirow's (1978) ten-step process for transformative learning into the Creating Collaborative Care (C3) curriculum at Medical University of South Carolina; which includes "genuine experience of dilemmas that require the development of new roles and new ways of acting; clearly, developing the interprofessional team skills necessary to succeed in a complex health care system encompasses this type of learning" (Blue et al. 2010, 1291–92).

COMPETENCIES, COMPETENCY FRAMEWORKS, AND LEARNING OBJECTIVES

Today, students enrolled in health professions education programs must demonstrate proficiency working within their individual areas of expertise as well as when working across disciplines to improve individual and population health outcomes (Greiner and Knebel 2003; Institute of Medicine 2008; Lancet 2010; World Health Organization 2006). Accordingly, many U.S. accreditation bodies now require health professions education programs to provide students with opportunities to learn about, from, and with one another to varying degrees (Zorek and Raehl 2013).

Competencies describe measurable or observable knowledge, skills, abilities, and behaviors deemed critical to successful job performance. Competencies as applied to health professions education programs describe what graduates have to be able to do independently and consistently in practice; as compared to what they know or are capable of doing under supervision, such as occurs during training (Fernandez et al. 2012).

Thistlewaite and colleagues (2014) recently described the relevance of competency frameworks across the collective group of health professionals working together in the health system and suggest they are useful for educators introducing IPE into their courses or programs, "as a guide to inform curricula in combination with appropriately aligned learning activities and assessments" (2014, 869). A number of organizations have adopted competency frameworks for interprofessional education, including the University of British Columbia (University of British Colombia 2008), the Canadian Interprofessional Health Collaborative (2010), and the Interprofessional Education Collaborative in the United States (IPEC 2011). Increasingly, IPE activities are being aligned with these competencies and assessment approaches are being developed to verify that learners have attained stated competencies (Thistlewaite et al. 2014).

The Core Competencies for Interprofessional Collaborative Practice (IPEC 2011) were developed in the United States to describe education and practice domains necessary to work effectively across professions to advance accessible, high-quality healthcare for individuals and communities. These include:

- Values/Ethics for Interprofessional Practice: Work with individuals of other professions to maintain a climate of mutual respect and shared values.
- Roles/responsibilities for Collaborative Practice: Use the knowledge of one's own role and those of other professions to appropriately assess and address the healthcare needs of the patients and populations served.
- Interprofessional Communication: Communicate with patients, families, communities, and other health professionals in a responsive and responsible manner that supports a team approach to the maintenance of health and the treatment of disease.
- Team and Teamwork: Apply relationship-building values and the principles of team dynamics to perform effectively in different team roles to plan and delivery patient- and population-centered care that is safe, timely efficient, effective, and equitable.

Representatives of the American Association of Colleges of Nursing, American Association of Colleges of Osteopathic Medicine, American Association of Colleges of Pharmacy, American Dental Education Association, Association of American Medical Colleges, and Association of Schools of Public Health developed these competencies as a basis for establishing learning objectives and designing learning activities to teach interprofessional collaborative practice at the prelicensure-certifying level, emphasizing the importance of informing interprofessional learning experiences by a theoretical framework.

While competencies describe standards that specify the knowledge, skills, and abilities required for success in the work place, objectives state intended outcomes for a specified learning activity, course, or module of instruction. Anderson and Krathwohl's adaptation of Bloom's Cognitive Taxonomy (2001, 67–78) classifies learning objectives into three domains knowledge/cognitive; psychomotor, and affective/attitudinal. Within these domains, learning at higher levels can be predicated on fundamental concepts and skills acquired and demonstrated at lower levels. Learning objectives are best framed in terms of active verbs that clarify how the learner is to demonstrate knowledge, skill, or affect. Well-written objectives provide clarity to the learner (and educator) about what is to be accomplished, how it is to be demonstrated and within what time frame. These learning objectives should also guide the assessment of learning outcomes. This taxonomy provides a useful framework for learning objectives describing the intended outcomes of IPE.

USING THEORY TO GUIDE PROGRAM DEVELOPMENT

In consideration of theoretical underpinnings of IPE and how to apply these to curriculum development, several authors (Benner et al. 2009; Blue et al. 2010; Charles, Bainbridge, and Gilbert 2010; Hean et al. 2012) have referenced the value of scaffolding and use of a developmental approach to IPE. With scaffolding, learners progress along a continuum of learning and professional development is explicitly recognized, with learning contexts (settings, objectives, tasks, characteristics of colearners, etc.) paired with the learner's phase of development. Similar to the milestone approach in medical resident education (Caverzagie et al. 2013), acknowledging a developmental continuum assumes that a learner is prepared to demonstrate acquisition of increasingly complex knowledge, skills, and attitudes at certain points in time along a progression, and that learning should follow in tandem. The work of Baxter-Magolda is relevant to IPE scaffolding in consideration of how learners move along a continuum from the most fixed to the most flexible ways of knowing. Baxter-Magolda describe how learners' early education within any realm typically begins with absolute knowing, in which knowledge is conceived as "fixed," either right or wrong, more certain than uncertain, and within the purview of instructors, not peers. Through experience, learners progress to transitional knowing, in which knowledge is uncertain in some areas, acquired by understanding information, dependent on the instructor to direct its application to different contexts, and explored with peers. Students next move to independent knowing, in which knowledge is largely uncertain, held by both instructors and peers, and comes from thinking for oneself. This independent knowing requires open-mindedness, allowing that others have their own beliefs that may be different than one's own. Ultimately, professionals' learning is characterized by contextual knowing, in which knowledge is uncertain but can be formatively assessed and ultimately evaluated and judged. Information is acquired by synthesizing expert opinion and existing evidence, as well as the experiences of self and others. Another perspective on scaffolding is based on the work of Vygotsky (from Hean et al. 2010) and the concept of the "zone of proximal development" (ZPD). In this theory, it is argued that learners are able to learn concepts, with support, that they cannot comprehend in isolation. Support systems, such as facilitators, more experienced peers, and computer-based technology, serve as guides to learning acquisition. Following this theory, scaffolding in IPE must be mindful of the continuum of task complexity, with learning moving from simple observation in realistic settings with two professions to complex cases involving multiple professions in authentic settings. Bainbridge and Wood (2012) describe sequencing considerations when designing IPE; emphasizing the importance of learners having the opportunity to learn about one another prior to learning with and from one another.

IPE can include a variety of instructional methods, and some of these methods are more suited to one particular theoretical approach than to others. As examples, case-based learning, problem-based learning, and team-based learning all have roots in social constructivist theory in that learning occurs through social interaction, applying and sharing one's own knowledge, and developing new knowledge through exchange. In these approaches, cases and problems must be relevant for learners and when a scaffolding approach is assumed, cases and problems for early learners should not be as complex as those designed for more advanced learners. Frequently, clinical cases presuming knowledge of disease processes and specific treatment approaches are not well-suited for early learners. However, when learners are more advanced in training, clinical cases and problems that detail symptoms and therapeutics may be more manageable to them and therefore provide greater educational yield, because learners can effectively apply knowledge and place new information in an existing knowledge framework.

Simulation, whether low-fidelity with role play and the use of standardized patients or high-fidelity with the use of computer-based mannequins, provides another educational approach based upon experiential learning theory (Kolb 1984). In simulation the learner is given a scenario that mirrors real life by presenting a real-world challenge to manage, and, through this, experienced learners develop insight and acquire new skills. Using a scaffolding approach, interprofessional simulation for early learners may focus on the development of interpersonal and basic teamwork skills, such asapproaching a patient regarding a potential medication error (University of Washington 2015, for example), and for learners with more advanced clinical training, a high-fidelity simulation may require knowledge of diseases and medications to work through the simulation but also focus on the development of more advanced interpersonal and teamwork skills (Shrader et al. 2011).

Reflection in and on action have been recommended as best practices for interprofessional education (Clark 2009). The reflective practitioner is one who is well-trained in both the science and the art of practice (Schön 1987). The scientific dimensions of practice include the technical knowledge and skills of the profession. The artistic dimensions of professional practice include integration of understanding and applied reasoning across several dimensions of practice, even where moral ambiguity, value conflicts, and ethical dilemmas exist. Professional practice also includes reflection on and in action; from both the procedural and interactive views (Jensen et al. 2000). John Dewey defined reflection as "active, persistent and careful consideration of any belief or supposed form of knowledge in the light of the grounds that support it and the further conclusion to which it tends" (Dewey 1933, 9). Reflection has been further described as "that process of reconstruction and reorganization of experience which adds to the meaning of experience"

(Rodgers 2002, 848). Reflective practice requires a grasp of the cognitive and normative elements of the profession as well as an understanding of how other professions might approach a problem and incorporating these perspectives into one's own practice. Not surprisingly then, several authors have endorsed the importance of reflection in IPE (Blue et al. 2015; Barr et al. 2005; Clark 2009; D'Eon, 2005; Oandasan and Reeves 2005; Parsell and Bligh 1998; Tsang 1998) and some have described models and approaches for teaching and learning reflective practice in this context that include attending to the organizational context and the culture of patient-centeredness (Zarezadeh 2009) and setting aside a time, place, and space for reflection (Clark 2009). Reflection with learners, such as assignments to reflect on learning during case discussions, experiential learning, and service-learning activities provides learners opportunity to develop skills pursuant to become effective reflective practitioners.

LEARNING THEORY APPLIED TO INTERPROFESSIONAL EDUCATION PROGRAM DESIGN

Many interprofessional learning activities are single events for a selected group of learners but others occur longitudinally over time as part of an IPE program. Regardless, using learning theory to undergird instructional design and curriculum decisions is imperative. The Medical University of South Carolina provides an example of an institution that has moved beyond using theory to guide an individual learning activity to using educational theory to inform the development and sequencing of activities at both the programmatic and single-learning event levels (Blue et al. 2010). This program combined several adult learning theories including Mezirow (1978; 1997); Kegan (1994); and Baxter-Magolda (1999; 2000) in order to create a foundational context of transformative learning along a developmental continuum. These theories provided the context for multiple and varied learning activities within the IPE program so that students could develop knowledge and skills at appropriate levels and in various contexts to advance their learning. Additionally, based on the work of Anderson and Krathwol in revising Bloom's Taxonomy, the conceptual framework guiding program development was grounded on the argument that students should follow a recursive learning process based on an intentional progression of acquisition, application, and demonstration of their IPE knowledge and skills. Learning activities were planned at the programmatic and individual levels with this framework in mind: *acquisition* refers to learning associated with remembering and understanding; *application* refers to learning associated with applying and analyzing; and *demonstration* refers to learning associated with evaluating and creating. At the programmatic level, goals were designed based on this framework (Blue et al. 2010), and at the individual learning activity level, it was also applied (Blue et al. 2015). For example, in Blue and colleagues (2015), the authors describe how the IPE student fellowship was designed for students to complete learning activities in the three phases of acquisition, application, and demonstration.

SUMMARY

Using theory to guide program development provides educators a framework on which to design IPE and to allocate the resources to support these experiences. Reliance on theory can guide the reasoned development of a learning event/program and inform learning outcome assessment and program evaluation processes. IPE by definition is based upon adult learning theory and the premise of an active, self-directed learner who learns through engagement with others in relevant learning contexts and has opportunity to apply existing knowledge to new situations and problem-solving contexts. Experiential and social learning theories are two educational theories predominantly underpinning interprofessional learning. Health professions education emphasizes a competency approach to curriculum design to ensure that graduates have the knowledge and skills for professional practice. The IPEC developed Core Competencies for Interprofessional Collaborative Practice that provide IPE educators with competency domains and subcompetencies to guide curriculum development. Educational theories can inform design of multiple types of learning activities to address the competencies, including the value of scaffolding as a developmental approach to a learner's acquisition of interprofessional collaborative skills.

REFERENCES

Anderson, Lorin W., and David A. Krathwol. 2001. *A Taxonomy for Learning Teaching and Assessing: A Revision of Bloom's Taxonomy of Educational Objectives*. New York: Longman.

Bainbridge, Lesley, and Victoria Isobel Wood. 2012. "The Power of Prepositions: Learning With, From and About Others in the Context of IPE." *Journal of Interprofessional Care* no. 26: 452–58.

Bandura, Albert. 1963. *Social Learning and Personality Development*. New York: Hold, Rinehart, and Winston.

Barr, Hugh. 2002. *Interprofessional Education: Today, Yesterday, and Tomorrow; A Review*. London, UK: Higher Education Academy, Health Sciences and Practice Network.

Barr, H., I. Koppel, S. Reeves et al. 2005. *Effective IPE: Argument, Assumption, and Evidence*. Oxford, UK: Blackwell.

Barr, Hugh, and Helena Low. 2011. "Principles of IPE." CAIPE. January 2011. http://caipe.org.uk/resources/principles-of-interprofessional-education/.

Barrett, G., R. Greenwood, and K. Ross. 2003. "Integrating IPE into 10 Health and Social Care Programmes." *Journal of Interprofessional Care* 17, no. 3: 292–301.

Bartlett, D., D. Lucy, L. Bisbee, and A. Conti-Becker. 2009. "Understanding the Professional Socialization of Canadian Physical Therapy Students: A Qualitative Investigation." *Physiotherapy Canada.* 61: 15–25.

Baxter-Magolda, Marcia. 1999. *Creating Contexts for Learning and Self-Authorship: Constructive-Developmental Pedagogy*, first edition. Nashville, TN: Vanderbilt University Press.

———. 2000. "Teaching to Promote Intellectual and Personal Maturity: Incorporating Students' Worldviews and Identities into the Learning Process." *New Directions for Teaching and Learning* 82. San Francisco: Jossey-Bass.

Becher, Tony. 1989. *Academic Tribes and Territories: Intellectual Enquiry and the Cultures of Disciplines*. Bristol, PA: The Society for Research into Higher Education and Open University Press.

Benner, P., M. Sutphen, V. Leonard, and L. Day. 2009. "Educating Nurses: A Call for Radical Transformation." Carnegie Foundation for the Advancement of Teaching. San Francisco: Jossey-Bass.

Blue, A. V., B. Chesluk, L. Conforti, and E. Holmboe. 2015. "Assessment and Evaluation in IPE: Exploring the Field." *Journal of Allied Health* 44, no. 2 (Summer): 73–82.

Blue, A. V., A. W. Chessman, C. Thiedke et al. 2014. "Student Observations and Ratings of Preceptors' Interactions with Patients: The Hidden Curriculum." *Teaching and Learning in Medicine* 16, no. 4: 312–16.

Blue, A. V., M. Mitcham, Y. Koutalos, D. Howell, and A. Leaphart. 2005. "Attaining Interprofessional Competencies through a Student Interprofessional Fellowship Program." *Journal of Interprofessional Care* 29, no. 3 (May): 253–55.

Blue, A. V., M. Mitcham, T. Smith, J. Raymond and G. Greenberg. 2010. "Changing the Future of Health Professions: Embedding IPE within an Academic Health Center." *Academic Medicine* 85, no. 8: 1290–95.

Breitbach, A., D. Sargeant, P. Gettemeier et al. 2013. "From Buy-In to Integration: Melding an Interprofessional Initiative into Academic Programs in the Health Professions." *Journal of Allied Health* 42, no. 3: e67–e73.

Canadian Interprofessional Health Collaborative. 2010. *A National Interprofessional Competency Framework.* August. http://www.cihc.ca/files/CIHC_IPCompetencies_Feb1210.pdf.

Caverzagie, K. J., W. F. Iobst, E. M. Aagaard, S. Hood, D. A. Chick, and G. C. Kane. 2013. "The Internal Medicine Reporting Milestones and the Next Accreditation System." *Annals of Internal Medicine* 158, no. 7: 557–59.

Centre for the Advancement of IPE (CAIPE). 1997. *IPE—a definition*. London: CAIPE Bulletin 13: 19.

Charles, Grant, Lesley Bainbridge, and John Gilbert. 2010. "The University of British Columbia Model of Interprofessional Education." *Journal of Interprofessional Care* 24, no. 1: 9–18.

Clark, Phillip G. 2006. "What Would a Theory of IPE Look Like? Some Suggestions for Developing a Theoretical Framework for Teamwork Training." *Journal of Interprofessional Care* 20, no. 6: 577–89.

———. 2009. "Reflecting on Reflection in IPE: Implications for Theory and Practice." *Journal of Interprofessional Care* 23, no. 3: 213–23.

Coster, S., I. Norman, T. Murrels, S. Kitchen, E. Meerabeau, E. Sooboodoo, and L. d'Avray. 2008. "Interprofessional Attitudes Amongst Undergraduate Students in the Health Professions: A Longitudinal Questionnaire Survey." *International Journal of Nursing Studies* 45, no. 11: 1667–81. doi: 10.1016/ijnurstu.2008.Epub, 18 April 2008.

Craddock, D., C. O'Halloran, A. Borthwick, and K. McPherson. 2006. "IPE in Health and Social Care: Fashion or Informed Practice?" *Learning in Health and Social Care* 5, no. 4: 220–42.

D'Amour, Danielle and Ivy Oandasan. 2005. "Interprofessionality as the Field of Interprofessional Practice and IPE: An Emerging Concept." *Journal of Interprofessional Care*, Suppl 1: 8–20.

D'Eon, Marcel. 2005. "A Blueprint for Interprofessional Learning." *Medical Teacher* 26, no. 7: 604–9.

Dewey, J. 1933. *How We Think. A Restatement of the Relation of Reflective Thinking to the Educative Process* (Revised edn.). Lexington, MA: D C Heath & Co.

Drinka, Theresa J. K., and Phillip G. Clark. 2000. *Health Care Teamwork: Interdisciplinary Practice and Teaching*. Westport, CT: Auburn House/Greenwood.

Duncan, M., M. Alperstein, P. Mayers, L. Olckers, and T. Gibbs. 2006. "Not Just Another Multi-Professional Course! Part 1. Rationale for a Transformative Curriculum." *Medical Teacher* 28, no. 1: 59–63.

Fernandez, N., V. Dory, G. Ste-Marie, M. Chaput, B. Charlin, and A. Bouchere. 2012. "Varying Conceptions of Competence: An Analysis of How Health Sciences Educators Define Competence." *Medical Education* 46: 357–65.

Freeth, Della, Marilyn Hammick, Scott Reeves, Ivan Koppel, and Hugh Barr. 2005. *Effective IPE: Development, Delivery & Evaluation*. Oxford: Blackwell.

Freeth, Della, and Maggie Nicol. 1998. "Learning Clinical Skills: An Interprofessional Approach." *Nurse Education Today* 18: 455–61.

Frenk, Julio, Lincoln Chen, Zulfiqar A. Bhutta et al. 2010. "Health Professionals for a New Century: Transforming Education to Strengthen Health Systems in an Interdependent World." *Lancet* 376: 1923–58.

Gora, Jo Ann. 2007a. "Ivory Towers No More." *University Business* (October): 52–53. http://www.universitybusiness.com/article/ivory-towers-no-more.

———. 2007b. "Ball State University's Immersive Learning." *University Business*. http://www.universitybusiness.com/article/ball-state-universitys-immersive-learning.

Greene, R. J., G. F. Cavell, and S. H. D. Jackson. 2006. "Interprofessional Clinical Education of Medical and Pharmacy Students." *Medical Education* 30, no. 2: 129–33.

Greiner, Ann C. and Elisa Knebel. 2003. Committee on the Health Professions Education Summit." *Health Professions Education: Abridge to Quality*. Washington, DC: Institute of Medicine.

Hammick, M., D. Freeth, I. Koppel, S. Reeves, and H. Barr. 2008. "A Best Evidence Systematic Review of IPE BEME Guide No. 9." *Medical Teacher* 29, no. 8: 735–51.

Hean, S., D. Craddcock, M. Hammick, M. Hammack, and M. Hammick. 2012. Theoretical Insights Into Interprofessional Education: AMEE Guide No. 62. *AMEE Guide: Theories in Medical Education*, 78–101.

Howkins, Elizabeth and Althea Allison. 1997. "Shared Learning for Primary Health Care Teams: A Success Story." *Nurse Education Today* 17: 225–31.

Institute of Medicine. 2008. *Retooling for an Aging America: Building the Healthcare Workforce*. Washington, DC.

IPE Collaborative Expert Panel. 2011. "Core Competencies for Interprofessional Collaborative Practice: Report of an Expert Panel." Washington, DC. http://www.aacn.nche.edu/educationresources/ipecreport.pdf. Accessed August 17, 2015.

Jensen, G. M., J. Gwyer, K. F. Shepard, and L. M. Hack. 2000. "Expert Practice in Physical Therapy." *Physical Therapy* 80, no. 1: 28–43.

Kegan, Robert. 1994. *In Over Our Heads: The Mental Demands of Modern Life*. Cambridge, MA: Harvard University Press.

Ker, J., L. Mole, and P. Bradly. (2014). "Early Introduction to Interprofessional Learning: a Simulated Ward Environment." *Medical Education* 37: 248–55.

Kettenbach, G., I. Ruebling, N. Westhus, et al. 2011. "Comparison of Pre- and Post-Course Attitudes and Perceptions of an Interprofessional Course." *Collaborating Across Borders III: Interprofessional Collaboration: From Concept to Preparation for Practice*. Tucson, AZ: Elsevier Sciences.

Knowles, M. 1990. *The Adult Learner: A Neglected Species*, 4th Edition. Houston, TX: Gulf Publishing.

Knowles, M. S. et al. 1984. *Andragogy in Action. Applying Modern Principles of Adult Education*. San Francisco: Jossey Bass.

Kolb, David. 1984. *Experiential Learning: Experience as the Source of Learning and Development*. Hillsdale, NJ: Prentice Hall.

Konrad, Shelley Cohen, and David M. Browning. 2012. "Relational Learning and Interprofessional Practice: Transforming Health Education for the 21st Century." *Work* 41, no. 3: 247–51.

Kuhn, Thomas S. 1970. *The Structure of Scientific Revolutions*, second edition. Chicago: University of Chicago Press.

Maine, Lucinda. 2012. "Educating for Practice: Improving Health by Linking Education to Practice using IPE." Global Forum on Innovation in Health Professional Education Washington, DC: Institute of Medicine. http://www.iom.edu/~/media/Files/Activity%20Files/Global/InnovationHealthProfEducation/2012-AUG-29/0105-Maine.pdf Accessed on 4/2/2014.

Mann, K. V., J. McFetridge-Durdle, R. Martin-Misener et al. 2009. "IPE for Students of the Health Professions: The 'Seamless Care' Model." *Journal of Interprofessional Care* 23, no. 3: 224–33.

Mayers, P., M. Alperstein, M. Duncan, L. Olckers, and T. Gibbs. 2006. "Not Just Another Multi-Professional Course! Part 2: Nuts and Bolts of Designing a Transformed Curriculum for Multi-Professional Learning." *Medical Teacher* 28, no. 2: 152–57.

Mezirow, Jack. 1978. "Perspective Transformation." *Adult Education* 28: 100–10.

———. 1997. "Transformative Learning: Theory to Practice." *New Directory for Adults and Continuing Education*, 74: 5–12.

Morison, S., M. Boohan, J. Jenkins, and M. Moutray. 2003. "Facilitating Undergraduate Interprofessional Learning in Healthcare: Comparing Classroom and Clinical Learning for Nursing and Medical Students." *Learning in Health and Social Care* 2, no. 2: 92–104.

Mu, K., C. Chao, G. Jensen, and C. Royeen. 2004. "Effects of Interprofessional Rural Training on Students' Perceptions of Interprofessional Health Care Services." *Journal of Allied Health* 33, no. 2: 125–31.

Oandasan, Ivy, and Scott Reeves. 2005. "Key Elements for IPE. Part 1: The Learner, the Educator and the Learning Context." *Journal of Interprofessional Care* Suppl 1: 21–38.

Parsell, Glennys, and John Bligh. 1998. "Educational Principles Underpinning Successful Shared Learning." *Medical Teacher* 20: 522–29.

Piaget, Jean. 1972. "The Epistemology of Interdisciplinary Relationships." *Interdisciplinarity: Problems of Teaching and Research in Universities*, 127–13. Paris, France: Organization for Economic Cooperation and Development (OECD).

Reeves, S, M. Tassone, K. Parker, S. Wagner, and B. Simmons. 2012. "IPE: An Overview of Key Developments in the Past Three Decades." *Work* 41: 233–45.

Rodgers, Carol. 2002. "Defining Reflection: Another Look at John Dewey and Reflective Thinking." *Teachers College Record* 104: 842–66.

Ruebling, Irma, and Charlotte Royeen. 2010. "Saint Louis University IPE Program." *Journal of Allied Health* 39, Suppl 1: e123–24.

Sanyal, Rajib. 2012. "Dean's forum." *American Journal of Business* 27, no. 2: doi:10.1108/ajb.2012.54027baa.002.

Schmidt, M., J. Gilbert, B. Brandt, and R. Weinstein. 2013. "The Coming of Age of IPE and Practice." *American Journal of Medicine* 126, no. 4: 284–88.

Schön, Donald. 1987. *Educating the Reflective Practitioner*. San Francisco: Jossey-Bass.

Shepard, Katherine, and Gail Jensen. 1990. "Physical Therapist Curricula for the 1990s: Educating the Reflective Practitioner." *Physical Therapy* 70, no. 9: 566–73.

Shrader, Sarah, L. McRae, W. M. King 4th, and D. Kern. 2011. "A Simulated Interprofessional Rounding Experience in a Clinical Assessment Course." *American Journal of Pharmacy Education* 75, no. 4: 61.

Thistlewaite, Jill E. 2012. "IPE: A Review of Context, Learning and the Research Agenda." *Medical Education* 46: 58–70.

Thistlewaite, J. E., D. Forman, L. R. Matthews, G. D. Rogers, C. Steketee, and T. Yassine. 2014. "Competencies and Frameworks in IPE: A Comparative Analysis." *Academic Medicine* 89, no. 6: 869–75.

Tsang, Nai Ming. 1998. "Re-examining Reflection: A Common Issue of Professional Concern in Social Work, Teacher and Nursing Education." *Journal of Interprofessional Care* 12: 21–32.

University of British Columbia, College of Health Disciplines. 2008. *The British Columbia Competency Framework for Interprofessional Collaboration*. Vancouver: University of British Columbia. http://www.chd.ubc.ca/files/file/BC%20Competency%20Framework%20for%20 IPC.pdf.

University of Washington Center for Health Science IPE, Research, and Practice. 2015. "Error Disclosure Toolkit." Available from: http://collaborate.uw.edu/educators-toolkit/error-disclosure-toolkit/error-diclosure-toolkit.html. Accessed April 9, 2014.

Walsh, C. I., M. F. Gordon, M. Marshal, F. Wilson, and T. Hunt. 2005. "Interprofessional Capability: A Developing Framework for IPE." *Nurse Education Practice* 5: 230–37.

World Health Organization. 2006. "Working Together for Health Report." The 59th World Health Assembly (WHA.59.23). 237. Geneva, Switzerland.

———. 2010. "Framework for Action on IPE & Collaborative Practice." Geneva: World Health Organization. April. http://whqlibdoc.who.int/hq/2010/WHO_HRH_HPN_10.3_eng.pdf.

Zarezadeh, Yadolah. 2009. "The Teaching and Learning Reflective Practice in Medicine, Nursing, and Physiotherapy: A Grounded Theory Study." PhD thesis Newcastle University.

Zorek, Joseph, and Cynthia Raehl. 2013. "IPE Accreditation Standards in the USA: A Comparative Analysis." *Journal of Interprofessional Care* 27, no. 2: 123–30.

Chapter Four

Interprofessional Education as Organizational Change

Alan Dow, Colleen Lynch,
John Cyrus, and Tanya Huff

Although interprofessional education (IPE) is seen as essential for expanding and enhancing teamwork in healthcare and improving health outcomes (Institute of Medicine 2001; 2003), implementing effective IPE faces many barriers (Jones et al. 2012; Lawlis, Anson, and Greenfield 2014). These barriers exist at many levels, ranging from systematic prioritization and resource allocation to individual resistance at the level of faculty, practitioners, and students. In order to overcome these barriers and implement successful IPE experiences, educational leaders need to be adept at navigating the process of organizational change.

To help navigate this organizational change, this chapter outlines the barriers to IPE defined in the literature, describes two frameworks of organizational change including presenting a model of how their concepts overlap, and applies this model through two case studies. The goal of this chapter is to provide educational leaders with a roadmap for navigating the organizational change implicit in implementing IPE.

BARRIERS TO INTERPROFESSIONAL EDUCATION

The factors that influence the success of IPE efforts, both positively and negatively, have been conceptualized across three levels: macro, meso, and micro (Oandasan and Reeves 2005). The macro level includes interactions with senior institutional leaders as well entities external to the institution. The meso level includes interactions at the level of students, faculty, and staff involved in interprofessional activities. Finally, the micro level includes interactions within the individual. Although the three levels are interconnected, defining them separately helps to describe the challenges facing interprofessional educators. At each level, the barriers involve different stakeholders for whom the value of IPE may be calculated differently, and, hence, the approach to achieving buy-in and implementing organizational change may vary.

The Macro Level

At the broadest level, a number of barriers face leaders of IPE. As a newly emphasized curricular element, IPE competes with existing curriculum for prioritization. This competition is driven by external forces such as the accreditors, licensing examinations, and professional certification as well as internal forces such as institutional strategic planning and, perhaps most importantly, resource allocation. For example, building on the call from the Institute of Medicine (2003), accreditors have implemented requirements for IPE in almost all health professions (Zorek and Raehl 2013). In response, a number of institutions have created centers for IPE to coordinate campus-wide efforts (Dow et al. 2014), integrated IPE into institutional strategic plans, and added an interprofessional emphasis to faculty advancement protocols. Many of these institutional actions have been supported by an allocation of resources to expand offerings in interprofessional education. Indeed, many of the macro barriers to IPE have waned as IPE has become accepted as a standard part of health professions education.

Yet, other areas in the macro level have been slower to adopt an interprofessional emphasis. Licensure and certification processes have not pivoted toward interprofessional models. As a result, while educators seek to train interprofessionally collaborative graduates, the models of care in which most learners train and most graduates will practice remain decidedly uncollaborative (Josiah Macy Jr. Foundation 2013). This conflict between the desired and current state is a substantive barrier to effective health professions education, especially to IPE.

The Meso Level

The meso level is where faculty, students, and staff interact in IPE curriculum. Here, a number of additional barriers to IPE exist. Curriculum can be seen as having several components: learning goals, learning activities, assessment, and situational factors (Fink 2013). At each of these components, interprofessional educators can face barriers, and delineating these barriers is essential for curriculum planning and implementation.

Learning goals to guide interprofessional education can be difficult to articulate. While interprofessional competencies such as the Competencies for Interprofessional Collaborative Practice (Interprofessional Education Collaborative Expert Panel 2011) have sought to create overarching competencies, educators have noted continued challenges with defining them to shape the instruction and assessment of specific experiences (Reeves 2012; Thistlewaite et al. 2014). In addition, most educational research in interprofessional education examines only short-term and superficial outcomes (Abu-Rish et al. 2012). As such, the evidence base for effective interprofessional education, from which educators can draw to develop new programs, is limited (Institute of Medicine 2015). Educators often struggle to link the clearly articulated problems with communication in healthcare to curriculum and have to rely on personal experience to develop the goals, activities, and assessments of IPE programs.

In addition, IPE faces some unique situational factors. Because IPE inherently involves bringing together students from different programs, IPE often brings to light differences in scheduling or the length of degree programs. Similarly, IPE may be emphasized differently by various participating programs, such as whether activities are compulsory or required or how individual performances figures into grades. All of these factors can lead to IPE ironically accentuating differences rather than the commonalities on the healthcare team. Finally, IPE, by combining large numbers of students, may present unique challenges in the size of educational spaces and number of instructors needed for educational activities.

The Micro Level

At the micro or individual level, IPE faces barriers as well. All professionals are socialized into their profession-specific culture. This socialization inherently leads to biases, which in turn can lead to real or perceived disrespect. In addition, conceptualization about expertise—either clinical or educational—can be challenged by similar expertise in other professions. As such, attitudes of students, staff, and faculty toward IPE may be fraught with insecurity. When added to the curricular constraints of already full curricula and a debated theoretical basis, students, staff, and faculty may be understandably reluctant to embrace IPE. Even for educators willing to embrace IPE, the opportunities for faculty development are limited and guiding principles have only been recently established (Hall and Zierler 2015).

IPE can thus be seen as an endeavor of overcoming barriers. Although some of the macro level barriers have begun to become enablers, educators still face significant barriers at the meso level that can reinforce resistance at the micro level. How then could an educator faced with such barriers succeed at implementing effective interprofessional education? Some frameworks for organizational change can guide this work.

FRAMEWORKS FOR ORGANIZATIONAL CHANGE

During the 1940s, social scientist Kurt Lewin conducted research on group interactions and attitude change at the University of Iowa and the Massachusetts Institute of Technology's Center for Group Dynamics and described four broad themes: field theory, group dynamics, action research, and planned change. While often treated separately in discussions of his work, Lewin saw these four areas as inextricably linked in understanding and implementing change. Each area reinforced and supported each other (Bargal 2006; Lewin 1943).

Lewin's field theory holds that the key to understanding group behavior is the "quasi-stationary equilibrium," a state of continuous small-scale adaptation maintained by a complex system of interacting forces or fields. These fields, such as social habit or organizational culture, constitute the group environment in which an individual or an institution functions (Burnes 2004). According to field theory, understanding and potentially altering the way groups and organizations act would require an analysis of the dynamic balance of forces working in opposing directions.

Lewin's work in group dynamics describes the influence of groups over the individual. It acknowledges that many of these forces from field theory are most visible at the group level, but deeply influence actions and beliefs at the individual level (Lewin 1947). Therefore, Lewin believed, the focus of any change effort must begin at the group level. By creating new norms, removing obstacles to individual change, and reinforcing individual change as group culture, overall change in groups can occur.

Action research represents the process by which a group or organization analyzes the forces that maintain the equilibrium. The group identifies driving and restraining forces, and, through identification of these forces, change can occur by upsetting the equilibrium between these forces. Change can be accomplished either by adding conditions favorable to the change or by reducing the forces opposed to the sought after change (Bozak 2003).

Lewin's research on planned change can be summarized by his three-step change process of "unfreeze," "change," and "re-freeze" (figure 4.1, outer ring). The "unfreeze" step is achieved by disrupting the status quo by either strengthening the driving forces or by weakening the opposing forces to change. In this step, it is often necessary, as Lewin writes, to "break open the shell of complacency and self-righteousness" by "bring[ing] about deliberately an emotional stir up" (Lewin 1947). The "change" step identifies and implements the most acceptable methods available to move a group from the previous status quo to a new desired state. Achieving desired change often requires several methods. Finally, the "refreeze" step of Lewin's model represents the attempt to ensure that any gains made during the "change" step are secured and not prone to backsliding. This final step in the process relies heavily on Lewin's previously stated belief that successful change must be solidified at the group level for individuals to be affected (Burnes 2004). Lewin believed that change efforts often fail because they achieve only short-term, individual results and are not cemented into a new status quo in the group or organizational culture.

Other researchers have built on Lewin's work on group and organizational change. In 1996, John Kotter added a major contribution to the field of change management with a practical, eight-step roadmap for organizational change (Kotter 1996) (inner ring of figure 4.1). The first four steps challenge the status quo and make the case for change (Lewin's "unfreeze"). Steps five through seven capture the process of actual change including its iterative

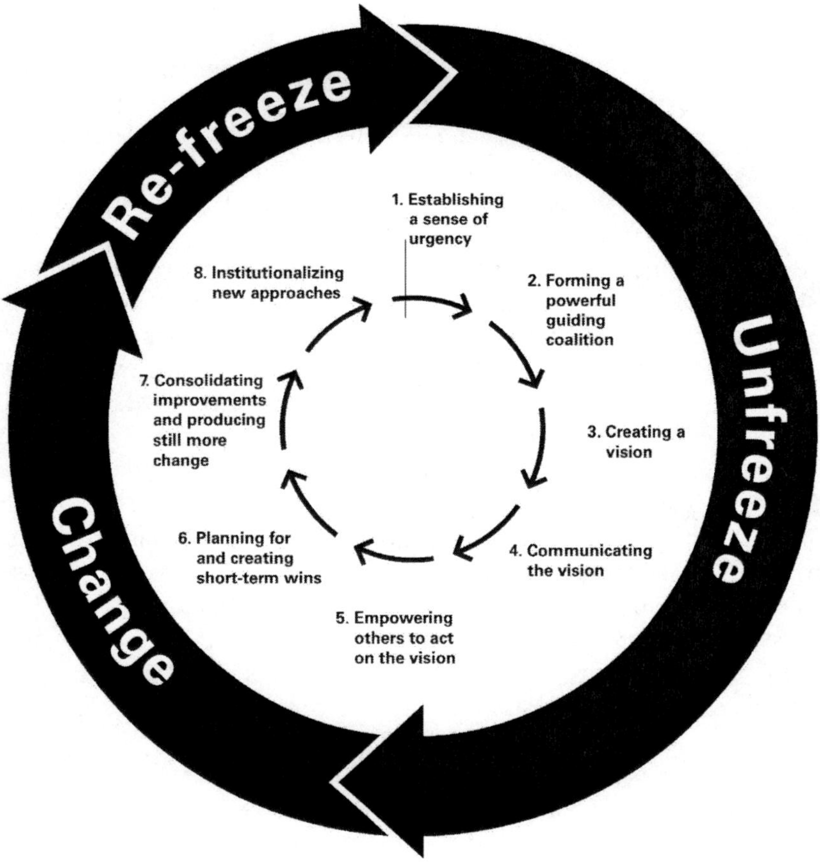

Figure 4.1. The Process of Group or Organizational Change as Described by Lewin (outer) and Kotter (inner), Depicted as Concentric Processes and Showing Overlap between the Models. Photo by author.

nature (Lewin's "change"). Step eight institutionalizes the change (Lewin's "refreeze"). In Kotter's words:

> The first four steps in the transformation process help defrost a hardened status quo. If change were easy, you wouldn't need all that effort. Phases five to seven then introduce many new practices. The last stage grounds the changes in the corporate culture and helps make them stick. (Kotter 1996, 22)

Aside from this quote that undoubtedly owes much to Lewin, Kotter's eight steps reflect additional application of Lewin's theory. Kotter stresses the importance of creating an environment where change can be successful. He describes mentally preparing the group to undertake the process by "establishing a sense of urgency." Framing the change as an organizational crisis similar to Lewin's "emotional stir up" disrupts group complacency and paves the way for the following steps. Many organizations make the mistake of failing to establish a sense of urgency regarding the need for change (Borkowski 2011). This phase is critically important for successful change efforts, as this initial phase of Kotter's change process is responsible for approximately 50 percent of failed change efforts (Kotter 2007). According to Kotter, urgency becomes optimal for successful change at the point when roughly 75 percent of the management of an organization becomes convinced that business as usual is completely unacceptable.

Building on the opportunity created by the crisis mentality, Kotter stresses the significance of "gathering a guiding coalition" of key players from across the organization that will minimize resistance from internal groups and enable creation of change at the group level so that it can be passed down to the individual. Though many transformational change processes initially begin with only one or two individuals, it is important for the leadership coalition to grow and to strengthen over time. Kotter (2007) indicates failure is likely at this step if a critical mass of supporters is not achieved early in the effort. Additionally, Antoni (2007) found that outcomes of change processes were positively influenced by stakeholder participation in change processes. This coalition is essential for "creating a vision" or shared mental model of the necessary change and "communicating the vision" of the coalition more broadly. The importance of vision transfer from the coalition to the larger group and specific individuals is further demonstrated in Kotter's fifth step, "empowering other to act on the vision," wherein structural, personnel, attitudinal, or other obstacles are removed so that the desired change can be taken up on a broader scale. Steps six and seven focus largely on maintaining organizational momentum by using short-term wins to demonstrate the value of the change, drive further change, and avoid a relapse into complacency. Kotter (2007) states that until changes sink deeply into organizational culture, new approaches are fragile and subject to regression. This process can often take five to ten years. Instead of prematurely celebrating the effects of change, leaders should use the credibility gained by the initial victory to continue to implement the change. The final step, "institutionalizing new approaches," emphasizes the necessity of anchoring changes in the culture of the organization due to the ability of a culture to influence individual behavior. This step relies on the idea that culture is exerted by the group on the individual without conscious intent, influencing the individual as they work in the organization (Kotter 1996).

These models are presented as overlapping frameworks for organizational change that can be used to understand the process of implementing innovations in interprofessional education and practice. Breaking through the silos that define education and practice in healthcare is a challenge, but these frameworks provide an outline for how to approach this challenge. Using these two complementary models that describe the change process as a backdrop, this chapter provides two examples of how interprofessional education was implemented using these models at our institution, Virginia Commonwealth University.

CASE STUDY ONE: INTERPROFESSIONAL CRITICAL CARE SIMULATIONS

In the fall of 2010, a medicine faculty member realized his critical care simulation sessions with medical students lacked realism. Though the students spent eight hours in the session, he did not feel they left the session prepared to care for critically ill patients as interns. He contacted two nursing faculty members who were also clinical nurses at the academic medical center. The nursing faculty had identified a similar need for their upper-level nursing course. While their students had a good grasp of basic concepts, they had trouble integrating the concepts in the care of actual patients. The faculty shared a recognized need for better collaboration around the acutely ill patient. In particular, this included the need for the students to have a better understanding of how to escalate care to each other and to rapid response teams, code teams, or more experienced practitioners.

The faculty worked together to create a two-hour series of simulations that built upon the content of the Fundamentals of Critical Care course. They added triggers within the simulations to teach competency in interprofessional collaboration in addition to critical care skills and developed a feedback form to guide teaching of the students after each simulation. They sought support from the directors of simulation centers in each school allowing staff to program the simulators and run the simulations. They also worked with the leaders of the two degree programs to enroll students in a pilot experience. The simulations were trialed with about twenty students near gradua-

tion in the spring of 2011. Evaluation of the simulations showed that the sessions were well-received by students.

As course directors for specific sections of the undergraduate curricula, the three faculty members were then able to develop and implement a three-session, six-hour curriculum of interprofessional simulation scenarios with all of the 350 fourth-year medical students and senior undergraduate nursing students. The curriculum was integrated into the nursing school as a requirement for the Senior Clinical Practicum course and the medical school as a requirement for the Critical Care experiences. Evaluation of these sessions revealed an increase in students' self-efficacy in both critical care skills and interprofessional collaboration. These results led the presentations in local and national forums. The simulations have continued for four years, and faculty now have defined effort for teaching the simulations.

Let's examine this case study in the context of Lewin's and Kotter's models.

Unfreezing

Establishing a Sense of Urgency

The faculty were spurred to develop the program by a recognized need for better training of their graduates in interprofessional collaboration. Although national and international organizations had been advocating for increased interprofessional education, the urgency in this case study came from the belief of frontline faculty that abilities in interprofessional practice were necessary for their students. These faculty can be thought of as local champions, likely influenced by the national dialogue around the need for increased interprofessional education. Often, IPE begins because of the passion of a few faculty.

Form a Powerful Coalition

The faculty were united by a shared urgency of improving the education of their students. In addition, they had responsibility for course oversight in their respective programs. Previous success as educators and practitioners granted them additional informal authority to be able to lead and innovate.

Create a Vision

The faculty formalized their vision for the simulation experiences by developing the curriculum. This curriculum began with desired topics borrowed from the Fundamentals of Critical Care course with interwoven interprofessional content. They created specific learning objectives, scenarios, and feedback forms.

Communicate the Vision

Once the curriculum was developed, the faculty reached out to several key organizational units necessary for the success of the simulation experience. The main resources needed were access to students and support from each school's simulation center. Faculty spoke with the leaders of the relevant degree programs in each school to gain their approval and to provide access to students. Likewise, the simulation leadership of each school agreed to support the simulation experiences. Both groups saw the experience as an opportunity to be innovative and enhance both the educational and scholarly achievements of the institution.

Change

Empower Others

The leaders of the simulation centers directed their staff to program the simulators and help refine the simulation-based education. This engagement increased the quality of the course and also engaged the simulation centers as co-developers of the learning experience. In a similar way, the interprofessional simulations provide the leaders of the degree programs an example of educational innovation to trumpet.

Plan for and Create Short-Term Wins

The initial two-hour simulation session was implemented with about twenty students. The faculty evaluated student responses to the sessions while also noting their own impressions of the value of the sessions.

Consolidate Improvements

The data from the evaluations of the initial simulations proved valuable. First, it allowed the faculty to refine the session for future use. In addition, it provided the foundation to propose expansion of the sessions. The faculty developed and proposed a three-session, six-hour experience for all graduating medical and nursing students.

Freeze

Institutionalize Change

The new experience was proposed to and approved by the program leadership for both professions. Each program implemented it as part of a required experience for their students. For the past four years, over a thousand students have participated in the program and outcomes have been presented in several national forums. Faculty now have supported faculty effort for teaching in the simulation experiences.

CASE STUDY TWO: FOR-CREDIT INTERPROFESSIONAL COURSES

Inspired by the successful interprofessional education innovations like the interprofessional critical care simulations as well as increasing accreditation requirements, university leadership incorporated interprofessional education into the university's strategic plan and allocated resources to create a Center for Interprofessional Education and Collaborative Care. The Center was a convening entity for faculty and leaders in the health professions from across the campus charged with expanding and improving interprofessional initiatives. In order to meet educational and accreditation goals, these individuals decided to develop two campuswide, for-credit IPE courses embedded as curricular requirements within the various health professions schools.

To negotiate the university and programmatic approval process, the faculty under the Center took the following steps. First, an interprofessional group of faculty developed the course offerings. This faculty group included content experts as well curricular leaders from each profession. Guided by the Core Competencies of Interprofessional Collaborative Practice (Interprofessional Education Collaborative Expert Panel 2011), *this group crafted the learning objectives, lesson plans, and assessments for the courses. The course offerings were then submitted to and approved by the university as elective courses under the Center.*

Then, each individual health science program considered whether to adopt the elective courses as curricular requirements through their program-specific curriculum approval process. This proved to be challenging. One challenge was that only a small number of faculty had been exposed to earlier IPE efforts on the health science campus, yet approval of curricular changes required endorsement by the entire faculty. For many faculty, interprofessional education was a new concept and it was difficult to conceptualize how the new courses could be operationalized within the existing curricular framework. In these instances, faculty champions anticipated barriers and worked proactively to anticipate and respond to concerns, such as making other curricular adjustments to keep the entire program "credit neutral." In addition, communication with strategic faculty occurred before the faculty voting process in some of the schools to support passage.

Once approved by the individual health sciences schools, the course leadership identified learning spaces, found a common educational time for participating programs, and recruited faculty. The first course launched in the fall of 2015 with nearly five hundred students representing five health science schools and seven degree programs.

This case study represents a broader example of Lewin's and Kotter's frameworks. For this discussion, we will focus on the central efforts of the Center and the organizational change process within the school of nursing. Notably though, each school had its own specific and substantial challenges.

Unfreezing

Establishing a Sense of Urgency

In contrast to the first case study, the urgency for large scale curricular reform must be felt by a greater number of the faculty for change to be endorsed. Urgency for large change usually comes from external sources. In the specific case of interprofessional education, a number of publications have cited the imperative for more effective interprofessional practice over the past four decades (Institute of Medicine 2003; World Health Organization 2010). For programs that train health professionals, these reports have led to the implementation of accrediting standards. For example, Essential VI of the Essentials of Baccalaureate Education for Professional Nursing Practice (American Association of Colleges of Nursing [AACN] 2008), Interprofessional Communication and Collaboration for Improving Patient Health Outcomes states:

> Effective communication and collaboration among health professionals is imperative to providing patient-centered care. All health professions are challenged to educate future clinicians to deliver patient-centered care as members of an interprofessional team, emphasizing communication, evidence-based practice, quality improvement approaches, and informatics. Interprofessional education is defined as interactive educational activities involving two or more professions that foster collaboration to improve patient care. Teamwork among healthcare professionals is associated with delivering high quality and safe patient care. Collaboration is based on the complementarities of roles and the understanding of these roles by the members of the healthcare teams. Interprofessional education enables the baccalaureate graduate to enter the workplace with baseline competencies and confidence for interactions and with communication skills that will improve practice, thus yielding better patient outcomes. Interprofessional education can occur in a variety of settings. An essential component for the establishment of collegial relationships is recognition of the unique discipline-specific practice spheres. Fundamental to effective interprofessional and intra-professional collaboration is a definition of shared goals; clear role expectations of members; a flexible decisionmaking process; and the establishment of open communication patterns and leadership. Thus, interprofessional education optimizes opportunities for the development of respect and trust for other members of the healthcare team.

Additional influences include the Future of Nursing Report (Institute of Medicine 2011), which outlined the significant transformation of the healthcare system over the past century—from a healthcare system built on an acute model of care, to a system much more focused on chronic conditions in the twenty-first century—and further emphasized that training methods from the twentieth century were inadequate to meet the challenges of the present day healthcare environment. The Future of Nursing Report (Institute of Medicine 2011, 13) called for a collaborative effort among health professions schools to design and implement "early and continuous interprofessional collaboration through joint classroom and clinical training opportunities." Amid health reform's focus on cost, quality, and access, the methods of educating health professionals to meet the demand of twenty-first-century healthcare play a central role in the national discussion and cannot be overlooked (Thibault 2013).

The national and global emphasis on interprofessional education also stimulates formal institutional urgency. In our example, interprofessional education was incorporated into the university's strategic plan and performance evaluations of leaders, such as deans, included elements related to interprofessional programming (Virginia Commonwealth University 2011).

Forming a Powerful Guiding Coalition

Implementing a successful interprofessional education program that spans multiple health science schools and involves hundreds of students requires skilled and respected change agents who can span the different units of the organization. Although the Center had been formed to coordinate interprofessional efforts, the proposed courses were expected to include five hundred students from five health science schools, and no one individual could singlehandedly lead such a critical change process across the campus (Appelbaum et al. 2012). Developing interprofessional education courses as curricular requirements requires involving those key stakeholders in the curriculum design process to help craft the desired future state; for example, faculty who currently teach potential interprofessional course content uniprofessionally, or faculty in leadership roles within their respective curriculum committees that can help navigate the curriculum change process are both be very important stakeholders. Interpersonal relationships within schools play an important role in the ability to overcome resistance to change (Battilana and Casciaro 2012). As such, the coalition in our case study included content experts from multiple professions as well as leaders within the programs that could help shepherd the curriculum through the programmatic approval process. All of this was coordinated centrally through the Center, but the initiative was truly a collaboration between the degree programs in each school and the Center.

Creating a Vision

A clear, consistent and well-articulated vision is critical for directing change efforts (Kotter 2007). Here, the vision involved developing courses that built upon the imperative articulated by the Institute of Medicine, World Health Organization, and accreditors. This vision was further supported by the overarching university strategic plan and resources allocated by the university. Pulling from the Core Competencies for Interprofessional Collaborative Practice, the faculty coalition sought to develop the first course, a foundational course about interprofessional practice. The faculty expanded content and instructional methods piloted in a shorter experience to develop a course focused on the individual and their professional identity, how that identity overlaps and interacts with other professions to form teams, and how those teams exist within the complex systems of healthcare. Once the faculty had completed outlining both courses and felt comfortable with their approaches, the process of trying to implement change began.

Communicating a Vision

Implementing the change needed to incorporate the courses required communication on many fronts. First, the courses had to be approved as electives under the Center by the university. Otherwise, approval would be a piecemeal process with each curriculum committee suggesting modifications, muddying ownership of the courses. To accomplish approval of the two new courses under the Center required working with university administrators to develop an approval process for Center-based courses. Linking the courses with the university's strategic plan and winning the support of key university leaders was essential.

In addition, members of the coalition began working with their programmatic leadership to win approval and integration of the course. In the School of Nursing example, adding the two one-credit courses would require removing two credits elsewhere in the curriculum. Coalition faculty approached this challenge by beginning to describe the interprofessional activities that were already taking place and how the curriculum could be revised to further integrate this approach. Faculty members brought up IPE in department meetings as a needed concept for future courses citing the Future of Nursing (Institute of Medicine 2011) and other reports. They noted how current course content could be taught via IPE, allowing for a credit-neutral and content-neutral approach to integration. While many of these faculty were supportive, some hesitations remained as a key curriculum meeting approached to discuss the course.

Empowering Others to Act on the Vision

Worried about the level of support for, and difficulty involved with, the curriculum change, the coalition faculty sought out some of the informal leaders of the school of nursing. These leaders had long tenures as faculty and were also engaged with the development and training of more junior faculty. In conversations in hallways and their offices with these key faculty, the coalition faculty worked to ensure their buy-in. They listened to the concerns of these informal leaders and sought to allay them or address them with the broader coalition. In addition, the university approval of the courses as electives demonstrated the university's commitment to IPE and also raised the possibility that the other programs might participate without nursing. Having presented the situations and discussed the faculty members' concerns, the coalition faculty asked them to speak in support of the curricular change.

Change

Planning for and Creating Short-Term Wins

The initial step of the curriculum change process in the School of Nursing was endorsement of the two new IPE courses by the curriculum committee. During the designated curriculum meeting, the faculty champions presented the vision for IPE across the campus. They described how the experiences would shape the education of nursing students and students from other health professions. The supportive key faculty were scattered across the room and helped field concerns from skeptics. The courses were endorsed by the curriculum committee and recommended forward for approval by the full faculty.

The next step was to bring the courses to the entire faculty for approval. The IPE vision was presented at the meeting of the faculty. Once again, faculty champions were present to answer all questions and present information in a positive way. In addition, since the curriculum meeting, the School of Pharmacy had adopted the course as a curricular requirement. In the context of this urgency, vision, and support, the courses were approved by School of Nursing faculty.

Consolidating Improvements and Producing Still More Change

In this second case study, many barriers to a successful IPE experience still remained after course approval. Center faculty needed to identify the best learning space for the team-based activities they had planned for the five hundred potential students. They also needed to find a common time across academic calendars for course meetings. And, they had to recruit additional faculty from all the participating professions to teach the course. To accomplish all of these goals, the faculty relied on the momentum from the initial course approval to implement additional change.

Refreezing

Institutionalizing the Change

The goal of this step is to anchor the new approaches into organizational culture (Appelbaum et al. 2012). Each faculty member must be supported with knowledge, skills, and abilities to effectively convey the content and teach with other health professions. Making the connection between the new behaviors of the faculty, the overarching success of interprofessional education on the health science campus, and the urgent needs of our healthcare system was an important final step in the complex, systematic undertaking of improving health professions education across the campus.

SELF-REINFORCING CYCLES OF INTERPROFESSIONAL CHANGE

Stepping back from these two descriptions of integrating interprofessional change provides a broader view of the importance of this type of approach. While the victories of change are won through frontline work on critical issues such as buy-in and overcoming logistical barriers, the most widespread impact of these victories is felt in how the culture of an organization is changed by increasing interprofessional education and practice. This culture change is the dividend of the hard work of interprofessional leaders.

Organizational culture is the values, beliefs, and assumptions that guide the behaviors of people in the organization (Schneider, Ehrhart, and Macey 2013). Organizational culture is an aggregate concept, derived from the experience of individuals, the stories they hear about people within the organization, and their observation of what succeeds within the organization. Organizations can have a unifying culture or many separate subcultures, which may provide substrate for conflict or inefficiency.

The concept of organizational culture—or perhaps hoped for organizational culture—has implications for leaders of interprofessional education and practice. Individuals within our organizations, whether they are students, faculty, practitioners, staff, or even patients and their families, are active participants in defining the culture of the organization. They are living the experiences, hearing and telling the stories about components of the organization, and being observed by others who are developing impressions about the organization. For people within the organization, these exposures to the culture of the organization are internalized and recirculated through these people as further manifestations of the organizational culture. As such, culture is a self-reinforcing concept where cultural impressions beget other cultural impressions.

Interprofessional culture change then is about trying to strategically influence the individuals in the organization to promote interprofessional ideals. The "unfreezing" process—establishing urgency, forming a coalition, creating and communicating a vision—is about building the substrate upon which culture change can begin to happen. The "change" process—empowering others, creating short-term wins, and consolidating improvements—is about realizing the culture change. And, the "refreezing" process—institutionalizing change—is about ensuring that the culture change is sustained.

The interprofessional critical care simulations began as a collaboration between a few passionate faculty with little institutional support. They believed in the interprofessional mission and did not expect traditional rewards, such as course credit or promotion, based on this work. A well-articulated vision and curriculum won them the capacity to pilot the simulations, and success of the pilot brought them access to greater opportunities including conference presentations and protected educational effort. But the real value to the organization was that the program proved large-scale interprofessional education could work. Through individual effort, they created change in the larger culture and became an exemplar of how interprofessional education could provide a well-regarded, meaningful experience to students.

In the second example, development and adoption of the university's first credit-bearing IPE courses as curricular requirements, the leaders built upon the foundation established by the first program. The vision for large-scale interprofessional education already existed, and some of the members of the coalition that developed the courses were veterans of the first program. Yet, the leaders in the second example took these ideas a step further. Leveraging the evolving accreditation standards for interprofessional education, the inclusion of interprofessional education in the strategic plan for the university, and the curricular policies and bodies of the individual academic programs, the leaders sought to create broader learning experiences that would reinforce an organizational culture supportive of interprofessional education. Here, it was not just leading by example; rather it was negotiating with numerous other leaders to collaborate on a sustainable structure for interprofessional education as permanent curricular experiences. In a sense, if the individuals involved in the first program were trailblazers, the individuals involved in the second program laid the asphalt for an avenue of interprofessional education. This work—creating the procedures and structures necessary for sustainable interprofessional education—can support further innovation in interprofessional education, reinforcing interprofessional innovation as part of the culture of the university.

What are the implications for organizational leaders who seek to create a culture supportive of interprofessional education and practice? Organizational change that increases interprofessional education and practice must begin with individuals who believe in this ideal. Often, they pursue it without a desire for traditional academic reward. Leaders should recognize and seek to support these individuals with a specific attention to removing the barriers they face to accomplishing their goals. As these innovators succeed, the success must be leveraged into broader organizational change that is integrated more formally into the broader culture of the organization. This integration occurs by weaving the new ideal into existing policies, procedures, and processes of the organization, for example emphasizing interprofessional work in tenure and promotion guidelines. Leaders should support this integration by working with organizational leaders from other professions to adapt organizational structure so that they remain effective yet also incorporate approaches supportive of the desired change. This institutionalization of the ideal—in this case interprofessional education and practice—will then serve to stimulate further innovation in this area. In this way, the interprofessional spirit of some initial advocates spreads to broader organizational change and engenders a culture infused with the ideals of interprofessional education and practice.

REFERENCES

Abu-Rish, E., S. Kim, L. Choe et al. 2012. "Current Trends in Interprofessional Education of Health Sciences Students: A Literature Review." *Journal of Interprofessional Care* 26, no. 6: 444–51.

American Association of Colleges of Nursing. 2008. *The Essentials of Baccalaureate Education for Professional Nursing Practice.* Washington, DC: American Association of Colleges of Nursing.

Antoni, C. H. 2007. "A Motivational Perspective on Change Processes and Outcomes." *European Journal of Work and Organizational Psychology* 13, no. 2: 197–216.

Appelbaum, S. H., S. Habashy, J. Malo, and H. Shafig. 2012. "Back to the Future: Revisiting Kotter's 1996 Change Model." *Journal of Management Development* 31, no. 8: 764–82.

Bargal, D. 2006. "Personal and Intellectual Influences Leading to Lewin's Paradigm of Action Research." *Action Research* 4, no. 4: 367–88.

Battilana, J and T. Casciara. 2012. "Overcoming Resistance to Organizational Change: Strong Ties and Affective Cooptation." *Management Science* 59, no. 4: 819–36.

Borkowski, N. 2011. *Organizational Behavior in Health Care*, second edition. Boston: Jones and Bartlett.

Bozak, M. G. 2003. "Using Lewin's Force Field Analysis in Implementing a Nursing Information System." *CIN: Computers, Informatics, Nursing* 21, no. 2: 80–85.

Burnes, B. 2004. "Kurt Lewin and the Planned Approach to Change: A Re-Appraisal." *Journal of Management Studies* 41, no. 6: 977–1002. doi:10.1111/j.1467-6486.2004.00463.x.

Dow, A., D. DiazGranados, P. Mazmanian, and S. Retchin. 2014. "An Exploratory Study of an Assessment Tool Derived from the Competencies of the Interprofessional Education Collaborative." *Journal of Interprofessional Care* 28, no. 4: 299–304.

Fink, L. 2013. *Creating Significant Learning Experiences.* San Francisco: Wiley.

Hall, L., and B. Zierler. 2015. "Interprofessional Education and Practice Guide No. 1: Developing Faculty to Effectively Facilitate Interprofessional Education." *Journal of Interprofessional Care* 29, no. 1: 3–7.

Institute of Medicine, 2001. *Crossing the Quality Chasm. Crossing the Quality Chasm: A New Health System for the 21st Century*. Washington, DC: National Academy Press.

———. 2003. *Health Professions Education: A Bridge to Quality*. Washington, DC: National Academies Press.

———. 2011. *The Future of Nursing: Leading Change, Advancing Health*. Washington, DC: The National Academies Press.

———. 2015. *Measuring the Impact of Interprofessional Education IPE on Collaborative Practice and Patient Outcomes*. Washington, DC: National Academies Press.

Interprofessional Education Collaborative Expert Panel. 2011. *Core Competencies for Interprofessional Collaborative Practice: Report of an Expert Panel.* Washington, DC: Interprofessional Education Collaborative.

Jones, K., D. Blumenthal, J. Burke, M. Condren, R. Hansen, M. Holiday-Goodman, and C. Peterson. 2012. "Interprofessional Education in Introductory Pharmacy Practice Experiences at U.S. Colleges and Schools of Pharmacy." *American Journal of Pharmaceutical Education* 765: 80.

Josiah Macy Jr. Foundation. 2013. Transforming Patient Care: Aligning Interprofessional Education with Clinical Practice Redesign. Report.

Kotter, J. P. 1996. *Leading Change*. Boston: Harvard Business School Press.

———. 2007. "Leading Change: Why Transformation Efforts Fail." *Harvard Business Review* 851: 96–103.

Lawlis, T. R., J. Anson, and D. Greenfield. 2014. "Barriers and Enablers that Influence Sustainable Interprofessional Education: A Literature Review." *Journal of Interprofessional Care* 284: 305–10.

Lewin, K. 1943. "Defining the "Field at a Given Time." *Psychological Review* 50: 292–310.

———. 1947. "Frontiers in Group Dynamics: Concept, Method and Reality in Social Science; Social Equilibria and Social Change." *Human Relations* 11: 5–41. doi:10.1177/001872674700100103

Oandasan, I., and S. Reeves. 2005. "Key Elements of Interprofessional Education. Part 2: Factors, Processes, and Outcomes." *Journal of Interprofessional Care* 19, Suppl. 1: 39–48.

Reeves, S. 2012. "The Rise and Rise of Interprofessional Competence." *Journal of Interprofessional Care* 264: 253–55.

Schneider, B., M. Ehrhart, and W. Macey. 2013. "Organizational Climate and Culture." *Annual Review of Psychology* 64: 361–88.

Thibault, G. E. 2013. "Reforming Health Professions Education Will Require Culture Change and Closer Ties Between Classroom and Practice." *Health Affairs* 3211: 1928–32.

Thistlewaite, J., D. Forman, L. Matthews, G. Rogers, C. Steketee, and T. Yassine. 2014. "Competencies and Frameworks in Interprofessional Education: A Comparative Analysis." *Academic Medicine* 896: 869–75.

Virginia Commonwealth University. 2011, August 15th. *Quest for Distinction.*

World Health Organization. 2010. *Framework for Action on Interprofessional Education and Collaborative Practice.* Geneva: World Health Organization.

Zorek, J., and C. Raehl. 2013. "Interprofessional Education Accreditation Standards in the USA: A Comparative Analysis." *Journal of Interprofessional Care* 272: 123–30.

Chapter Five

Designing an Interprofessional Education Program from Planning to Implementation

Jean P. Shipman, Susan Chase-Cantarini, Rebecca D. Wilson, and Alice I. Weber

UNIVERSITY OF UTAH IPE'S EXPERIENCE

Recognizing early on the importance of health sciences students learning about each other's practice domains and professional boundaries, the University of Utah (UU) started exploring interprofessional education (IPE). In 2002, the initial IPE course consisted of four hybrid modules with in-person sessions cofacilitated by faculty in health, medicine, nursing, and pharmacy. This evolved into a more clinically focused, interactive learning activity that incorporated interprofessional student teams interacting individually with a standardized patient, followed by faculty-facilitated team debriefing. New opportunities for IPE presented themselves with the opening of a thirty-bed acute and ambulatory care high-fidelity simulation center.

The UU is unique in that its development of IPE programs was, for the first decade, led by health sciences library directors. The reason for such leadership is that the health sciences administration saw the health sciences library as a neutral entity that partnered with every health sciences program. The Spencer S. Eccles Health Sciences Library (EHSL) was also appointed to be the manager of a five-story Health Sciences Education Building (HSEB) that was built in 2006 to house a majority of the health sciences programs' classes and special events. The EHSL was placed in charge of administrating this building, again as it was neutral and had the ability to technologically support the classroom infrastructure. Through planning the special events for the HSEB, the EHSL staff learned how to apply scheduling software and provided the technical support for HSEB's simulated clinical patient exam suites. Librarians from EHSL became schedulers of the initial ambulatory care simulation IPE event, which used the HSEB suites; thus, EHSL became even a more integral partner with the IPE program.

As the UU IPE program became more simulation-based, the library director quickly realized that her expertise lacked special knowledge with conducting simulated clinical experiences and an understanding of how the academic student enterprise worked, due to not directly instructing matriculated students. She also could not dedicate the time that was required to run an IPE program that had grown from one event to multiple events per year. It became clear that a dedicated director for IPE needed to be hired. This new director has added much to the UU program as she has a strong background with simulation and also a PhD in education technology.

The current UU IPE program consists of six simulation-based courses set in acute care, ambulatory care and telehealth/rural care across dentistry, health, medicine, nursing, pharmacy, and social work programs. The IPE program trains over 1,200 students per year, involving a cadre of sixty faculty facilitators and twelve faculty governance committee members. It is from this collective experience and recent literature that the authors provide the following tips for initiating an effective and productive IPE program.

TIPS FOR INITIATING AN INTERPROFESSIONAL EDUCATION PROGRAM

Designing, planning, and implementing an IPE program is highly context-dependent; however, there are some common approaches to consider and pitfalls to avoid. In general, the goal is to assist healthcare students to learn from, with, and about each other in order to promote collaboration and improve patient care (World Health Organization 2010). For the purposes of this chapter, we define design as creating the infrastructure and curricular elements, planning as determining the logistics of bringing students together, and implementation as activities needed to prepare faculty to work with students within the interprofessional curriculum. Although addressed separately, the elements of designing, planning, and implementing are highly interconnected and iterative. Oftentimes, what you can accomplish logistically will inform the types of program outcomes that can be achieved by students and how those outcomes will be assessed.

The following lessons were learned the hard way. We quickly developed a simulation pilot soon after a new simulation center was opened in the College of Nursing at our higher education administration's request. We piloted the course in record time without going through any formal curricular committee review of any school or college due to the strong encouragement of one dean. We applied the course credit from a previous interprofessional course in order to be able to assess a student fee. This fee is used to financially support the program. As many schools and colleges were unaware of the course's offering until the final hour, several decided to cover the fee for the first semester to be able to have their students participate. Programs that have set student fees and not credit hour courses had to compensate for their equivalent student credit hour contributions. Schedulers of the various scenario student groups had to hustle to obtain student names and assign them to the correct group configuration. Faculty had to be quickly trained in debriefing techniques, and a course management site (Canvas) had to be rapidly created to disseminate basic information about the course, course requirements and assignments, and expectations for professional conduct. Students also had to be informed about how they would be assessed and graded, and a process for assigning grades, accepting incompletes, and waiving student fees in some cases had to be outlined. Despite learning the hard way, we realize that we gained a lot of knowledge about how to better create an IPE program that we are sharing tips to others.

Offering new and innovative changes, such as an IPE program, across a health science center can seem overwhelming at first; starting small with strategic planning will lead to great rewards in the end. Having the "big picture" or goal in mind will help ease some potential challenges. Synergy will develop as you gain support, develop your team, and design your program.

Tip #1 Gain Support (Design)

Program design includes creating the infrastructure: gaining support and creating the leadership and governance structures required to move forward. This includes generating both grassroots and administrative champions at each participating school. Including clinical partners early in the process may also be beneficial. Consider sustainability and impact while designing: How will the program be funded and sustained with long-term support? Is there an internal grant funding process you could apply to for initial seed support? Can you identify local foundations that might be interested in funding an IPE program? Work with your development office to identify and approach potential donors who are interested in supporting IPE training. Collect patient and provider stories that touch donors' hearts and that indicate the impact IPE can make on offering improved and safer patient care. Is there a source of funding available from higher administration for at least initial support of an IPE program? Are there other unique funding opportunities available within your community?

It is important that deans of the health sciences schools support IPE, and recognize it as a service to their students. Currently, there is movement toward including competence in interprofessional collaboration as part of accreditation standards in order to promote and advance IPE (Zorek and Raehl 2013). Initiatives across the country are underway offering new approaches, models, and frameworks for implementation (Barr 2013; Pardue 2015; Thistlethwaite et al. 2014). Deans are instrumental in providing financial support and allocating faculty time (Bridges et al. 2011). Deans can also stress the importance of being involved to their faculty and assist with incorporating involvement in IPE programs as part of faculty contracts and integrating IPE program participation into criteria for promotion and tenure. In addition, deans can request financial support from their institutions for IPE programs and for staffing. They can build costs within their school budgets and help with identifying donors who may want to sponsor an IPE program.

Another key ingredient to success is to identify early on who can be champions of such programs and to harness the energy of these individuals to encourage others to engage with planning the program, to assist with teaching, and with endorsing it to others (Bridges et al. 2011). Champions are found in unexpected places and will be the early adopters that help others to see the value of interprofessional learning. There may be faculty close by that are easily influenced to participate as they believe in the philosophy of IPE to improve the future of healthcare.

Tip #2: Develop Your IPE Team (Design)

Bring your champions together to develop your program's model. Establish a governance structure once you have outlined the program with the needed committees and advisors. For example, the program at the UU has an IPE Advisory Committee, which sets overall direction, and three subcommittees that coordinate efforts through the Advisory Committee: Curriculum, Faculty Development, and Research/Scholarship. Be willing to adjust your governance structure as the program grows. Look for participants from all the health sciences programs, including the health sciences library, as this entity can help to reach out to known individuals and to coordinate committee activities and document their progress with technological support and organization skills.

Librarians have experience with organizing and prioritizing information and knowledge and can offer an overarching perspective on IPE program goals. Providing foundational evidence from the literature is important for establishing and maintaining a rigorous IPE program that addresses both academic and clinical aspects. Health literacy is an important component of providing excellent patient care. Health sciences librarians have training on this important topic and are in an excellent position to share their knowledge with students, faculty, and clinicians. Librarians are also neutral parties within an IPE team, which can become politically polarized. They are in a unique position to facilitate connections between people in a variety of associated fields and can call upon their established relationships to encourage initial and continued participation in IPE programs.

Balanced representation from all participating programs is essential to ensure that all voices are heard, and that decisions incorporate the visions, needs, and concerns of these areas. Decide how many individuals are needed, what skills are required, and who can contribute effectively to the efforts, and who can influence and create needed impact. Appoint members that fit best with your institution and try to get such appointments recognized by your promotion and tenure process. Consider including a student member on key committees, as they bring a unique perspective as to what is desired by health sciences students and can provide insight into scheduling and other curricular demands. Promote the committees and their composition publicly to encourage others to learn more about IPE and for them to give consideration to joining in the future, as it is important to keep committee membership fresh and engaged.

Once the teams or committees are formed and members are appointed, create guidelines for these committees or teams. Begin developing common understanding about working definitions, goals, and program frameworks. Members will come from a diversity of perspectives and organizational cultures, and will bring their own professional language, culture, and expectations, which adds to the beauty of an IPE program. Such variations, however, can lead to early confusion or conflict if it isn't clearly articulated early in the proceedings what is meant by IPE and its related competencies. Take time to articulate what key terms mean and carefully review the verbiage of the team charters to reach agreement early in the process. As you create guidelines, common understanding, terminology, and team charters, you will notice that you are leveling the playing field of members, recognizing each one's contributions, and thus, living the experience of forming an interprofessional team. Your team is a microcosm of future team development.

Knowledge management can be a challenge when bringing participants together across schools and campuses. Establishing a common document sharing site is an essential part of the communication plan. Listing committees, their charges, membership, and associated terms of appointment, is also critical for informing others of the IPE program and how it functions. In addition, consider conducting update meetings for all interested faculty to share experiences and knowledge. This is a great area for health sciences librarians to take a lead, as they can apply their organizational and communication skills as well as their technical expertise. Course management software can be used, as well as content management systems (e.g., Drupal), or websites can also be a common way of sharing information about IPE programs.

Tip #3 Use a Conceptual Framework (Design)

It is important when developing an IPE program to take the time to create or adopt a conceptual model for the program from the beginning. Over the years, there have been many efforts to provide team-based education; most formal models and frameworks have evolved during the last decade. Many reflect on the interdependence between health professionals' education, practice, and competence domains. The Interprofessional Education Collaborative (IPEC) Expert Panel reported three frameworks that captured the interdependence between health professionals' education and practice to improve patient and community-based care. These included: (1) D'Amour and Oandasan's "The Interprofessionality as the Field of Interprofessional Practice and Interprofessional Education: An Emerging Concept," (2) the World Health Organization Study Group's "Framework for Action on Interprofessional Education and Collaborative Practice" (2010), and (3) the Commission on Education of Health Professional's "Health Professionals for a New Century: Transforming Education to Strengthen Health Systems in an Interdependent World" (2011).

Meanwhile, several organizations around the world began publishing competency frameworks, statements, and domains capturing the essence of interprofessional practice. These frameworks offer attributes required of healthcare students and professionals to practice effectively in interprofessional teams. Some common attributes or competence domains consist of the following: ethical practice, conflict resolution, teamwork, communication, collaboration, and role clarification (Thistlethwaite et al. 2014). IPE models and frameworks can serve as a basis for your program outcomes and develop into system-wide activities in education and practice settings. The development of assessment and evaluation tools should also complement these frameworks and competencies.

Tip #4 Frame Curricular Parameters (Design)

Prior to developing curricular elements, it is helpful to determine what givens or constraints will be placed on your program based upon your education or practice setting. Larger questions to address include whether your curriculum will be embedded in current courses or if will it be offered as separate credit-bearing courses (e.g., didactic, simulation, or clinical), or separate noncredit bearing seminars/workshops that each health sciences program may require its students to attend.

Building interprofessional experiences into service-learning opportunities is another potential venue that gives students a chance to connect within their communities The University of California, San Diego (UCSD) has a well-established program called the UCSD Student-Run Free Clinic Project (Beck 2005). New York University uses online courses as one way to deliver IPE instruction along with simulation and virtual patients (Djukic et al. 2012). University of Florida offers an interdisciplinary family health course that is featured in chapter 6 of this book and at http://education.health.ufl.edu/pff/. Whatever you offer, you will want to consider overlap in shared content across curricula and provide opportunities for students to gather, despite their complex and varied schedules.

Tip #5 Plan Early for Program Evaluation (Design)

Early in your planning, explore methods for evaluating your IPE program. More health sciences accrediting bodies require IPE in curricula (Zorek and Raehl 2013); incorporating accreditation criteria can guide the development of program outcomes, which drive your evaluation plan. Once your program outcomes are determined, consider using a logic model to guide a comprehensive evaluation plan (McCawley, n.d.). These models include diagraming how both input and processes will lead to the desired program outcomes. As with any large-scale program it is important to consider the stakeholders. In particular, determine what documentation the participating programs need to demonstrate inclusion of IPE competencies for accreditation purposes.

Evaluation data should be gathered from a variety of stakeholders to provide a more comprehensive view. Chapter 10 of this book offers information about assessing IPE programs. Consider using both quantitative and qualitative data, as either alone often does not provide sufficient information. Data can be solicited via pre-post surveys, open-ended questions during interviews, focus groups, incorporated as part of formal course evaluations, and other methods. Depending on the questions to be answered, there are several assessment tools available that can contribute to program evaluation. These include: (1) the Interdisciplinary Education Perception Scale—IEPS (Zanotti, Sartor, and Canova 2015), (2) Team Objective Structured Clinical Exam—TOSCE (Emmert and Cai 2015), (3) Kirkpatrick's evaluation outcome mode (Anderson, Smith, and Hammick 2015), and (4) Readiness for Interprofessional Learning Scale—RIPLS (Murphy and Nimmagadda 2015).

Recognize students and faculty as lead contributors to the evaluation process; engage them in both formative and summative feedback. Formative feedback includes information gathered during planning and implementation as a basis for continuous improvement. Summative feedback is a holistic approach that gathers information about the entire program, often for the purposes of determining if the program should be continued.

Tip #6 Curriculum (Design)

There is no one right way to approach IPE curriculum design; current available models are as individual as the institutions themselves. However, one place to start is exploring content that is similar across participating programs. Consider shared content, such as patient-centered care planning or systems-based care; and high-risk care elements that require coordination, such as discharge planning or resolution of conflict or ethical dilemmas. Involving clinically savvy educators from each participating discipline will help ensure the relevance of the education for the various student types. Be sure to look for places where IPE may already be happening. Determine where students from different professions are currently gathering and interactivity already occurs. Opportunities may be closer than you think; follow the energy. For instance, at the UU, the HSEB building led to the formation of an interprofessional Health Sciences Student Council (HSSC) that developed out of the sheer interest in learning more about other professional students that were seen within the building. Students took it upon themselves to develop a means for them to learn more about each other's professions, practice parameters, and curricular structures.

Best practices of adult learning suggest that students be actively engaged. There are several ways to accomplish this including using networking opportunities, innovative technologies, and simulation methodologies. Although, optimum approaches to teaching IPE are not well understood, new and innovative strategies are emerging (see chapter 3 for pedagogical perspectives for IPE). The Society for Simulation in Healthcare (SSH) has developed simulation-enhanced IPE models that have been endorsed by accrediting agencies and healthcare organizations (2013). They recommend keeping the focus on evidence-based care and highlighting safe quality patient-centered outcomes.

Students can complete reflection activities addressing what they learned, what they observe in practice, and how they can improve future practice. Current practitioners can reflect on core tenants of adding value to patient-centered care, improving care quality, and enhancing patient safety through interprofessional practice competencies.

Students find it meaningful to encounter IPE sessions that will translate into their current and future practice. A common situation is for students to learn about IPE within their curricula only to find it not being practiced when they move into their clinical work settings. Having students make a connection between these ideas and applications to practice, while helping them to learn about themselves, creates opportunities for significant learning (Fink 2003). IPE faculty can enhance the value of student learning experiences by tying IPE competencies to improvements in healthcare delivery.

As you design your curriculum, you will want to make choices regarding assessment of student gains in interprofessional competence. Several tools exist to evaluate student readiness, knowledge, attitude, and skills regarding interprofessional competencies (Blue et al. 2015). The National Center for Interprofessional Practice and Education Resource Page (https://nexusipe.org/resource-exchange) is an excellent place to start when searching for currently available tools. This site is updated regularly by members and includes references to aid in decision making.

Tip #7 Do Not Underestimate Logistics (Plan)

Thoughtful planning and preparation helps to ensure that all needed IPE program components are in place and will be sustained over time. Establishing short-term goals congruent with long-term goals is important. No doubt, one of the biggest challenges to be addressed is scheduling IPE events and activities. Having a dedicated time for IPE would be invaluable for multicollege and multicampus-wide programs; few windows of opportunity exist, however, with the different program calendars and already established demands on time. It may be worthwhile to have a subcommittee or team focus on the logistics of bringing students together, whether in person or virtually, as this is one of the most common barriers faced by IPE programs. Look for technological solutions as well, such as scheduling software, to aid in scheduling both students from various health sciences programs and grade years within these programs, and also faculty. Librarians can help with finding appropriate scheduling software, and with ensuring that the mix of students scheduled is correct for different IPE events, depending on the experience needed.

Tip #8 Develop Your Faculty (Implement)

Faculty development and active involvement will enhance IPE program strength and endurance. Build upon current faculty who demonstrate collaborative approaches and those who express interest in being involved. Capitalize on those who already exhibit appropriate strengths, who can, in turn, become future champions of IPE. Recognize and mentor local IPE champions from each profession, pulling them in for their creative ideas and potential leadership in program planning teams.

Bringing together multiple perspectives, experiences and areas of expertise will benefit future program growth. Cultivate faculty who express enthusiasm for your program. Prepare faculty teams by building a culture of interprofessional collaboration, capitalizing on role modeling to students. Provide training opportunities that reinforce IPE best practices (Hall and Zierler 2015). Training can be accomplished during scheduled team meetings, via special workshops or tailored training sessions. Utilize team-building strategies to develop faculties' own strengths, both personally and professionally, and while teaching important content to faculty and staff. Content areas to consider in the training include: (1) the language and components of IPE, (2) benefits of developing interprofessional teams to foster safe patient care, and (3) facilitation skills in leading teams. Establish common ground and consistency. Adopt and use a framework to guide and teach facilitation and debriefing with faculty, including librarians. There may be faculty already familiar with this process. Take advantage of individuals who already possess these skills and ask them to be instructors. If facilitating and debriefing are new skills for faculty, several resources can be found in the literature (LeGros et al. 2015), particularly the healthcare simulation literature, to assist them with learning more about how to develop these skills. Both junior and senior faculty can benefit from skill development efforts. For the most part, faculty see themselves as life-long learners and can contribute in different ways. Find those with strength in collaboration, communication, program planning, and evaluation, and encourage them to be champions to corral other faculty to get involved.

As your program grows and evolves, celebrate and share your successes with faculty along the way. Build excitement and enthusiasm for your work across your organization. Be sure to promote your program's achievements and efforts through local venues and publications. Share student feedback that supports continuation of your program and generate faculty interest. Faculty, staff, and students can be ambassadors and will spread their positive experiences through conversations with others. Partner with public relations, clinical educators, student government, and supervisors to share feedback and program successes.

Consider early on how faculty may be recognized for their contributions, particularly in regard to retention and promotion. As the field of IPE grows, there are opportunities for collaborative projects to enhance their teaching, service, and scholarship. Without this recognition, faculty may lose interest or decide to redirect their efforts if IPE is not contributing to their career development portfolios.

Tip #9 Communicate Early around Implementation (Implement)

One shortfall IPE programs often experience is that they strive to create a perfect program, without ensuring that all parties involved are truly comfortable with the implementation plan. As with any change in an organization, communication is critical to building and sustaining commitment. Keeping communications open among the governance teams and committees is a key component of a successful program, especially in the early formation days. Anticipate how the program will affect students, faculty, and programs. Understanding the potential barriers and scope of resources will bolster system-wide support (Lawlis, Anson, and Greenfield 2014; Ogrinc et al. 2012).

Ensure lines of responsibility among the various governance teams are clear and understood. Provide a forum for sharing questions that can be addressed quickly and from reputable sources.

A common problem IPE programs face is who has the ultimate authority for making key decisions and for program development. IPE programs' inherent nature of encouraging cooperation and collaboration among disparate programs that are accustomed to setting their own decision-making processes and techniques can be difficult. Getting these individual programs to conform to a shared governance style may be a challenge, but is one of the development experiences faculty can gain from participating in an IPE program. Learning how to share and how to compromise are invaluable lessons for anyone to gain.

Tip #10 Document Your Process and Disseminate Your Results (Implement)

Many IPE programs have been formulated over time, but very few have documented their developmental journey, or their experiences with creating their programs. The University of Washington has done a great job with this (Willgerodt et al. 2015). Grand Valley State University also has described its IPE program in great detail in the literature (Grapczynski et al. 2015). The lack of reporting is usually due to a lack of time as just getting programs created tends to absorb most free time of faculty. There are several ways to ensure that the process is recorded. One immediate step is to take minutes of all meetings and to centrally house these minutes for all to view. This not only records when decisions are made, but who has actually made them. Minutes also give a timeframe for when certain activities occurred as well as when milestones were reached. A second way to ensure that your program's development is properly recorded is to appoint a committee to archive decisions and to be responsible for coordinating what publications and presentations come out of your program's participants. Early on discussions should be held as to who will share authorship for publications as there are many health sciences schools represented. Will all schools be included or is it ok to have some authors with the rest of participants highlighted in a publication's acknowledgments. Some specific professional topics may need to be targeted and written about by all IPE program developers, whereas other topics might be okay to be shared at various health sciences programs' professional conferences by the IPE professionals that are members of the professional associations hosting the conferences (i.e., it is ok for medical libraries to present at the Medical Library Association annual meeting about the IPE program as other members of the IPE team probably will not be in attendance). Deciding how to distribute the intellectual property gathered and who gets credit for such early on will hopefully prevent misunderstandings and hurt feelings among IPE program participants.

ENJOY THE RIDE

Students love the opportunity to learn from, with, and about each other, particularly in clinically relevant settings. IPE has a unique place in providing this opportunity. Based on our experiences with building an IPE program at the UU, we highly recommend that you "just do it." It is worth the challenges and barriers you might face in creating an IPE program at your institution. Every problem seems to melt when you see the students' reactions and enthusiasm, as ultimately they are what make all of your efforts worth it. Enjoy the ride and the rewards that come from learning about each other at all levels of an organization.

REFERENCES

Anderson, Elizabeth, Roger Smith, and Marilyn Hammick. 2015. "Evaluating an Interprofessional Education Curriculum: A Theory-Informed Approach." *Medical Teacher* 16 (June): 1–10. (Epub ahead of print.)

Barr, Hugh. 2013. "Toward a Theoretical Framework for Interprofessional Education." *Journal of Interprofessional Care* 27: 4–9.

Beck, Ellen. 2005. "The UCSD Student-Run Free Clinic Project: Transdisciplinary Health Professional Education." *Journal of Health Care for the Poor and Underserved* 16: 207–19.

Blue, Amy V., Benjamin J. Chesluk, Lisa N. Conforti, and Eric S. Holmboe. 2015. "Assessment and Evaluation in Interprofessional Education: Exploring the Field." *Journal of Allied Health* 44, no. 2 (Summer): 73–82.

Bridges, Diane R., Richard A. Davidson, Peggy S. Odegard, Ian V. Maki, and John Tomkowiak. 2011. "Interprofessional Collaboration: Three Best Practice Models of Interprofessional Education." *Medical Education Online* 16: 1–10.

Djukic, Maja, Terry Fulmer, Jennifer G. Adams, Sabrina Lee, and Marc M. Triola. 2012. "NYU3T: Teaching, Technology, Teamwork: A Model for Interprofessional Education Scalability and Sustainability." *Nursing Clinics of North America* 47, no. 3 (September): 333–46.

Emmert, Michelle C., and Li Cai. 2015. "A Pilot Study to Test the Effectiveness of an Innovative Interprofessional Education Assessment Strategy." *Journal of Interprofessional Care* 19 (June): 1–6. (Epub ahead of print.)

Fink, L. Dee. 2003. *Creating Significant Learning Experiences: An Integrated Approach to Designing College Courses*. San Francisco: Jossey-Bass.

Grapczynski, Cynthia A., Shelley Schuurman, Andrew D. Booth, Deborah Bambini, and Cynthia Beel-Bates. 2015. "The Integrated Model for Interprofessional Education: A Design for Preparing Health Professions' Students to Work in Interprofessional Teams." *Journal of Allied Health* 44, no. 2 (Summer): 108–14.

Hall, Leslie W., and Brenda K. Zierler. 2015. "Interprofessional Education and Practice Guide No. 1: Developing Faculty to Effectively Facilitate Interprofessional Education." *Journal of Interprofessional Care* 29, no. 1 (January): 3–7.

Interprofessional Education Collaborative Expert Panel. 2011. *Core Competencies for Interprofessional Collaborative Practice: Report of an Expert Panel.* Washington, DC: Interprofessional Education Collaborative.

Lawlis, Tanya R., Judith Anson, and David Greenfield. 2014. "Barriers and Enablers that Influence Sustainable Interprofessional Education: A Literature Review." *Journal of Interprofessional Care* 28, no. 4: 305–10.

LeGros, Theresa A., Helen M. Amerongen, Janet H. Cooley, and Ernest P. Schloss. 2015. "Using Learning Theory, Interprofessional Facilitation Competencies, and Behavioral Indicators to Evaluate Facilitator Training." *Journal of Interprofessional Care* (July 31): 1–7. (Eprint ahead of pub.)

McCawley, P. F. (n.d.). "The Logic Model for Program Planning and Evaluation." University of Idaho Extension Program. Accessed August 3, 2015. http://www.cals.uidaho.edu/edcomm/pdf/CIS/CIS1097.pdf.

Murphy, Judy I., and Jayashree Nimmagadda. 2015. "Partnering to Provide Simulated Learning to Address Interprofessional Education Collaborative Core Competencies." *Journal of Interprofessional Care* 29, no. 3 (May): 258–59.

Nelson, Sioban, Maria Tassone, and Brian D. Hodges. 2014. *Creating the Health Care Team of the Future: The Toronto Model for Interprofessional Education and Practice*. Ithaca, NY: Cornell University Press.

Ogrinc, Gregory S., Linda A. Headrick, Shirley M. Moore, Amy J. Barton, Mary A. Dolansky, and Wendy S. Madigosky. 2012. *Fundamentals of Health Care Improvement: A Guide to Improving your Patient's Care*, second edition. Oakbrook, IL: Joint Commission Resources and Institute for Healthcare Improvement.

Pardue, Karen T. 2015. "A Framework for the Design, Implementation, and Evaluation of Interprofessional Education." *Nurse Educator* 40, no. 1: 10–15.

Society for Simulation in Healthcare (SSH). 2013. Interprofessional Education and Healthcare Simulation Symposium. February. http://www.ssih.org/LinkClick.aspx?fileticket=FQKvyEp0k3k%3d&portalid=48.

Thistlethwaite, Jill E., Dawn Forman, Lynda R. Matthews, Gary D. Rogers, Carole Steketee, and Tagrid Yassine. 2014. "Competencies and Frameworks in Interprofessional Education: A Comparative Analysis." *Academic Medicine* 89, no. 6: 869–75.

World Health Organization. 2010. *Framework for Action on Interprofessional Education and Collaborative Practice*. Geneva, Switzerland: WHO Press.

Willgerodt, Mayumi A., Erin Abu-Rish Blakeney, Douglas M. Brock, Debra Liner, Nanci Murphy, and Brenda Zierler. 2015. "Interprofessional Education and Practice Guide No. 4: Developing and Sustaining Interprofessional Education at an Academic Health Center." *Journal of Interprofessional Care* (July 14): 1–5. (Epub ahead of print.)

Zanotti, Renzo, Giada Sartor, and Christina Canova. 2015. "Effectiveness of Interprofessional Education by On-Field Training for Medical Students, with a Pre-Post Design." *BMC Medical Education* 15, no.1 (July 29): 121.

Zorek, Joseph, and Cynthia Raehl. 2013. "Interprofessional Education Accreditation Standards in the USA: A Comparative Analysis." *Journal of Interprofessional Care* 27, no. 2: 123–30.

Chapter Six

Engaging Service Learning in Interprofessional Education

The University of Florida Experience

Erik W. Black, Nichole Stetten, and Amy V. Blue

The 1998 Pew Health Professions Commission report "Recreating Health Professional Practice for a New Century" identified twenty-one different critical competencies for the twenty-first-century health professional. Included among these competencies was the ability to work as a member of an interdisciplinary team of healthcare providers. Since the report's release, health professions accrediting bodies echoed the Pew report's recommendations for preparing a new generation of health professionals. Seemly overnight, interprofessional education has become a mainstream topic and an area of burgeoning interest (IPEC 2011). Addressing the needs of diverse student bodies, each with jam-packed curricula, is a formidable challenge. Many institutions have adopted intersession activities or other brief experiences to meet the needs of accreditation; others have built complex experiences that provide students with early access to clinics and patients (e.g., Vanderbilt's VPIL experience [Schorn et al. 2014]). The University of Florida has a robust history of interprofessional learning, its marquee activity is a service-learning activity that all first-year students within the health science center participate in (Davidson and Waddell 2005). The purpose of this chapter is to describe how interprofessional education can be incorporated into a service-learning experience through a description of a unique service-learning experience for first-year students from each of the six University of Florida Health Science Center (UFHSC) colleges. The learning experience, Putting Families First (PFF), was conceived as a vehicle for interprofessional learning among students from diverse colleges and programs at large academic health science center. Since its inception in 1997, over 7,500 students have participated, completing nearly fourteen thousand home visits to over 2,500 local families. This chapter will begin with a brief overview of PFF, define service learning and interprofessional education, and then explore interprofessional service learning in the health sciences education; finally the chapter will describe PFF in greater detail, including outcomes data from students and recommendations for faculty and administrators who wish to promote interprofessional service-learning opportunities in their own health science institutions.

OVERVIEW OF PUTTING FAMILIES FIRST: AN INTERDISCIPLINARY FAMILY HEALTH EXPERIENCE

PFF is a required course for first-year health professions students that has provided a foundational learning experience for University of Florida Health Sciences students since 1997 (Davidson and Waddell 2005). Central to the PFF experience is a service-learning requirement in which interprofessional teams of students participate in home visits with local families. Other institutions (e.g., Jefferson College of Health Sciences, Florida International University [Arenson et al. 2015; Rock et al. 2014]) have adopted similar service-learning outreach programs that incorporate local members of the community, but PFF is recognized as the first and largest interprofessional health sciences service-learning course in the world. Over the years PFF has evolved to incorporate prevailing perspectives on interprofessional education, health promotion, disease prevention, and teams and teamwork, yet service learning has remained an enduring component of the experience.

Service Learning

Service learning is a community-based education that allows students to obtain a deeper level of learning in their field of interest by engaging with members of the community (Borges and Hartung 2007; Moely, Furco, and Reed 2008). Service learning is an experiential opportunity that comprises formal learning opportunities that connect academic or classroom-based experiences to authentic structured public-service activities (Furco 2007). These structured experiences allow students to apply what they learn in settings outside the classroom, as well as instill teamwork and leadership skills among students who might not normally work together (Borges and Hartung 2007; Buff et al. 2011). Service learning's ability to encourage diverse students to interact and work together in diverse settings facilitates unique opportunities for students to confront preexisting stereotypes about communities and the individuals within them. For example, a study by Sauer (2006) provides evidence that students who participated in service learning shed stereotypes they held about specific or vulnerable populations, and obtained a deeper and richer understanding of the community that surrounded them. Numerous studies have detailed positive outcomes associated with student service-learning experiences in higher education, identifying increases in participant's moral and ethical development, development of personal identity, and increases in communication skills (Astin and Sax 1998; Rockquemore and Schaffer 2000; Schmidt 2000). Further, studies report that student service-learning experiences have a positive effect on reducing stereotypes, increasing cultural and racial understanding, promoting critical thinking, and increasing learners' sense of social responsibility (Astin and Sax 1998; Eyler et al. 2001; Vogelgesang and Astin 2000). In addition to helping students grow as community members, service learning promotes student reflection. Reflection provides a means for students to make sense of their personal observations and experiences, furthering their growth as learners (Arndell et al. 2014; Borges and Hartung 2007; Yorio and Ye 2012).

Interprofessional Education (IPE)

Interprofessional education is an emergent topic in the health professions education, and while there are multiple definitions of IPE, they all incorporate a similar thematic structure that asserts that IPE occurs when two or more professions learn or work together toward a common goal. According to Benner, Benner, Sutphen, and Leonard (2009) the goal of IPE is to create cultures where systems-based decision makers collaborate as a community to solve complex problems and address issues that exceed the reach of any one profession. In 2003, the Institute of Medicine (IOM) published data that indicated patients are more likely to receive quality care when health professionals work together (Knebel and Greiner 2003). Since this publication, the IOM has recommended that health professional students work together in order to learn from each other in order to improve healthcare delivery, interdisciplinary respect, and health outcomes (Bridges et al. 2011; De Los Santos, McFarlin, and Martin 2014; Iachini et al. 2015; Mulholland, Barnett, and Spencer 2013). To this end, in 2011, the Interprofessional Education Collaborative (IPEC 2011), representing multiple health professions societies, identified four core competency domains within the context of patient care that are key to interprofessional education; these include values/ethics, roles/responsibilities, interprofessional communication, and interprofessional teamwork and team-based care. The IOM and IPEC recommendations, coupled with evolving societal, economic, and academic expectations have redefined our understanding of best practices in health professions education and prompted many to endorse interprofessional education as a way to provide healthcare that is safe, high-quality, and patient-centered. In a relatively short time, the competencies domains identified by the IPEC collaborative have become core expectations of twenty-first-century healthcare providers (Baker et al. 2005; Commission on Collegiate Nursing Education 2003; the Joint Commission 2008) , students (Vlasses et al. 2008; Kirsch and Aron 2008; National League for Nursing Accrediting Commission 2008), and resident physicians (Van Zanten et al. 2008).

Since the initial 2003 IOM report, multiple studies have shown that interprofessional teams can better address complex and challenging health problems, provide increased quality care, decrease medical errors, improve patient satisfaction, and improve the overall resources available for marginalized/vulnerable populations (Acquavita et al. 2014; Bridges et al. 2011; Iachini et al. 2014; Mulholland, Barnett, and Spencer 2013). In the classroom, IPE allows students to learn about healthcare from a variety of health professionals' perspectives. This type of interaction facilitates a more holistic understanding of healthcare, as well as improved communication and leadership skills when students interact with professionals from other healthcare fields (Acquavita et al. 2014; Buckley, Vu, and Remedios 2014).

Interprofessional Service Learning in the Health Sciences

Given the experiential and contextualized nature of health professions education, which has traditionally included a focus on community-based education and outreach (Seifer 1998), the shift from uniprofessional to interprofessional service learning is not novel. In fact, there are multiple publications describing interprofessional service-learning activities during the last ten years (e.g., Buff et al. 2011; Dacey et al. 2010; Freeth et al. 2001; Gillespie et al. 2010; Mareck et al. 2005; Pilon et al. 2015; Schorn et al. 2015). A closer look at these activities reveals several commonalities: a limited number of students participating, short duration, the activity's classification as elective or volunteer and a lack of longitudinal institutional commitment to the activity; that is, a majority of the activities are funded through extramural or intramural temporary or exploratory grant monies (Bridges et al. 2011). Yet, a non-systematic analysis of the outcomes data associated with these studies provides evidence of multiple successful student-led quality improvement projects, positive impact upon patient satisfaction, increased feelings of patient well-being, and perceived increases in patients' ability to self-manage their care (Dacey et al. 2010; Gillespie et al. 2010; Lee et al. 2013; Mareck et al. 2004; Pineda-Herrero et al. 2015; Schorne et al. 2015). Further, there is evidence that the incorporation of service learning and IPE into an integrated experience negates a health science curriculum's tendency to devalue service and also increases quality of healthcare overall (Arndell et al. 2014; Borges and Hartung 2007; Buff et al. 2011).

PUTTING FAMILIES FIRST: AN INTERDISCIPLINARY FAMILY HEALTH EXPERIENCE

Putting Families First has been a community-based interprofessional learning experience since 1997. PFF was conceived and launched by Dr. Richard Davidson and Dr. Rhondda Waddell and initially funded with grant money from the Pew Foundation. In 2001, the University of Florida Health Science Center provided full funding for the program, ensuring the program would continue to exist regardless of extramural funding status. At present, there are no extramural funds used for the operation of PFF. PFF is housed in the Office of Interprofessional Education within the Office of the Senior Vice-President for Health Affairs. It is a required course for all first-year students in the Colleges of Medicine, Dentistry, Pharmacy, and Veterinary Medicine students; the traditional nursing students (four-year bachelor of science) in the College of Nursing; the physical therapy, health administration and clinical and health psychology students from the College of Public Health and Health Professions; and nutrition graduate students from the Institute for Food and Agricultural Sciences. For the 2014 to 2015 academic year, the course comprised 694 students, eighty-eight faculty facilitators and more than two hundred volunteer families from the local community. Curricular goals and specific objectives for PFF are detailed in tables 6.1 and 6.2; they primarily focus on introducing students to concepts and skills related to teamwork, interprofessional practice, and public health issues. Students will later build upon these concepts and skills in uniprofessional activities associated with their program's curriculum.

Logistical Structure

PFF runs from September to March, during which students meet on six different occasions for two hours in small, interprofessional groups facilitated by two interprofessional faculty during the fall and spring semesters. The first-year student participants are subdivided into interprofessional groups of sixteen students for the in-class sessions, with two interprofessional faculty facilitators assigned to each group. Groups are then further divided into four interprofessional teams of four (see figure 6.1) to work with the assigned volunteer family. Students are required to complete four home visits with a local volunteer family, learning about the family's health and working with the family on a health improvement project that is of interest to the family. Team assignments to family volunteers is made in a semirandom manner, taking into account volunteer preferences and needs, and student professional program. For example, if the Office of Interprofessional Education is aware of a poly-pharmacy concern associated with a volunteer, efforts are made to include a pharmacy student in their volunteer team. Demographics of the

Table 6.1. PFF Goals and Taxonomic Classification.

PFF Course Goals	Goal #
The goals of Putting Families First: An Interprofessional Family Health Experience are for students to be able to:	
Explain how cultural, social, economic, and political determinants affect individual, animal, and population health. (Knowledge—content)	1
Use the knowledge of one's own role and those of other professions to address the healthcare needs of populations and patients served. (Knowledge—IPE)	2
Propose a patient-centered interprofessional health improvement plan based upon the patient's perceived needs. (Skill)	3
Communicate with other health professionals in a respectful and responsible manner. (Skill)	4
Demonstrate interprofessional teamwork in a variety of roles (e.g., team member, team leader, and role model). (Skill)	5
Advocate a patient-centered approach in healthcare. (Attitude)	6
Recognize the importance of interprofessional collaboration in healthcare. (Attitude)	7

volunteer families closely match those of the surrounding county in a geographically diverse fashion (see figure 6.2) and the distribution of families within groups is systematic; the Office of Interprofessional Education strives to provide a range of family types within each small group. For example, one group may include an uninsured family with adult children living at home, a widowed elder living alone, a retired affluent professional couple, and a middle-class family whose child has cystic fibrosis. Volunteer families sign Health Insurance Portability and Accountability Act (HIPPA) releases at the time of their recruitment into the program.

Each of the six small-group sessions has a different theme and the faculty are responsible for covering content related to teams and teamwork, cultural competencies, professional roles and responsibilities, the U.S. healthcare system, and social determinants of health, in addition to discussing the students' volunteer families in a case conference format. Table 6.1 features goals and objectives associated with PFF. Course content associated with each small-group session is delivered using blended instructional methods. All course content is housed on the Canvas Learning Management System (see figure 6.3) and students are able to access each of the seven content modules (one for each small group visit and an orientation module) from anywhere on or off campus. Short reading assignments, quizzes, and other activities must be completed as individuals or as a team prior to or following the small-group

Table 6.2. PFF Objectives by Module.

Module	*Month*	*Module Topic*	*Objectives*
1	Prior to September Meeting	Orientation	-Describe the goals of the PFF experience. -Describe what is expected of students during the PFF experience. -Explain the principles of patient-centered care. -Articulate the importance for advocating for patient-centered care.
2	September	Interprofessional Teamwork in Healthcare	-Describe effective teamwork behaviors. -Recognize different professions' roles in healthcare and a team. -Apply communication skills to establish rapport with another individual (e.g., active listening, use of open-ended questions, facilitation, summarizing). -Prepare for first home visit.
3	October	Social Determinants of Health	-Describe social determinants of health. -Evaluate how social determinants of health influence PFF families. -Define health literacy. -Appraise the level of health literacy associated with the team's PFF patient. -Describe how health interventions must be adapted to meet the health literacy of patients. -Analyze possible health improvement projects for PFF families. -Prepare for second home visit.
4	November	Access to Care	-Discuss the structure of the U.S. healthcare system. -Evaluate how healthcare access issues influence PFF families. -Identify community resources applicable to PFF families. -Develop possible health improvement projects for PFF families. -Evaluate peer's teamwork skills as a member of a team. -Evaluate self as a team member.

5	January	Cultural Influences on Health	-Discuss how culture influences health behavior. -Evaluate how culture influences PFF families' health behavior. -Prepare for third home visit. -Work on health improvement project for PFF families.
6	February	Roles and Responsibilities in Healthcare	-Describe the roles and responsibilities of professions other than your own. -Advocate for the role of your profession in healthcare. -Apply effective techniques to maintain patient boundaries, terminate professional relationship, and if pertinent, transition care with PFF families. -Evaluate health needs of PFF families. -Work on health improvement project for PFF families. -Prepare for fourth home visit
7	March	Improving Health	-Demonstrate completion of a health improvement project for an individual, family, or animal. -Analyze the use of interprofessional communication and teamwork to complete a health improvement project. -Assess individual professional growth during the PFF experience. -Evaluate peer's teamwork skills as a member of a team. -Evaluate self as a team member.

meetings and home visits. From September through March (with the exception of December), small groups meet on a monthly basis, traditionally the third Tuesday of the month from 10:40 a.m. to 12:30 p.m. This means that the Office of Interprofessional Education is tasked with the logistical challenge of organizing and reserving meeting space for forty-four small groups on each of the six small-group meeting dates.

Volunteer Families

The primary focus of PFF is the volunteer families. Students are encouraged to think of these volunteers as their first patients. While students are strictly forbidden to provide invasive care to volunteers, viewing the volunteer as a

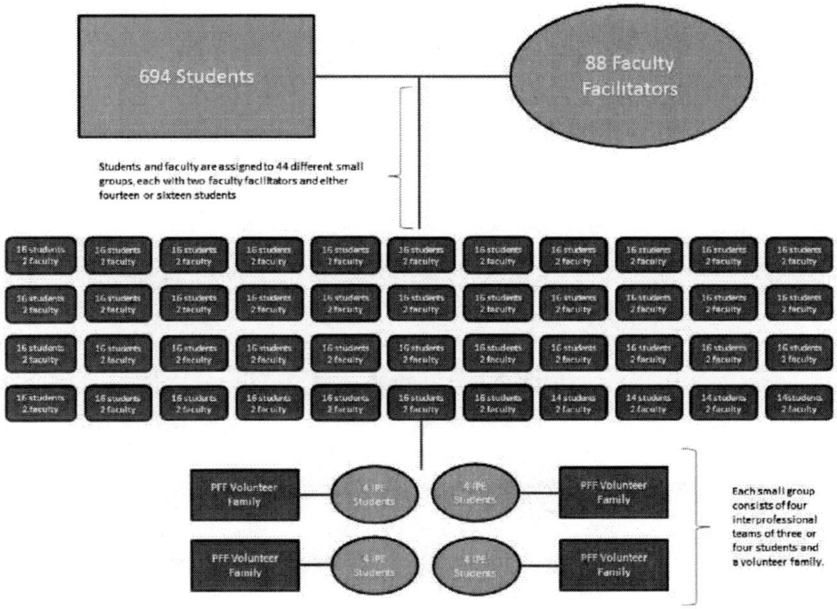

Figure 6.1. 2014 to 2015 PFF Student/Faculty Logistics. Photo by author.

patient confers a sense of duty and responsibility to the students that encourages them to place the needs and desires of the volunteer ahead of their own. Each student team is responsible for completing four home visits, two per semester, with their assigned volunteer families. Home visits follow the first and second small-group meeting in the fall semester and the fourth and fifth small-group meeting in the spring semester. Students are challenged to collaboratively plan their home visit with their volunteer family at a time when all students can be present. Home visits to volunteer families are scheduled by team members, who contact the family and arrange an appropriate and mutually convenient time. During home visits, students initially learn about the family through use of health-related instruments and then broaden visit topics to address particular health needs of the family. Students are to implement a project that addresses a health improvement need of the family. Health improvement is defined broadly; examples may include education about a particular health condition, recipes for a healthier diet, assistance with completing disability forms, creating a garden for a family, or providing information on low-cost health or pet services.

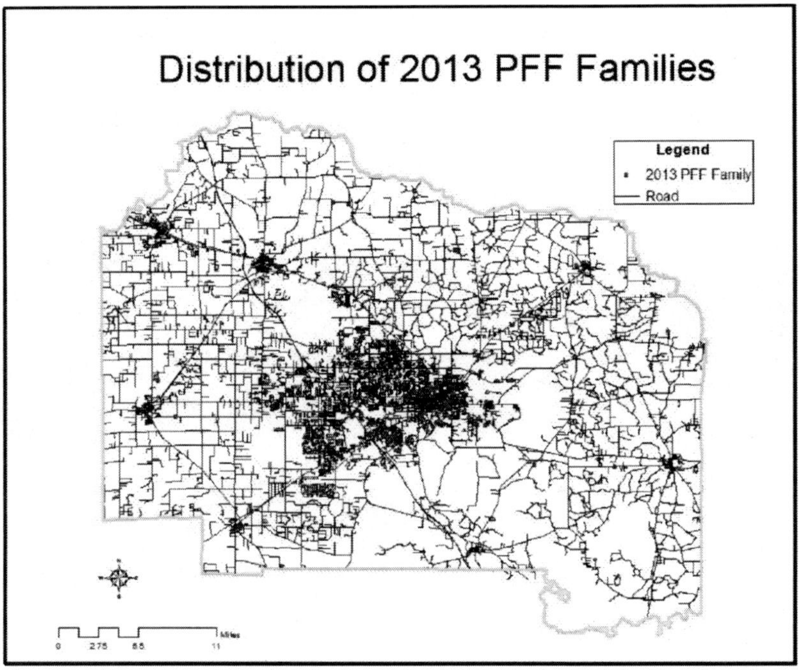

Figure 6.2. Geographic Distribution of PFF Volunteers (2013–2014). Photo by author.

Faculty Facilitators

A cadre of core faculty representing each of the involved Health Science Center colleges works in collaboration with the faculty and staff in the Office of Interprofessional Education to provide curricular guidance for PFF and ensure content is addressing subjects of value within the respective academic programs. The eighty-eight faculty facilitators who act as small-group leaders are recruited from across the health science center. Participating colleges are expected to provide sufficient faculty resources to enable PFF to function. As interprofessional education has emerged as a more prominent topic in the health sciences, the office's ability to recruit and retain faculty has sufficiently increased. In order to provide an equitable experience across the many different small groups, PFF operates with a standardized curriculum. Faculty are provided with a facilitation guide for each small-group meeting that provides "talking-points" to guide faculty through the required materials to be covered during each meeting and how to link session topics with home visit tasks (i.e., what are cultural influences on the health of your family for the session focused on cultural issues in healthcare). Thus, small-group lead-

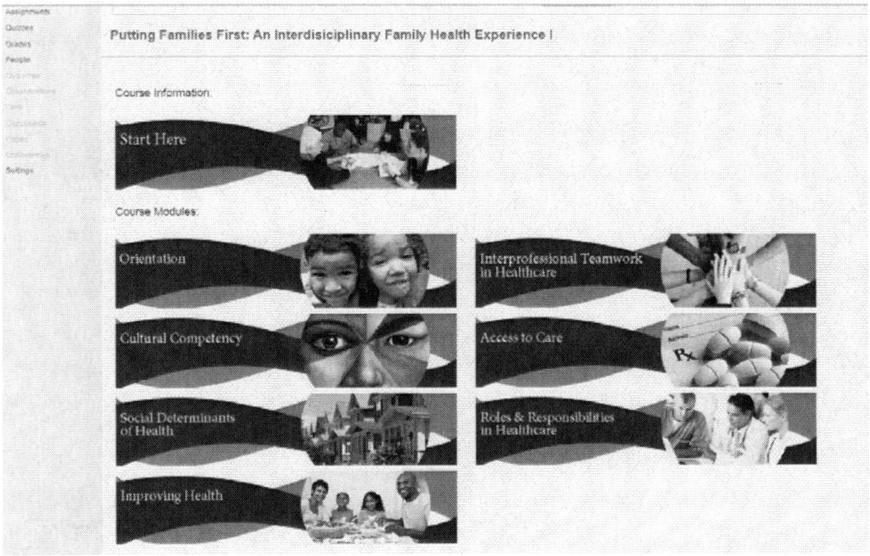

Figure 6.3. PFF Course Site hosted on the Canvas LMS. Photo by Author.

ers are responsible for leading their groups and interacting with their students. Each year the Office of Interprofessional Education hosts two faculty development kick-off sessions. During these sessions the PFF curriculum is reviewed, faculty are made aware of changes to the course and are provided strategies for successful small-group instruction. Additionally, the Office of Interprofessional Education offers one-on-one support for faculty who may have specific concerns or questions about facilitations.

Student Evaluation and Grading

Students earn points for completing individual assignments and assignments as part of their team. As individuals, students are required to complete short quizzes on each module's content, complete a home visit report for each home visit, assess their team members' teamwork skills, reflect on the results from their team members' feedback on their own teamwork skills, determine personal learning goals for the experience, and complete a reflection at the end of the experience reflecting on learning goals and the overall experience. As a team, students complete questionnaires based on information obtained from the family during the home visits and must also present a Family Health Presentation at the end of the year summarizing their work with the family. The small-group facilitators also evaluate each student's performance in the small-group sessions. Because of the myriad differences in the operation of the various different programs associated with PFF, PFF does not exist as a course entity. Rather, PFF is a component of a course within each of the different participating program's curriculum. For example, PFF makes up a component of the BMS 6810 and BMS 6812 Introduction to Clinical Medicine course in the College of Medicine and is part of VEM 5008 Professional Development in the College of Veterinary Medicine. Students' final grades are determined by each college. For example, in the colleges of dentistry, medicine, pharmacy, and veterinary medicine, the course is part of a larger first-year course in terms of credit. Grades earned in the PFF course represent a proportion of total grade for the larger courses.

Since its inception, PFF has included a peer evaluation component. Historically, this peer evaluation has been nominally effective. Often, students provided survey based feedback with little variance that was highly negatively skewed. In essence, the evaluations informed us that nearly all students are excellent peers and productive members of their respective teams. Data derived from this traditional evaluation process, in addition to being unwieldy (providing student feedback on their peer evaluations for seven hundred students is not a small undertaking) did not align with students' students reflections, which provided evidence of conflict and challenges within some groups. In addition to being unwieldy, providing student feedback on their peer evaluations for seven hundred students is not a small undertaking; students' evaluations were not supported by qualitative evidence from students reflections. In 2014, the PFF administration decided to pilot the Comprehensive Assessment of Team Member Effectiveness (CATME) online system (Ohland et al. 2012) for peer evaluation. CATME allows for anonymous online peer evaluation of self and team competencies and behaviors. Team members assessed themselves and their peers across three different teamwork competencies: Contributing to the Team's Work, Interacting with Teammates, and Keeping the Team on Track. The assessed competencies were scored from one to five. These ratings were summed to provide a composite score for each of the competencies, which could range from four to twenty. In addition, team members provided feedback about team satisfaction providing five-point Likert-style (strongly disagree to strongly agree) responses to the following prompts: I am satisfied with my present teammates; I am pleased with the way my teammates and I work together; I am very satisfied with working in this team. Initial responses show increased variance compared with prior methods of peer evaluation, though in a strong majority of cases, students described themselves and their peers in very positive terms. This data was also supported by students' satisfaction with their team. Perhaps equally important, CATME's automated nature eliminated the logisticaly hurdles associated with providing timely peer feedback to students.

CATME will continue to be a component of the PFF evaluative process; future studies will employ mixed-method procedures to evaluate students' peer evaluations and corresponding reflective statements.

Lessons Learned and Recommendations for Health Science Educators

PFF serves as a conduit for student exposure, growth, and development at an early stage in their clinical education. Data exists indicating that participation raises student awareness of the scope of access and disparities issues in the local community. Students experience firsthand the interdependent relationship between an individuals' health and their lived environment (Estrada et al., forthcoming). Through the experience, they also acquire fundamental teamwork skills and knowledge of the roles and responsibilities of a variety of health professions, thus the experience provides an in-depth interprofessional education experience. PFF is a mature interprofessional service-learning program whose success has been facilitated by multiple factors known to effectively guide the development and implementation of interprofessional education and service-learning programs. These include institutional leadership commitment, administrative structure and resources, broad faculty support, established schedule, and faculty development.

Since its inception, health science leadership has been committed to PFF, and over the years, as noted above has been supported by institutional funding. Interprofessional education has been a component of the health science center's 2010 to 2015 strategic plan and remains a central component of the education portion of the 2015 to 2020 strategic plan. Leadership commitment is recognized as a key element for the success of interprofessional education programs (Blue et al. 2010; Bridges et al. 2011).

Administrative resources, including an office with professional staff and faculty dedicated toward interprofessional education is also described as an essential factor for inculcating a culture that appreciates and is able to advance interprofessional education (Bridges et al. 2011; Oandasan and Reeves 2005) The University of Florida Office of Interprofessional education includes two faculty for a 1.5 full time equivalents (FTE) commitment, including a director, two professional staff, and an administrative assistant.

Faculty support is necessary for the successful implementation of IPE at an institution. Given the history of the PFF program and the institutional commitment, faculty recognize the value of participating in the program. Through a structure of core faculty from each academic program to guide curricular revisions and program improvement, faculty are engaged in shaping the students' learning experience.

Scheduling is often cited as challenge in IPE and for good reason, given that academic programs have full curricula and often varying academic calendars within an institution. Agreement was reached several years ago that PFF in-class sessions would be held on a particular schedule and all participating academic programs need to respect that. Programs work with their own faculty for the release time needed from other classes and ensure that students' schedules allow them to attend the PFF sessions.

Faculty development is recognized as essential for effective interprofessional education. In PFF, new and experienced faculty attend orientation and training sessions held every year so they are familiar with the overall PFF experience and any changes made for the upcoming year. Additionally, faculty receive a facilitator guide to provide important information and teaching points, including points on how to address profession-specific perspectives on content. For example, with the cultural issues in healthcare, facilitators are briefed that different cultures view owning a pet differently than others.

In addition to recommendations related to interprofessional education, several recommendations related to service learning are derived from our unique experience. While many service-learning activities exist within a co-curricular or elective learning environment for students, a required service-learning activity necessitates several considerations. These include support for participating family members and students, recruiting sites (suitable families) for students, and addressing student safety issues.

While students in the program provide support for participating families through their health improvement projects, in some cases the nature of the family's need is such that students are limited in their ability to address particular needs. These may involve medical, dental, or other healthcare advice from a provider, more substantive assistance with navigating local, state, or federal agencies, or assistance with accessing tangible support items (such as a walker). The office employs a full-time case manager who provides additional assistance to families, and in turn to students, when a family's need is above what students are able to help to facilitate or provide. In this manner, our students know that a back-up system exists to further help families. For example, if a student team suspects that a family needs medical attention, the case manager can intervene and ensure a visit to a physician.

Recruiting sites, or in the case of PFF, volunteer families, is a time-consuming effort and two of the staff (one being the case manager) have established numerous community contacts over the years as venues through which to recruit families. Branding the program with a specific identity and developing materials to distribute to agencies and at community events is essential. The Office of Interprofessional Education worked with marketing professionals to ensure that materials are attractive (i.e., succinct, colorful, etc.).

Student safety is an utmost concern. All families are carefully screened at intake, and a home visit by the case manager is conducted to ensure that the environment is safe for the students. Specific instructions are provided to students about home visits, including that the entire team makes the visit together, no one should drive alone to the home, and that if a safety suspicion arises, to leave the home or neighborhood. We have a twenty-four-hour pager that students can use if they need to reach the office during after-hours and weekends regarding any concerns about a family visit. We also ask students to inform the office if a family has moved to another residence in the area and not conduct the home visit until that new residence has been vetted by the case manager.

CONCLUSION

In conclusion, PFF represents a unique learning opportunity that integrates service learning within an interprofessional education context. Through working as an interprofessional team with a local family, students learn about the social determinants of health in relation to a specific patient and engage in teamwork to improve the patient's health.

REFERENCES

Acquavita, S. P., M. A. Lewis, E. Aparicio, and E. Pecukonis. 2014. "Student Perspectives on Interprofessional Education and Experiences." *Journal of Allied Health* 43, no. 2: 31E–36E.

Arenson, C., E. Umland, L. Collins, S. B.Kern, L. A. Hewston, C. Jerpbak, R. Antony, M. Rose, and K. Lyons. 2015. "The Health Mentors Program: Three Years Experience with Longitudinal Patient-Centered Interprofessional Education." *Journal of Interprofessional Care* 29, no. 2: 138–43.

Arndell, C., B. Proffitt, M. Disco, and A. Clithero. 2014. "Street outreach and shelter care elective for senior health professional students: An interprofessional educational model for addressing the needs of vulnerable populations." *Education for Health* 27, no. 1: 99.

Astin, A. W., and L. J. Sax. 1998. "How undergraduates are affected by service participation." *Service Participation* 39, no. 3: 251.

Baker, D. P., E. Salas, H. King, J. Battles, and P. Barach. 2005. "The Role of Teamwork in the Professional Education of Physicians: Current Status and Assessment Recommendations." *The Joint Commission Journal on Quality and Patient Safety* 31, no. 4: 185–202.

Benner, P., M. Sutphen, V. Leonard, and L. Day. 2009. *Educating Nurses: A Call for Radical Transformation* 15. New York: John Wiley & Sons.

Blue, A., M. Mitcham, T. Smith, J. Raymond, and G. Greenberg. 2010. "Changing the Future of Health Professions: Embedding Interprofessional Education Within an Academic Health Center." *Academic Medicine* 858: 1290–95.

Borges, N. J., and P. J. Hartung. 2007. "Service Learning in Medical Education: Project Description and Evaluation." *International Journal of Teaching and Learning in Higher Education* 19, no. 1: 1–7.

Bridges, D. R., R. A. Davidson, P. S. Odegard, I. V. Maki, and J. Tomkowiak. 2011. "Interprofessional Collaboration: Three Best Practice Models of Interprofessional Education." *Medical Education Online* 16.

Buckley, E., T. Vu, and L. Remedios. 2014. "The REACH Project: Implementing Interprofessional Practice at Australia's First Student-Led Clinic." *Education for Health* 27, no. 1: 93.

Buff, S. M., P. Y. Gibbs, O. Oubré, J. C. Ariail, A. V. Blue, and T. S. Greenberg. 2011. "Junior Doctors Of Health©: An Interprofessional Service-Learning Project Addressing Childhood

Obesity and Encouraging Health Care Career Choices." *Journal of Allied Health* 403: 39E–44E.

Dacey, M., J. I. Murphy, and D. C. Anderson. 2010. An Interprofessional Service-Learning Course: Uniting Students Across Educational Levels and Promoting Patient-Centered Care. *Journal of Nursing Education, 49*, no. 12: 696–99

Dacey, M., J. I. Murphy, D. O. Anderson, and W. W. McCloskey. 2010. "An Interprofesional Service Learning Course: Uniting Students across Educational Levels and Promoting Patient-centered Care." *Journal of Nursing Education* 4912: 696–99.

Davidson, R. A., and R. Waddell. 2005. "A Historical Overview Of Interdisciplinary Family Health: A Community Based Interprofessional Health Professions Course." *Academic Medicine* 804: 334–38.

De Los Santos, M., C. D. McFarlin, and L. Martin. 2014. "Interprofessional Education and Service Learning: A Model for the Future of Health Professions Education." *Journal of Interprofessional Care* 28, no. 4: 374–75.

Estrada, A., Behar-Horenstein, Estrada, D., Black, E. W., Kwiatkowski, A., Bzoch, A., Blue, A. (accepted). Incorporating interprofessional education into a veterinary medical curriculum. *Journal of Veterinary Medicine Education.*

Eyler, J., D. E. Giles Jr., C. M. Stenson, and C. J. Gray. 2001. At a Glance: What We Know About the Effects of Service-Learning on College Students, Faculty, Institutions and Communities, 1993–2000.

Freeth, D., S. Reeves, C. Goreham, P. Parker, S. Haynes, and S. Pearson. 2001. "'Real life' Clinical Learning on an Interprofessional Training Ward." *Nurse Education Today* 215: 366–72.

Furco, A. 2007. "Institutionalising Service-Learning in Higher Education." *Higher Education and Civic Engagement: International Perspectives* 65.

Gillespie, J., R. Whiteley, W. Watts, L. Dattolo, and D. Jones. 2010. "Interprofessional Education in Child Welfare: A University-community Collaboration between Nursing, Education, and Social Work." *Relational Child and Youth Care Practice* 231.

Iachini, A. L., M. E. Warren, J. W. Splett, M. W. George, L. K. Taylor, and M. D. Weist. 2015. "Exploring the Impact of a Pre-Service Interprofessional Educational Intervention for School Mental Health Trainees." *Journal of Interprofessional Care* 29, no. 2: 162–64.

Kirsh, S. R., and D. C. Aron. 2008. "Integrating the Chronic-Care Model and the ACGME Competencies: Using Shared Medical Appointments to Focus on Systems-Based Practice." *Quality and Safety in Health Care* 17, no. 1: 15–19.

Knebel, E., and A. C. Greiner, eds. 2003. *Health Professions Education: A Bridge to Quality.* Washington, D.C.: National Academies Press.

Lee, M. L., P. A. Hayes, P. McConnell, R. M. Henry. 2013. "Delivering Health Care to a Vulnerable Appalachian Population Through Interprofessional Service-Learning." *Gerontology and Geriatrics Education, 34*, no. 1: 43–59.

Marek, K. D., L. Popejoy, G. Petroski, D. Mehr, M. Rantz, and W. C. Lin. 2005. "Clinical Outcomes of Aging in Place." *Nursing Research* 54, no. 3: 202–11.

Moely, B. E., A. Furco, and J. Reed. 2008. "Charity and Social Change: The Impact of Individual Preferences on Service-Learning Outcomes." *Michigan Journal of Community Service Learning* 15, no. 1: 37–48.

Mulholland, P., T. Barnett, and J. Spencer. 2014. "Interprofessional Learning and Rural Paramedic Care." *Rural and Remote Health* 14, no. 3: 1–13.

National League for Nursing Accrediting Commission, and National League for Nursing Accrediting Commission. 2008. NLNAC accreditation manual. New York.

Oandasan, I., and S. Reeves. 2005. "Key Elements of Interprofessional Education. Part 2: Factors, Processes and Outcomes." *Journal of Interprofessional Care* 19, S1: 39–48.

Ohland, M. W., M. L. Loughry, D. J. Woehr, L. G. Bullard, R. M. Felder, C. J. Finelli, . . . and D. G. Schmucker. 2012. "The Comprehensive Assessment of Team Member Effectiveness: Development of a Behaviorally Anchored Rating Scale for Self-and Peer Evaluation." *Academy of Management Learning and Education* 11, no. 4: 609–30.

Panel, I. E. C. E. 2012. Core Competencies for Interprofessional Collaborative Practice: Report of an Expert Panel, 2011. Washington, D.C.: Interprofessional Education Collaborative.

Pilon, B. A., C. Ketel, H. A. Davidson, C. K. Gentry, T. D. Crutcher, A. W. Scott,. . . and S. T. Rosenbloom. 2015. “Evidence-Guided Integration of Interprofessional Collaborative Practice into Nurse Managed Health Centers.” *Journal of Professional Nursing, 31*, no. 4: 340–50.

Pineda-Herrero, P., C. Quesada-Pallarès, B. Espona-Barcons, and Ó. Mas-Torelló. 2015. “How to Measure the Efficacy of VET Workplace Learning: The FET-WL Model.” *Education+ Training* 57, no. 6: 602–22.

Rock, J. A., J. M. Acuña, J. M. Lozano, I. L. Martinez, P. J. Greer Jr., D. R. Brown, L. Brewster, L., and J. L. Simpson. 2014. “Impact of an Academic-Community Partnership in Medical Education on Community Health: Evaluation of a Novel Student-Based Home Visitation Program.” *Southern Medical Association* 1074: 203–11.

Rockquemore, K. A., and R. Harwell Schaffer. 2000. “Toward a Theory of Engagement: A Cognitive Mapping of Service-Learning Experiences.” *Michigan Journal of Community Service Learning* 7, no. 1.

Sauer, B. L. 2006. “Student-Directed Learning in a Community Geriatrics Advanced Pharmacy Practice Experience.” *American Journal of Pharmaceutical Education* 70, no. 3: G1.

Schmidt, B. C. 2000. “The Service Sojourn: Conceptualizing the College Student Volunteer Experience.” Unpublished doctoral dissertation, University of Utah, Salt Lake City, UT.

Schorn, M. N., A. Wu, H. A. Davidson, E. Black, and R. Rockhold. 2014. “Interprofessional Education IPE: Synchronous, Asynchronous, Clinical Practice, Simulation across Disciplines, across Universities.” *Medical Science Educator* 241: 9–11.

Seifer, S. D. 1998. “Service-learning: Community-Campus Partnerships for Health Professions Education.” *Academic Medicine* 733: 273–77.

Van Zanten, M., J. J. Norcini, J. R. Boulet, and F. Simon. 2008. “Overview of Accreditation of Undergraduate Medical Education Programmes Worldwide.” *Medical Education* 42, no. 9: 930–37.

Vlasses, P. H., J. W. Wadelin, and D. V. Travlos. 2008. “Accreditation Council for Pharmacy Education: Annual Report.” *American Journal of Pharmaceutical Education* 72, no. 2.

Vogelgesang, L. J., and A. W. Astin. 2000. “Comparing the Effects of Community Service and Service Learning.” *Michigan Journal of Community Service Learning* 7, no. 1.

Yorio, P. L., and F. Ye. 2012. “A Meta-Analysis on the Effects of Service-Learning on the Social, Personal, and Cognitive Outcomes of Learning.” *Academy of Management Learning and Education* 11, no. 1: 9–27.

Chapter Seven

Interprofessional Education and Patient Care

Supporting Patient Safety

Karen McDonough and Brenda Zierler

The complexity of modern healthcare demands that health professionals practice in teams. The explosion of medical knowledge and available interventions, combined with the aging population and the prevalence of chronic illness, means that no single practitioner can provide high-quality care alone. Unfortunately, the complexity of modern healthcare has also increased the likelihood of error. The Institute of Medicine's (IOM) "To Err Is Human," published in 1999, attributed the deaths of ninety-eight thousand Americans per year to medical error. This report focused the attention of healthcare organizations, accrediting bodies, and the public on patient safety, which is now recognized as a major public health issue. Based on a detailed review of more contemporary medical records, James estimated that the number of Americans dying prematurely because of preventable adverse events is four times higher than the 1999 IOM report and suggests that over 400,000 hospitalized patients per year suffer some type of preventable harm that contributed to their death (James 2013).

The worst type of error affecting patient safety, a sentinel event, can have multiple causes. A sentinel event is defined by the Joint Commission as "an unexpected occurrence involving death or serious physical or psychological injury, or the risk thereof" (Joint Commission 2013, SE-1). The Joint Commission publishes an annual report of the most frequently identified root causes (Joint Commission 2015) of sentinel events, which focuses on systems and processes of care delivery. Human factors, communication, and leadership have been the top three contributing factors of sentinel events in

U.S. hospitals in 2013, 2014, and 2015. Although these data are self-reported, they are used to identify areas for improvement and to prevent similar patient safety events in the future. Improving the safety of patients is not only a priority in clinical settings, but must be a priority in academic settings. Interprofessional education (IPE) provides an opportunity for health professions students to not only learn about, from, and with each other, but also to understand the rationale for why working together is essential.

Human error is inevitable in a system as complex as modern healthcare. Historically, medical errors have been attributed to failures of individual clinicians, whose competence or attention were less than adequate (Wachter 2016). In the last twenty years, most experts have adopted a systems approach, which assumes that preventable adverse events are caused by predictable human errors occurring in the context of poorly designed systems. These systems either facilitate the error or fail to prevent it from impacting the patient. Figure 7.1 illustrates the differences between adverse events, medical errors, and preventable adverse events (Wachter 2016).

Patient safety is defined as the prevention of injury due to errors occurring in the course of healthcare (Wachter 2016). These may be errors of

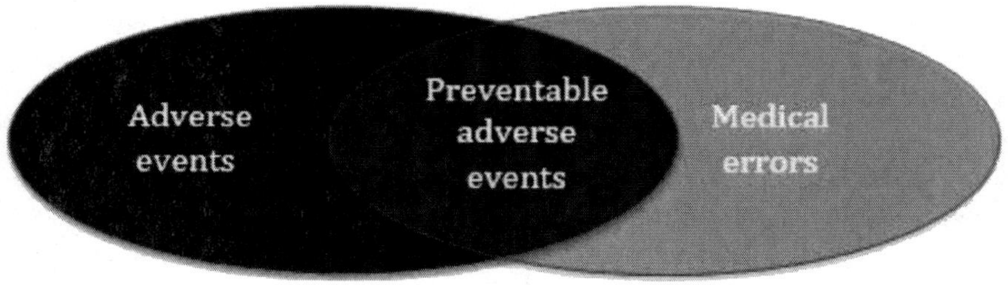

Figure 7.1. ***Adverse events*** **are any unfavorable occurrence caused by medical treatment, rather than the patient's underlying condition. Some adverse events, such as a drug rash in a patient without a known drug allergy, are not due to error and are not preventable.** ***Medical error*** **is defined as the failure of a planned action to be completed as intended or the use of a wrong plan to achieve an aim. Some medical errors do not cause harm to the patient, either because of luck or because a system or health professional prevented the harm. Medical errors that result in adverse events are** ***preventable adverse events.*** **Adverse events are any unfavorable occurrence caused by medical treatment, rather than the patient's underlying condition. Some adverse events, such as a drug rash in a patient without a known drug allergy, are not due to error and are not preventable. Medical error is defined as the failure of a planned action to be completed as intended or the use of a wrong plan to achieve an aim. Some medical errors do not cause harm to the patient, either because of luck or because a system or health professional prevented the harm. Medical errors that result in adverse events are preventable adverse events. Photo by author.**

commission, such as wrong site surgery, or errors of omission, such as failure to prescribe a needed medication. The injury may be immediate, or especially with errors of omission, may occur years later.

Safety is one of six key characteristics of high quality healthcare outlined in an IOM report "Crossing the Quality Chasm: A New Health System for the 21st Century" (Institute of Medicine 2001) that focused on redesigning the American healthcare system by providing six "Aims for Improvement":

1. Safety;
2. Effectiveness;
3. Equity;
4. Timeliness;
5. Patient-centeredness;
6. Efficiency.

Although IPE may impact all of these domains, patient safety has become a key focus of IPE. Preventable adverse events are rarely caused by the action or inaction of a single clinician. In order to impact a patient, a typical error must pass through multiple systems and clinicians from multiple professions.

In studies of errors that have led to patient harm or malpractice claims, communication and teamwork failures were major contributors over half of the time (Rabol et al. 2011; Singh et al. 2007). Errors happen in teams, and improvements in safety and quality must also happen in teams. Interprofessional education aims to prepare health professions students with the knowledge, skills, and attitudes needed to provide safe and high quality team-based care.

THE IMPACT OF IPE ON PATIENT SAFETY

In practice, interprofessional teams have been shown to improve patient safety in many ways. For example, team-based depression management in primary care improved mortality in patients with multiple other chronic illnesses (Gallo et al. 2015). Collaborative care improved glycemic control in patients with diabetes (McAdams-Marx et al. 2015). Heart failure teams reduced the risk of hospitalization (McAlister et al. 2004) and readmission (Eastwood 2014). Interprofessional geriatric team consultation improved six-month mortality in frail hospitalized elders (Deschodt et al. 2013). Palliative care teams improved symptom control and decreased hospital admissions (Higginson and Evans 2010), reduced emergency department visits in the last month of life (Henson et al. 2015), and improved refractory breathlessness (Higginson et al. 2014). The literature is rich with other examples of interprofessional teams that provided safer and higher quality care than any single profession could alone.

Undergraduate health professions education must prepare students for an interprofessional collaborative approach to practice. Many IPE activities have been shown to improve learners' knowledge, attitudes, and skills toward other professions and collaborative practice (Balogun et al. 2015; Darlow et al. 2015; Gould et al. 2015; Gunaldo et al. 2015). As with other educational interventions, demonstrating any impact of IPE on long-term patient and population outcomes has been more challenging. A 2013 Cochrane review identified fifteen controlled studies of objectively measured patient or healthcare process outcomes following an IPE intervention. Seven of these studies reported positive outcomes compared to controls, in randomized, time-interrupted, and controlled before-and-after trials. An additional four trials reported mixed outcomes, and four published trials were negative. The positive outcomes in these trials ranged from improved glycemic control and diabetes guideline adherence to improved motor function in stroke patients. The authors concluded that although the field of rigorous IPE research is growing steadily, the heterogeneity of the interventions and outcomes reported prevented them from drawing generalizable conclusions about the long-term impact of IPE on patient outcomes (Reeves et al. 2013).

INTERPROFESSIONAL COMPETENCIES AND PATIENT SAFETY

The Interprofessional Education Collaborative (IPEC 2011) outlined four key competency domains for interprofessional collaborative practice (see figure 7.2). All four of these domains impact the safety and quality of care provided by interprofessional teams.

Interprofessional Teamwork

Teamwork is the ability of a healthcare team to work together, communicate effectively, and coordinate action, to use the collective skills of team members to achieve their common goals. Teamwork clearly impacts the safety and quality of patient care: in the emergency room, the operating room, the intensive care unit, at hospital discharge, and in the outpatient setting (Lingard et al. 2004; Mazzocco et al. 2009; Reader, Flin, and Cuthbertson 2007). Failures in teamwork and team communication contribute to a majority of preventable adverse events. The key role of interprofessional teamwork in patient safety has led to the widespread adoption of a specific IPE strategy, team training in healthcare.

Team training has its origins in the Crew Resource Management programs developed in another high-risk industry, commercial aviation. These focused on leadership strategies, team communication, and situational aware-

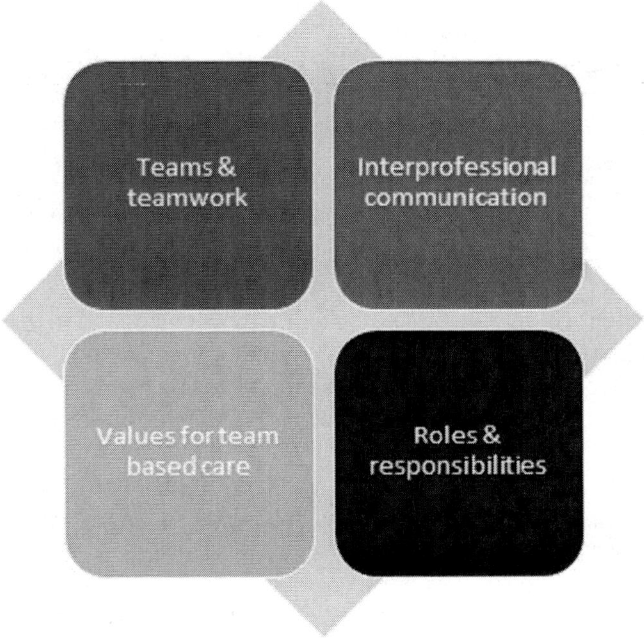

Figure 7.2. Interprofessional Competencies that Impact Patient Safety. Reprinted with permission from the National Academies Press.

ness, competencies that have been adapted and expanded for healthcare teams.

Team training programs, such as TeamSTEPPS® (TeamSTEPPS 2015), a program focused on improving communication and teamwork skills among healthcare professionals, and the Veterans' Administration Medical Team Training program (VA MTT), a program developed and implemented in forty-three VA medical centers from September 2003 to May 2007 are now widely used to improve interprofessional teamwork (Dunn et al. 2007). They include well-developed content, tools, and delivery methods that can be implemented and adapted for local groups of learners, as well as facilitator training programs and planning support.

Recent high-quality studies of team training have shown improvement in both process outcomes and patient outcomes (Weaver, Dy, and Rosen 2014). For example, in a controlled study of VA MTT, risk-adjusted surgical mortality was significantly lower in the hospitals that implemented team training (Young-Xu et al. 2011). The MTT hospitals also identified fewer handoff issues, fewer case delays, better adherence to antibiotic prophylaxis guidelines, and fewer equipment issues than those that had not implemented the program. Team training has been recommended by patient safety experts as a leading intervention to improve safety (Shekelle et al. 2013).

Usually implemented with practicing professionals, team training has also been offered to students and other trainees, with improvements in team behaviors and attitudes following training (Brock et al. 2013). Training has shown positive effects in both consistent, established teams as well as ad hoc teams that form and disband quickly, suggesting that skills learned in team training are transferable (Weaver et al. 2010).

Team Communication

Team communication, whether verbal, written or electronic, is the underpinning of patient safety and teamwork. Information sharing positively predicts the performance of teams in medical settings (Mazzocco et al. 2009; Weller 2014). Teams that share information well make fewer errors than those that do not.

Specific communication practices can help clinicians share information accurately and improve patient safety. Examples of interprofessional communication strategies include:

- Closed loop communication, a key element of team training. The sender clearly identifies the recipient of the information, ideally by name, and the recipient acknowledges it by repeating back the key points. Closed loop communication is used frequently in direct patient care, for example, when a clinician makes a request of another team member and the recipient acknowledges the request. It is also applicable to clinician-patient communication.
- Graded assertion is another skill emphasized by both the TeamSTEPPS and the VA's Medical Team Training program. This communication technique is used to respectfully share safety and quality concerns, with increasing force if the issue is not acknowledged and resolved. This approach is particularly helpful for team members speaking up against the hierarchy gradient that exists on medical teams.
- Handoffs within and between professions are major sources of information drop-off and error, and effective handoffs are another focus of team training. A structured approach to handoff communication has been shown to reduce the frequency of preventable adverse events (Starmer et al. 2014).
- Surgical checklists have been widely implemented to improve safety in the operating room. This structured approach to team communication levels the hierarchy present on many healthcare teams, and encourages information sharing by all members of the interprofessional surgical team. The most commonly used checklist, developed by the World Health Organiza-

tion (WHO), requires pauses at three points in the procedure (Haynes et al. 2009):

1. Before the patient is anesthetized, to confirm identity, procedure, surgical site, and consent.
2. Before the incision is made, to reintroduce all team members, again verify patient identity and planned procedure, and to plan for any anticipated critical events.
3. Before the patient leaves the operating room, to check instrument counts, and to identify key concerns for ongoing care.

Staff training and implementation of the WHO checklist has been associated with improved patient safety: mortality was 0.8 percent in hospitals that implemented the checklist versus 1.5 percent in matched controls, and the rate of complications per 100 procedures was 16.7 in implementation hospitals and 26.7 in controls (de Vries et al. 2010).

- Structured interdisciplinary rounds have been shown to decrease the frequency of preventable adverse events (O'Leary et al. 2011). This daily meeting encourages all hospital team members, including nurses, physicians, social workers, and pharmacists, to share information and review patient plans, following a consistent and well-defined format and process.

This model has been expanded to include the patient and family in structured interdisciplinary bedside rounds (SIBR). Stein, the associate vice chair for Quality at Emory School of Medicine described features of SIBR utilizing a TeamSTEPPS framework (retrieved from: http://www.crepatientsafety.org.au/seminars/designing_hospital_units/designinghospitalunits-dec11-jasonsteinsession2.pdf). The interprofessional team meets at the bedside of each patient to review interval events, identifies any safety issues, and formulates and communicates the plan for the day. Supporting the role of structured communication in encouraging inclusive teams, staff on a unit using SIBR were more likely to say they felt comfortable bringing up an issue for consideration, understood the plan for the day, and were working on a team than controls who were working on another unit (Gausvik et al. 2015).

At Emory University Hospital, where this model was developed, specific competencies have been identified for SIBR and training implemented. Nurses, medical students, and residents new to SIBR are observed by a nurse manager or attending physician in an "in-vivo" objective structured clinical examination (OSCE). Those who can demonstrate SIBR competencies in five of six consecutive patients are "certified," a status that has been met by all daytime nurses and rotating medicine residents who have participated in the program (Stein 2015).

Values and Ethics for Interprofessional Practice

Values across professions impact the patient safety culture of an organization, which is defined at a group level as shared values, beliefs, norms, and procedures about patient safety. Perceived organizational culture is an important predictor of clinicians' willingness to report an error (Linthorst 2012), and a more positive safety culture has been associated with a lower risk of adverse events. Interprofessional team training may improve the safety culture within an organization (Weaver et al. 2013).

Respect for the culture and expertise of all health professions can also promote inclusivity in teams. A democratic approach to problem solving, actively engaging the ideas and opinions of all team members, is associated with better team performance (Woolley 2010). Mutual respect, eliciting input from all when in a team leader role, and speaking up in a team member role are all encouraged by team training.

Roles and Responsibilities for Collaborative Practice

A clear understanding of each professional's roles, responsibilities, and skills allows clinicians to engage all appropriate professions in the care of a patient, and to distribute work appropriately. This can enhance patient safety by ensuring that the team member with the greatest expertise performs patient care tasks. Knowledge of the care other professionals can provide also increases the likelihood that unmet patient care needs will be identified and addressed.

MODELS OF IPE FOR SAFETY AND QUALITY

Interprofessional education to improve patient safety can occur in many different learning environments: small-group classrooms, standardized patient exercises, and simulation labs, as well as in the context of clinical care and project-based learning. Web-based activities, in some cases interspersed with classroom sessions, are an emerging way to overcome logistical barriers to IPE, such as cross-program scheduling and space requirements. In a 2010 report, the World Health Organization (2010) defined interprofessional education as occurring "iwhen students from two or more professions learn about, from, and with each other to enable effective collaboration and improve health outcomes."

Key features of IPE can occur in a variety of settings: interactive, experiential, and is relevant to the goals and experience of adult learners.

Examples of IPE by Approach and Setting

Classroom-based IPE

At the University of Washington, all third-year dental, second-year medicine, senior nursing, third-year pharmacy, first-year physician assistant, and dietetics masters students participate in a series of four interprofessional small groups over the course of an academic year. The primary goals of these small groups are to increase knowledge of professional roles and skills, to enhance attitudes toward interprofessional collaboration, and to practice team communication skills.

In the first session, students are presented with a patient admitted with heart failure, diabetes, and advanced periodontal disease. Although this patient's stated goal was to improve and go home, she declined most treatments offered, as well as nursing home placement and home care. She remained in the hospital for weeks, creating professional and ethical challenges for her team. As this case unfolds in text and video, students improve their understanding of professional roles as they create a team-based plan of care, consider the perspective of a profession other than their own in caring for a "difficult" patient, and practice communication and respectful disagreement as they attempt to resolve this challenging situation.

The second session focuses on roles and responsibilities in outpatient teams, assembled to address the care needs of a complicated patient. It also addresses an educational gap identified in across health sciences schools, asking about military service and eliciting a military history from patients. After students observe a faculty member elicit a military history from a classmate who served, they identify the care needs and the professional(s) who could meet each need in the cases of three veterans: a forty-three-year-old man with diabetes and chronic pain; a thirty-five-year-old woman seeking preconception counseling, and a twenty-two-year-old man who suffered traumatic brain injury.

The third session focuses on community health and the role each of the health professions can play in community health and public policy. Students develop a model of the patient and family contributors and the "upstream" community and policy level contributors to a major public health problem, pediatric caries. The students then consider interventions each profession could make at each level to impact the prevalence and severity of the problem.

In the fourth session, students focus on teamwork and team communication as they discuss a medical error—administration of an antibiotic to a patient with a known allergy, resulting in anaphylaxis. After reflecting on contributors to the error and on team performance, students practice disclosing a medical error to a patient actor with empathy and transparency.

Interprofessional standardized patient exercises

An interprofessional standardized patient exercise follows a series of classroom based IPE sessions at the University of California, San Francisco. In this half-day exercise, students work with a team to assess and treat a simulated patient with multiple chronic illnesses. After a brief orientation, they evaluate the patient. Team members observe each other as each performs his or her assessment. They then develop a team-based plan of care, and meet with a facilitator to present their plan of care and debrief the exercise. They also receive feedback on their communication and teamwork skills from the standardized patient and their peers. Both students and faculty value the exercise, and pre- and post-administration of the—attitudes toward healthcare teams—survey demonstrated overall improvement in scores for team value and team efficiency. In focus groups, students reported that the exercise allowed them to learn about the roles and skills of other team members, and improved their ability to collaborate with others (Wamsley et al. 2012).

Simulation

Simulation offers a realistic but low-risk opportunity for students to practice working as an interprofessional team. At the University of Missouri, groups of students from pharmacy, medicine, nursing, and health administration programs participate in a yearly simulation workshop. The student teams evaluate five simulated emergency department patients, representing lower acuity patients seen after a mass casualty event. Patients are portrayed by standardized patients and high-fidelity simulators. Patient safety issues, such as an unrecognized drug allergy, communication issues, pregnancy, or an unlocked bed, are embedded in each scenario. After ten minutes to form their team and plan how to approach their five patients, students assess and manage each. The students then present their assessment and plan, and debrief the experience with interprofessional facilitators, focusing on teamwork, communication, and the safety issues that the team did or did not identify. Facilitators concluded the debriefing by highlighting safety issues and safety goals. Almost all students agreed that the simulation had increased their understanding of the importance of interprofessional communication, of the roles of other professions, and of patient safety issues, and a pre- and post-survey demonstrated improvement in knowledge and attitudes about interprofessional teamwork (Vyas et al. 2012).

Educators at Louisiana State University developed a two-hour operating room-based simulation session for fourth-year medical students entering surgery, nurse anesthetist trainees, and nursing students. Teams of six students, two from each discipline, managed two patients: a trauma patient and a patient with a reaction to a local anesthetic. On a pre- and post-survey, participants demonstrated significant improvements in self-efficacy in most teamwork and communication skills. Observers also documented substantial improvement in team communication and teamwork between the first and second scenarios (Paige 2015).

At the University of Washington, senior nursing and medical students and third-year pharmacy students participate in a half-day workshop based on TeamSTEPPS training. After a one-hour didactic introduction, student teams evaluate then debrief their team's performance with three simulated patients: an elderly hospitalized man with dyspnea, a teenager in the emergency department with asthma, and a postoperative patient with supraventricular tachycardia. Results from the pre- and post-surveys demonstrated improved attitudes and self-efficacy for team communication and teamwork (Brock et al. 2013). The value of learning with other professions has been the most prominent theme in post-workshop debriefs and evaluations.

Shared clinical experiences

In the training ward model, interprofessional student teams care for a small number of patients in the hospital under the supervision of faculty from each profession. In one recently developed program in Melbourne, Australia, volunteer senior medical and nursing students care for patients in two beds of either an emergency department or a rehabilitation floor. Students take primary responsibility for these patients' care, working together and reporting to senior staff on the ward. On the rehabilitation unit, they were joined by students from other appropriate disciplines, such as social work, dietetics, or occupational therapy. Overall student satisfaction with this experience was rated highly. In focus groups, students described improved teamwork and collaboration, and a better understanding of other professions' roles (Morphet et al. 2014). Training wards have been established in Canada, Scandinavia, and other sites in Australia.

Shared clinical experiences can also occur in the outpatient setting. In one example, eight Australian Universities established the Capricornia Allied Health Project, in rural Queensland. Exercise physiology, dietetics, occupational therapy, pharmacy, podiatry, and social work students are placed in an ambulatory clinic focused on early interventions for clients with multiple chronic illnesses. Under the supervision of clinic preceptors, students spend two-thirds of their time in discipline-specific patient care, and the other third in interprofessional work, including shared initial intake evaluations and interprofessional communication and conferences. After completing this experience, most students reported improved understanding of team-based care and improved communication, as well as increased profession-specific knowledge (Frakes et al. 2014).

Online

Online education is emerging as a flexible approach to IPE with fewer time and space barriers to participation by students from multiple schools. At Virginia Commonwealth University, fourth-year medicine, nursing, and pharmacy students and second-year masters of social work students participate in a web-based interprofessional geriatrics module with a virtual electronic health record (EHR) (Dow et al. 2015). This is an online, asynchronous model, based on principles of team-based learning. Students are divided into interprofessional teams of about seven students. Each student receives a profession-specific narrative about an elderly woman, the information their profession would collect. Students document this information in the virtual EHR, then other students on the team can view it. Individual and team knowledge are assessed: students first answer multiple-choice questions independently, and then answer again as a team, collaborating online with a team-specific discussion board. Team members complete anonymous peer evaluations, and then receive a new chapter of the patient's story.

Teams that collaborated more, based on counts of log-ins and discussion board posts and views, had higher individual and team scores on the multiple-choice questions. Mean team scores were also significantly higher than mean individual scores, supporting the benefit of collaboration.

Grand Valley State University in Michigan uses a hybrid activity, in which a case is presented online and students meet once in person at a time and location of their choosing, without a need for facilitators or reserved space. Physician assistant, pharmacy, and physical therapy students are assigned to develop a written team-based plan of care for an online patient case, a middle-aged man with diabetic neuropathy.

In addition to their plan of care, they are asked to submit a brief reflection on their experience. Qualitative analysis of these reflections revealed three themes. The first was that the experience gave students a better understanding of the benefits of team-based care. The second theme was that the experience increased their knowledge of the scope of practice and roles of other professionals. The final theme was that the students felt better prepared to identify the need for consultation and felt more confident in collaborating with other professionals. Participating students also demonstrated improvement in self-assessed ability to communicate with other professionals and work with a team (Shoemaker et al. 2014).

CONCLUSION

Collaborative care, provided by interprofessional teams, clearly improves the safety of healthcare in many settings, from the emergency room to the ICU to the end of life. Undergraduate health sciences education can prepare students for their roles as collaborative team members with a variety of IPE strategies, many of which have been shown to improve students' knowledge, attitudes, and skills for working in interprofessional teams. All IPE should be interactive, experiential, and related to learners' real life goals, to maximize the educational impact for these adult learners.

REFERENCES

Balogun, S. A., K. Rose, S. Thomas, J. Owen, and V. Brashers. 2015. "Innovative Interprofessional Geriatric Education for Medical and Nursing Students: Focus on Transitions in Care." *QJM: Monthly Journal of the Association of Physicians* 108, no. 6 (June): 465–71.

Brock, D., E. Abu-Rish, C. R. Chiu, D. Hammer, S. Wilson, L. Vorvick, K. Blondon, D. Schaad, D. Liner, and B. Zierler. 2013. "Interprofessional Education in Team Communication: Working Together to Improve Patient Safety." *Postgraduate Medical Journal* 89, no. 1057 (November): 642–51.

Darlow, B., K. Coleman, E. McKinlay, S. Donovan, L. Beckingsale, B. Gray, H. Neser, M. Perry, J. Stanley, and S. Pullon. 2015. "The Positive Impact of Interprofessional Education: a Controlled Trial to Evaluate a Programme for Health Professional Students." *BMC Medical Education* 15 (June): 98,015-0385-3.

Deschodt, M., J. Flamaing, P. Haentjens, S. Boonen, and K. Milisen. 2013. "Impact of Geriatric Consultation Teams on Clinical Outcome in Acute Hospitals: A Systematic Review and Meta-Analysis." *BMC Medicine* 11 (February 22): 48, 7015-11-48.

de Vries, E. N., H. A. Prins, R. M. Crolla, A. J. den Outer, G. van Andel, S. H. van Helden, W. S. Schlack, et al. 2010. "Effect of a Comprehensive Surgical Safety System on Patient Outcomes." *New England Journal of Medicine* 363, no. 20 (November): 1928–37.

Dow, A. W., P. A. Boling, K. S. Lockeman, P. E. Mazmanian, M. Feldman, D. DiazGranados, J. Browning et al. 2015. "Training and Assessing Interprofessional Virtual Teams Using a Web-Based Case System." *Academic Medicine: Journal of the Association of American Medical Colleges* (September 11).

Dunn, E. J., P. D. Mills, J. Neily, M. D. Crittenden, A. L. Carmack, and J. P. Bagian. 2007. "Medical Team Training: Applying Crew Resource Management in the Veterans Health Administration." *Joint Commission Journal on Quality and Patient Safety*, 33, no. 6 (June): 317–25.

Frakes, K. A., S. Brownie, L. Davies, J. Thomas, M. E. Miller, and Z. Tyack. 2014. "Experiences from an Interprofessional Student-Assisted Chronic Disease Clinic." *Journal of Interprofessional Care* 28, no. 6 (November): 573–75.

Gallo, J. J., S. Hwang, J. H. Joo, H. R. Bogner, K. H. Morales, M. L. Bruce, and C. F. Reynolds 3rd. 2015. "Multimorbidity, Depression, and Mortality in Primary Care: Randomized Clinical Trial of an Evidence-Based Depression Care Management Program on Mortality Risk." *Journal of General Internal Medicine* (October 2).

Gausvik, C., A. Lautar, L. Miller, H. Pallerla, and J. Schlaudecker. 2015. "Structured Nursing Communication on Interdisciplinary Acute Care Teams Improves Perceptions of Safety, Efficiency, Understanding of Care Plan and Teamwork as well as Job Satisfaction." *Journal of Multidisciplinary Healthcare* 8 (January 14): 33–37.

Gould, P. R., Y. Lee, S. Berkowitz, and L. Bronstein. 2015. "Impact of a Collaborative Interprofessional Learning Experience upon Medical and Social Work Students in Geriatric Health Care." *Journal of Interprofessional Care* 29, no. 4: 372–73.

Gunaldo, T. P., S. C. Andrieu, D. Garbee, L. K. Giovingo, D. E. Mercante, S. Tortu, and R. English. 2015. "Student Perceptions about Interprofessional Education after an Elective Course." *Journal of Interprofessional Care* 29, no. 4: 370–71.

Haynes, Alex B., Thomas G. Weiser, William R. Berry, Stuart R. Lipsitz, Abdel-Hadi S. Breizat, E. P. Dellinger, Teodoro Herbosa et al. 2009. "A Surgical Safety Checklist to

Reduce Morbidity and Mortality in a Global Population." *New England Journal of Medicine* 360, no. 5: 491–99.

Henson, L. A., W. Gao, I. J. Higginson, M. Smith, J. M. Davies, C. Ellis-Smith, and B. A. Daveson. 2015. "Emergency Department Attendance by Patients with Cancer in Their Last Month of Life: a Systematic Review and Meta-Analysis." *Journal of Clinical Oncology: Official Journal of the American Society of Clinical Oncology* 33, no. 4 (February): 370–76.

Higginson, I. J., C. Bausewein, C. C. Reilly, W. Gao, M. Gysels, M. Dzingina, P. McCrone, S. Booth, C. J. Jolley, and J. Moxham. 2014. "An Integrated Palliative and Respiratory Care Service for Patients with Advanced Disease and Refractory Breathlessness: A Randomised Controlled Trial." *The Lancet. Respiratory Medicine* 2, no. 12 (December): 979–87.

Higginson, I. J., and C. J. Evans. 2010. "What is the Evidence That Palliative Care Teams Improve Outcomes for Cancer Patients and Their Families?" *Cancer Journal Sudbury, Mass.* 16, no. 5 (September–October): 423–35.

Institute of Medicine. 1999. "To Err Is Human: Building a Safer Health System." Retrieved from: http://www.nap.edu/catalog/9728/to-err-is-human-building-a-safer-health-system.

———. 2001. "Crossing the Quality Chasm: A New Health System for the 21st Century 2001." Retrieved from: http://www.nap.edu/catalog/10027/crossing-the-quality-chasm-a-new-health-system.

Interprofessional Education Collaborative Expert Panel. 2011. "Core Competencies for Interprofessional Collaborative Practice: Report of an Expert Panel." Washington, DC: Interprofessional Education Collaborative.

James, J. T. 2013. "A New, Evidence-Based Estimate of Patient Harms Associated with Hospital Care." *Journal of Patient Safety* 9, no. 3 (September): 122–28.

Joint Commission. 2013. Retrieved from:http://www.jointcommission.org/assets/1/6/CAMH_2012_Update2_24_SE.pdf

———. 2015. Retrieved from: http://www.jointcommission.org/assets/1/18/Root_Causes_Event_Type_2004-2Q_2015.pdf.

Lingard, L., S. Espin, S. Whyte, G. Regehr, G. R. Baker, R. Reznick, J. Bohnen, B. Orser, D. Doran, and E. Grober. 2004. "Communication Failures in the Operating Room: An Observational Classification of Recurrent Types and Effects." *Quality & Safety in Health Care* 13, no. 5 (October): 330–34.

Linthorst, G. E., B. L. Kallimanis-King, I. Douwes Dekker, J. B. Hoekstra, and J. C. de Haes. 2012. "What Contributes to Internists' Willingness to Disclose Medical Errors?" *Netherlands Journal of Medicine* 70, no. 5 (June): 242–48.

Mazzocco, K., D. B. Petitti, K. T. Fong, D. Bonacum, J. Brookey, S. Graham, R. E. Lasky, J. B. Sexton, and E. J. Thomas. 2009. "Surgical Team Behaviors and Patient Outcomes." *American Journal of Surgery* 197, no. 5 (May): 678–85.

McAdam-Marx, C., A. Dahal, B. Jennings, M. Singhal, and K. Gunning. 2015. "The Effect of a Diabetes Collaborative Care Management Program on Clinical and Economic Outcomes in Patients with Type 2 Diabetes." *Journal of Managed Care & Specialty Pharmacy* 21, no. 6 (June): 452–68.

McAlister, F. A., S. Stewart, S. Ferrua, and J. J. McMurray. 2004. "Multidisciplinary Strategies for the Management of Heart Failure Patients at High Risk for Admission: A Systematic Review of Randomized Trials." *Journal of the American College of Cardiology* 44, no. 4 (August18): 810–19.

Morphet, J., K. Hood, R. Cant, J. Baulch, A. Gilbee, and K. Sandry. 2014. "Teaching Teamwork: An Evaluation of an Interprofessional Training Ward Placement for Health Care Students." *Advances in Medical Education and Practice* 5 (June 25): 197–204.

O'Leary, K. J., R. Buck, H. M. Fligiel, C. Haviley, M. E. Slade, M. P. Landler, N. Kulkarni et al. 2011. "Structured Interdisciplinary Rounds in a Medical Teaching Unit: Improving Patient Safety." *Archives of Internal Medicine* 171, no. 7 (April 11): 678–84.

Paige, J. T., D. D. Garbee, K. M. Brown, and J. D. Rojas. 2015. "Using Simulation in Interprofessional Education." *Surgical Clinics of North America* 95, no. 4 (August): 751–66.

Rabol, L. I., M. L. Andersen, D. Ostergaard, B. Bjorn, B. Lilja, and T. Mogensen. 2011. "Descriptions of Verbal Communication Errors between Staff. An Analysis of 84 Root

Cause Analysis-Reports from Danish Hospitals." *BMJ Quality & Safety* 20, no. 3 (March): 268–74.

Reader, T. W., R. Flin, and B. H. Cuthbertson. 2007. "Communication Skills and Error in the Intensive Care Unit." *Current Opinion in Critical Care* 13, no. 6 (December): 732–36.

Reeves, S., L. Perrier, J. Goldman, D. Freeth, and M. Zwarenstein. 2013. "Interprofessional Education: Effects on Professional Practice and Healthcare Outcomes Update." *Cochrane Database of Systematic Reviews* 3 (March 28): CD002213.

Shekelle, P. G., P. J. Pronovost, R. M. Wachter, K. M. McDonald, K. Schoelles, S. M. Dy, K. Shojania et al. 2013. "The Top Patient Safety Strategies that can be Encouraged for Adoption Now." *Annals of Internal Medicine* 158, no. 5 Pt 2 (March) 5: 365–68.

Shoemaker, M. J., M. de Voest, A. Booth, L. Meny, and J. Victor. 2015. "A Virtual Patient Educational Activity to Improve Interprofessional Competencies: A Randomized Trial." *Journal of Interprofessional Care* 29, no. 4: 395–97.

Shoemaker, M. J., C. M. Platko, S. M. Cleghorn, and A. Booth. 2014. "Virtual Patient Care: An Interprofessional Education Approach for Physician Assistant, Physical Therapy and Occupational Therapy Students." *Journal of Interprofessional Care* 28, no. 4 (July): 365–67.

Singh, H., E. J. Thomas, L. A. Petersen, and D. M. Studdert. 2007. "Medical Errors Involving Trainees: A Study of Closed Malpractice Claims from 5 Insurers." *Archives of Internal Medicine* 167, no. 19 (October 22): 2030–36.

Starmer, A. J., N. D. Spector, R. Srivastava, D. C. West, G. Rosenbluth, A. D. Allen, E. L. Noble et al. 2014. "Changes in Medical Errors after Implementation of a Handoff Program." *The New England Journal of Medicine* 371, no. 19 (November 6): 1803–12.

TeamSTEPPS®: Strategies and Tools to Enhance Performance and Patient Safety. September 2015. Agency for Healthcare Research and Quality, Rockville, MD. http://www.ahrq.gov/professionals/education/curriculum-tools/teamstepps/index.html.

Vyas, D., R. McCulloh, C. Dyer, G. Gregory, and D. Higbee. 2012. "An Interprofessional Course Using Human Patient Simulation to Teach Patient Safety and Teamwork Skills." *American Journal of Pharmaceutical Education* 76, no. 4 (May 10): 71.

Wachter, R. 2016. Chapter 12: Quality of Care and Patient Safety, in Goldman-Cecil Medicine, twenty-fifth edition, Elsevier 2016.

Wamsley, M., J. Staves, L. Kroon, K. Topp, M. Hossaini, B. Newlin, C. Lindsay, and B. O'Brien. 2012. "The Impact of an Interprofessional Standardized Patient Exercise on Attitudes toward Working in Interprofessional Teams." *Journal of Interprofessional Care* 26, no. 1 (January): 28–35.

Weaver, S. J., S. M. Dy, and M. A. Rosen. 2014. "Team-Training in Healthcare: A Narrative Synthesis of the Literature." *BMJ Quality & Safety* 23, no. 5 (May): 359–72.

Weaver, S. J., L. H. Lubomksi, R. F. Wilson, E. R. Pfoh, K. A. Martinez, and S. M. Dy. 2013. "Promoting a Culture of Safety as a Patient Safety Strategy: A Systematic Review." *Annals of Internal Medicine* 158, no. 5 Pt 2 (March) 5: 369–74.

Weaver, S. J., R. Lyons, D. DiazGranados, M. A. Rosen, E. Salas, J. Oglesby, J. S. Augenstein, D. J. Birnbach, D. Robinson, and H. B. King. 2010. "The Anatomy of Health Care Team Training and the State of Practice: A Critical Review." *Academic Medicine: Journal of the Association of American Medical Colleges* 85, no. 11 (November): 1746–60.

Woolley, A. W., C. F. Chabris, A. Pentland, N. Hashmi, and T. W. Malone. 2010. "Evidence for a Collective Intelligence Factor in the Performance of Human Groups." *Science New York, N.Y.* 330 6004 (October 29): 686–88.

World Health Organization WHO. 2010. "Framework for Action on Interprofessional Education and Collaborative Practice." Geneva: World Health Organization. Retrieved from: http://whqlibdoc.who.int/hq/2010/WHO_HRH_HPN_10.3_eng.pdf.

Young-Xu, Y., J. Neily, P. D. Mills, B. T. Carney, P. West, D. H. Berger, L. M. Mazzia, D. E. Paull, and J. P. Bagian. 2011. "Association between Implementation of a Medical Team Training Program and Surgical Morbidity." *Archives of Surgery Chicago, Ill.: 1960* 146 12 (December): 1368–73.

Chapter Eight

Medical Libraries Supporting Interprofessional Education

Lauren M. Young, Susan B. Clark, Connie K. Machado, Elizabeth G. Hinton, and Mitzi R. Norris

From liaison programs to embedded librarians, medical libraries have supported the educational activities of the healthcare professions in their schools and programs through instruction, outreach, and access to resources. As interprofessional education (IPE) programs become incorporated into the institutions in which we work, there is a need to support them as we have other disciplines and activities.

Libraries are incredibly adept at gauging the needs of their communities, patrons, and institutions. More specifically, academic library initiatives are routinely founded upon the best practices and guiding principles of information literacy and access to information in conjunction with the didactic and accreditation needs of the institution. As libraries participate in accreditation and assessment conversations and activities on campus, they develop goals that reflect the programmatic needs of individual colleges and departments. By engaging with their units in these discussions, librarians demonstrate their interest in and ability to contribute to evolving needs within the institution. The outcomes of such relationships can be small and focused, such as working closely with a specific department to compile lists of the titles held in a discipline for inclusion in an accreditation review, or larger in scope such as ongoing instruction and collection development commitments. Support of IPE falls into the latter category; rather than being specific and finite in nature, these pursuits should be reflected throughout the library's offerings.

This chapter describes the ways in which librarians are supporting IPE with three primary emphases: instruction, space, and resources. Literature reviews highlighting activities at various institutions will be included.

SUPPORTING WITH INSTRUCTION

Traditional librarian roles have evolved, and outreach and innovation in instruction have become an important part of this evolution. This has been most notable for reference and instruction librarians. Librarians have the knowledge, tools, and resources to expand their roles and become an integral part of IPE initiatives at their respective institutions. Librarians are appropriate leaders in IPE because of their interest in education initiatives and their "neutral" position since they generally serve each school within their institution and have knowledge about all relevant programs.

The focus on IPE began in 1988 with the World Health Organization report *Learning Together to Work Together for Health* (World Health Organization 1988) that presented the concept of multiprofessional education as a means to improve the competence of health professionals. The Interprofessional Education Collaborative (IPEC) was formed in 2009 to promote and encourage substantive interprofessional learning experience to prepare healthcare professionals (Interprofessional Education Collaborative 2015). Leadership in IPEC includes six national associations of schools in the health sciences including the American Association of Colleges of Nursing, the American Association of College of Pharmacy, the American Dental Education Association, the Association of Schools and Programs of Public Health, the American Association of Colleges of Osteopathic Medicine, and the Association of American Medical Colleges. Additionally, several program-specific groups for healthcare professions require IPE as part of their accreditation and competency standards, to include:

- Medical (LCME Survey Report Template for Full Survey Visit Reports. http://www.lcme.org/publications.htm#guidelines/).
- Dental (Accreditation Standards for Advanced Education Programs in General Dentistry. http://www.ada.org/~/media/CODA/Files/aegd.ashx/).
- Nursing (The Essentials of Baccalaureate Education for Professional Nursing Practice. http://www.aacn.nche.edu/education-resources/BaccEssentials08.pdf/).
- Pharmacy (Accreditation Standards and Key Elements for the Professional Program in Pharmacy Leading to the Doctor of Pharmacy Degree. https://www.acpe-accredit.org/pdf/Standards2016FINAL.pdf/).
- Occupational Therapy (2011 Accreditation Council for Occupational Therapy Education (ACOTE®) Standards and Interpretive Guide. http://

www.aota.org/-/media/Corporate/Files/EducationCareers/Accredit/Standards/2011-Standards-and-Interpretive-Guide.pdf/).

- Physical Therapy (Standards and Required Elements for Accreditation of Physical Therapist Education Programs. http://www.capteonline.org/uploadedFiles/CAPTEorg/About_CAPTE/Resources/Accreditation_Handbook/CAPTE_PTStandardsEvidence.pdf/).

Because of the need for IPE and librarians' evolving roles in support of it, this section will examine ways in which librarians have become involved in IPE and will provide examples of how libraries can play vital roles in the development of new initiatives.

How Librarians Are Getting Involved

Examples of IPE instruction and outreach

Many librarians are using evidence-based practice (EBP) and problem-based learning (PBL) as models for teaching IPE. Library faculty develop curriculum, teach courses, create library resource guides, and employ other means to augment IPE at their institutions, working across disciplines to align their expertise and resources to fulfill institutional needs. In 2013, a team of librarians and medical faculty performed a review of the literature regarding evidence-based medicine (EBM) training and undergraduate medical education. Maggio and colleagues (2013) recommend teaching EBM in an IPE environment in order to expose students to a wider variety of evidence-based resources and to the challenges that other disciplines face. Further, the authors found several studies that incorporated medical librarians into the EBM teaching team and noted that medical librarians add authenticity to the EBM experience.

Librarians serve as evidence-based practice consultants at Northeastern Ohio Universities Colleges of Medicine and Pharmacy (McEwen, Bruce, and Sutton 2010). In one instance, second-year medical and pharmacy students were divided into groups of eight to ten and given a case study about a heart patient in an EBP component called "The Heart Disease Group Project." During the six-month course, the students gave oral presentations, submitted a group paper, and performed self and peer evaluations. The librarians' main roles included serving as an EBP consultant during six class sessions, providing reference services to the students, grading two sections of the written assignment, and attending all oral presentations. This project was considered successful because students attained a greater awareness and understanding of library resources, an appreciation for interprofessional (IP) teams, and an understanding of the need for IPE training. Additionally, students were able to recognize the medical librarian as an integral part of the interprofessional team. The authors concluded that the integration of IPE principles into the existing curriculum rendered the instruction more effective than one-shot library instruction on the topic.

Librarians at the University of Minnesota Bio-Medical Library teamed up with campus faculty members to present an interprofessional train-the-trainer workshop on evidence-based practice (Koffel and Reidt 2015). The workshop included twenty-five faculty members from the university's schools of medicine, nursing, pharmacy, allied health, dentistry, and veterinary medicine, with nine faculty members and librarians serving as instructors. After receiving two separate requests from faculty members for EBP faculty development opportunities, the library recognized a chance for developing EBP skills in an IPE environment. The workshop presented the basic EBP skills of literature searching, critical appraisal of sources, and application, and reinforced the idea that EBP belongs to all professions. Participating faculty members rated the workshop favorably and enjoyed the IP learning environment.

A problem-based learning IPE module was developed at the University College Dublin School of Public Heath, Physiotherapy and Population Science, Health Sciences Centre, in Ireland (Cusack and O'Donoghue 2012). An interdisciplinary team of health professionals, students, librarians, and an educational developer designed the PBL IPE module. Ninety-two students from medicine, physiotherapy, nursing, and diagnostic imaging evaluated the learning objectives, library information skills, and intellectual stimulation, among additional aspects of the module. Overall, students valued the unit. Regarding the library component of the module, 70 percent responded that the library information sessions were valuable, and 80 percent said the library information skills would be helpful throughout their programs of study and their future careers (Cusack and O'Donoghue 2012). Students reported that the best part of the module was working with and learning from students in other disciplines, which led to a better understanding of their own professional roles.

The Himmelfarb Health Science Library at George Washington University has embedded problem-oriented, case-based learning into the curriculum design process since 2000 (Butera, Gomes, and Kakar 2014). The library faculty are members of an interdisciplinary team that designed and implemented a problem-based learning course that is taken by first- and second-year medical students. Library faculty coteach small groups of medical students in a weekly course that instructs students how to best access information and locate evidence-based resources. Library faculty also provide lectures on professionalism and ethics, data searches, finding and evaluating resources, and evidence-based medicine. In addition, the library faculty monitor a blog for questions during the ethics lectures. In annual evaluations, the value of this librarian integration into the curriculum is consistently acknowledged as evident. The integration of library instruction into the medical curriculum is a core value of medical librarianship (Butera, Gomes, and Kakar 2014), and IPE lends itself perfectly to this initiative.

Library guides (LibGuides) are a web-publishing platform for libraries to collect and share information on a variety of topics. Several libraries have chosen to support IPE initiatives by incorporating IPE-based library guides into their subject guide listings. The University of Nebraska Medical Center McGoogan Library of Medicine, University of Massachusetts Medical School Lamar Soutter Library, Nova Southeastern University College of Osteopathic Medicine University Libraries, and University of Nevada, Reno University Libraries are a few examples of libraries that have embraced IPE by creating library guides (University of Nebraska Medical Center McGoogan Library of Medicine n.d.; University of Massachusetts Medical School Lamar Soutter Library 2015; Nova Southeastern University Libraries 2015; University of Nevada, Reno, University Libraries 2015).

Librarians have developed unique roles to promote IPE at their institutions. At the University of Southern California (USC) Norris Medical Library, librarians provide leadership in IPE. The school created an extensive IPE portal committed to providing information and resources for IPE. An IPE committee was formed with members representing a mixture of students and faculty from the seven schools within the institution including librarians. The library's representative provides a leadership role by scheduling and leading the meetings, maintaining communication between the committee members, and performing grant research (Brennan, Chatfield, and Eandi 2012). The USC IPE portal contains information regarding IPE initiatives at USC, upcoming IPE conferences, competencies and evaluation, and scholarly materials to support IPE teaching and research (University of Southern California Norris Medical Library 2011).

Another way librarians have led IPE programming is by creating narrative-based educational offerings such as the Common Read program. At Western Michigan University School of Medicine, a year-long lecture course was developed around a selected book (Lorbeer, O'Hagan, and Knuth 2015). A committee composed of healthcare professionals and a medical librarian found a way to incorporate IPE into the colleges of medicine, pharmacy, and nursing and allied health programs and two local hospitals. The first year of the program was successful; a diverse group of students, residents, faculty, and practitioners were able to share their thoughts on the reading and learn from one another in a structured IPE environment. Based on course evaluations, participants saw value in the program and expressed their desire to continue the program, albeit with shorter readings. This type of narrative course also incorporates the humanities, an emerging area of interprofessional education.

Consumer health librarians can help source interprofessional teams with patient information, and point learning teams to literature that addresses social issues in family care paired with clinical issues. Two of the library faculty at the University of Florida Health Science Center Libraries have been involved with the Putting Families First course, which was formerly known as Interdisciplinary Family Health (Edwards et al. 2015). Students from all six colleges participate in a year-long course that focuses on teamwork in healthcare. Small groups of students work with one family throughout the course with the goal of improving health in nonclinical ways. Library faculty lead discussion, give feedback to students, provide information on resources for students to use, and grade papers (Edwards et al. 2015). Because of increased involvement among the different colleges, the library is seeking ways to broaden the impact beyond two faculty members working with small groups. See chapter 6 of this book for a more in-depth discussion of the efforts being made at the University of Florida Health in the unique Putting Families First course.

In 2014, Olson and Bialocerkowski conducted a systematic review of interprofessional education in allied health. The authors' work suggests that the capacity for IP collaboration, understanding, and attitude improvement may be greater with more mature or experienced students. Similar findings emerged at Duquesne University in Pittsburgh, Pennsylvania, when librarians partnered with nursing, allied health, and pharmacy faculty to create an interprofessional health sciences version of an existing information literacy course (Nolfi et al. 2015). Ten first-year students from each school were enrolled in the course, and were required to create PICO (Patient/Intervention/Comparison/Outcome) questions, locate and evaluate scholarly material, and work in IP groups. Instructors administered pre- and post-class surveys and the Readiness for Interprofessional Learning Scale (RIPLS) Questionnaire (Latrobe Community Health Service and the Health and Socialcare Interprofessional Network 2009) at the beginning and end of the semester. Although the sample size was small, students in the IP group reported that the course had higher relevance to their studies and careers than either non-health sciences students or health sciences students in the regular information literacy course. Responses to the RIPLS survey were conflicting; students clearly understood the importance of IP learning, but many also felt that they would learn more in classes specific to their own discipline. The authors suggest that appreciation for IP takes time to develop, but starting IP learning early is beneficial to the student.

Identifying campus champions and forming relationships

So how have libraries found success in developing partnerships? Reaching out to nonlibrary colleagues is necessary, but librarians must focus on partnering with someone who is willing to be a champion of libraries in order to successfully implement a library-supported IPE curriculum.

Pritchard (2010) described the role of librarians in providing information literacy support to faculty teaching in the science curriculum. The author describes the commonalities and differences between "information literacy" and "academic literacy." Information literacy is the recognition of the need to understand, find, evaluate, and use information. Academic literacy is the competencies of successful students such as critical thinking, reading, writing, communicating, being part of a team, managing self, and life-long learning. Librarians are natural partners to effectively teach these skills. Pritchard emphasizes the need for librarians to identify and connect with specialists within their institutions. Additionally, she cautions against the passive role of the "patiently waiting librarian"; alternatively, librarians need to proactively seek and create opportunities for participation in IPE.

As stated by Cusack and O' Donoghue (2012), upper-level campus management must be invested in the support of IPE. Additionally, Butera, Gomes, and Kakar (2014) believe it is imperative that librarians form and strengthen relationships with key administrators on campus such as deans, directors, and other faculty members who are spearheading campus IPE curriculum initiatives. Librarians at the University of Florida HSCL also noted the importance of connecting with other groups to encourage IPE (Edwards et al. 2015). The authors stressed the importance of meeting with administrators to identify ways for librarians to be a part of IPE at their campus.

In 2010, two faculty librarians at the Health Sciences and Human Services Library, University of Maryland, Baltimore, were appointed to an academic task force along with the deans from the institution's seven academic schools (Betz and Raimondo 2015). The charge was to plan and implement a campus-wide IPE program for students and faculty. Librarian participation in the initiative led to an IPE library guide, campus-wide IPE days, a presentation to campus members about nationwide IPE centers, and a significantly strengthened relationship with senior faculty and deans. The librarians feel that involvement in campus IPE events has not only increased visibility on campus and credibility among fellow faculty members, but it has also positively influenced student opinions of the library faculty.

The University of Mississippi Medical Center's Rowland Medical Library participated in ACRL's 2014 to 2015 cohort of "Assessment in Action," a fourteen-month long assessment-based professional development program. The team, composed of two librarians and the executive director of Academic Effectiveness, chose a project focused on using library resources to improve student learning and to promote interprofessional growth (Hinton, Norris, and Young 2015). The library worked with the Office of Academic Affairs and the Interprofessional Subcommittee of the Associated Student Body to host an interprofessional student event in the library's Collaborative

Learning Center (CLC) with a clinician/library faculty-led discussion on Basic Life Support (BLS) and the role of interprofessionalism in life-saving care situations. Outcomes were measured by discussions and pre- and post-tests given to two separate focus groups. A nurse educator administered a BLS pre-test and library faculty administered an IP core competency survey. Following a short video clip depicting an interprofessional BLS event, students were asked to react to the video and share their opinions and feelings regarding the role of interprofessionalism in life-saving care situations. Finally, post-tests were administered in order to measure subjective interprofessional growth and the retention of BLS training. Notes were taken during the discussions so keywords could be analyzed for themes upon conclusion. The initial sample indicated growth in both objective and subjective measures. In both groups, BLS test results showed the potential for increased retention in an interprofessional education environment, and answers to the IP competencies clearly indicated a stronger appreciation for interprofessionalism after the sessions. The success of this endeavor was made possible by the support of key administrators on the institution's campus.

Conclusion

The value of IPE is increasingly being recognized and required by program-specific accreditation organizations. The accrediting standards are being driven by the realization that healthcare is a team effort and should be taught in an interdisciplinary manner in order to improve patient outcomes. As healthcare education demands the use of IPE, librarians are valuable resources.

Librarians must be willing to venture out from the library and forge relationships with other departments on campus in order to successfully support IPE. Librarians should look for opportunities to become involved with campus IPE initiatives. Curricula that employ problem-based learning or evidence-based practice present an ideal environment in which librarians can assume a role in embedding IPE. Many of the examples discussed in this section identify opportunities for partnership with other campus departments, and methods of embedding IPE into the existing curriculum.

SUPPORTING WITH SPACE

Planning for Space and Design

The library in an academic medical center serving numerous hospitals and schools has always been a solitary entity reaching out to all the divisions and missions on campus. Originally its main purpose was to house extensive print collections largely composed of bound journals required to support all of the health sciences curricula. As new technologies developed, electronic resources displaced print materials physically. These volumes are often removed to an off-site location; consequently, library floor space is opened up and can look vacant, rendering it vulnerable to reassignment by institutional administration to other divisions and offices not affiliated with the mission of the library. Not only have curriculum styles in the health sciences taken on new philosophies and practices (Barr 2013), but the role of the library as a physical space to house print resources and support solitary study has almost ceased to exist and become outdated (Webster 2010).

> "Our experts firmly believe that by 2015, while the manner in which health sciences libraries develop and deliver services and collections will drastically change, the health sciences library would continue to exist, even in an era of easy desktop access to information. . . . [B]y 2015, they predict that academic health sciences libraries will house and manage instructional spaces for activities such as distance-learning classrooms, media labs, presentation facilities including auditoriums, and configurable teaching spaces." (Ludwig and Starr 2005, 321)

Students from the various health-related schools have always gathered for the common purpose of study in the library. Before there were IPE initiatives, the University of Mississippi Medical Center's Rowland Medical Library's faculty observed that students from one discipline studied in proximity to students in other disciplines. "There was a time when study was always understood to be a solitary activity, and collaboration was often seen as a form of cheating" (Bennett 2007). This pattern of siloed study defined the library as the neutral gathering space that provided a common area for all students to "claim" as their own (Nordquist, Kitto, and Reeves 2013). This serves in today's educational environment to equate the library with a café, student union or any freely available space with great Wi-Fi; neutral to all where resources are available on personal devices without the need to be surrounded by voluminous bound volumes for reference.

Since the library has shed its role as "the physical storeroom of the collection of books and scientific journals" (Nordquist, Kitto, and Reeves 2013) and many resources are available electronically 24/7, it is imperative to redefine its direct role as a keeper of knowledge resources and transition to a viable physical learning space. The library acquires, manages, and makes accessible electronic resources, but these activities are not visible to the user (Nordquist, Kitto, and Reeves 2013). Warehoused print materials are available by request, while the newest materials are only a click away on their own personal devices. This is nothing new in the academic library world, but where do you begin to reimagine the use of the large vacant spaces left behind by this trend and remain relevant to the educational mission?

> "Designing and redesigning physical learning space is [of] strategic importance for leadership in education. We need to pay attention to it in order for us to stay relevant to society and prepare the best and most valuable health professional to serve society's needs." (Nordquist, Kitto, and Reeves 2013, 3)

We must survey the physical space, observe the patrons and their study patterns, and derive a new purpose and role for the library in medical education. As librarians have embraced new roles, such as liaison librarians and embedded librarians, the physical space of the library has not changed. What remains is the footprint of a library designed decades before to meet needs that no longer exist. With librarians now represented within the schools and departments, the "new" library must take an active role in curriculum design, teaching, and planning. Refer to Lewis's five steps toward redefining the academic library "at the end of the age of print academic libraries" (Lewis 2007, 2). He goes on to provide meaningful insight into managing this transition.

PARTS OF THE PUZZLE (SUMMARIZED)

1. Complete the migration from print to electronic resources.
2. Retire legacy print collections. . . . This will free space that can be repurposed.
3. Redevelop the library as the primary information learning space on the campus.
4. Reposition library and information tools, resources, and expertise so it is embedded into the teaching, learning, and research enterprises.
5. Migrate the focus of collections from purchasing materials to curating content.

(Lewis 2007, 3–4)

Finding effective methods to monitor all the educational facets and changes on campus, which would include interprofessional education initiatives, curriculum changes, new programs or degrees, and assessment activities, while continuing to meet the mission of the institution and the library, is a good first step. The interprofessional education initiative moves full circle to bring students back into the library for their collaborative study needs. Their needs are not for the print material, but for a neutral environment, fully equipped to facilitate their interprofessional and collaborative study needs. The library provides this space without being aligned with one program or school. It is "program neutral" and is available for longer hours than many other educational facilities within the various schools on the medical campus, and is open to all regardless of their school affiliation.

Where do we begin to put new life into the empty space left behind? What are the first things to consider as we move into the next century? And how can this space be redesigned to meet current medical education curriculum needs, while still serving the needs of the student/patrons and the mission of the library and university? These are some of the many questions Rowland asked as the print collections shrank or were relocated, and open space was becoming the new reality.

Transforming Existing Space into a Collaborative Student Space with an Interprofessional Mission: Rowland Medical Library's Experience

After considering these questions and many others, Rowland Medical Library incorporated some design changes to encourage IPE experiences and adapt to the ever changing role of libraries in an academic medical center. December 2013, Rowland, serving the University of Mississippi Medical Center, opened the doors of its newly created Collaborative Learning Center (CLC). Having identified outdated, underutilized space within the library floor plan, the librarians at Rowland endeavored to create a more functional, collaborative space for library patrons, and tied the initiative to the interprofessional didactic shift in which the institution was embarking. The following section frames best practices from the literature within the experience at Rowland.

Beginning the process

The first logical step for transforming space is research. The changing uses of library space have been the subject of many articles, dedicated issues of journals, books, and symposia for over twenty years. Research from other disciplines as well, such as interprofessional journals and websites, academic construction/building, and general educational publications comprises a significant body of materials for librarians gathering knowledge and information to move forward.

Gathering information about current educational needs from the students themselves is a key part of the process. When planning to collect input about the space transformation, consider a survey of students and patrons, and ask what they require for study (Jordan and Ziebell 2009). Don't forget to include library staff, faculty, and IT personnel in this planning stage. Based on the survey conducted by Jordan and Ziebell to investigate client behavior, Webster outlines a simple method for surveying students on the features of library learning spaces that support specific study activities (Webster 2010). IPE learning spaces should be designed and developed "with the express intention of supporting transparency, interactivity, and collaboration between the health professions. It is also recognized that new facilities must be able to adapt to changing needs" (Cleveland and Kvan 2015). Contact the IPE committee within your institution, or better, try to become part of the IPE initiative on campus as it plans space to facilitate this new learning environment. Questions to consider: On average, how many students would need to be accommodated in an IPE group? How many groups would be working simultaneously? Will this be the only space on campus? Does the IPE planning group envision a need for scheduling the space or just ad hoc use? Some answers to these basic questions will give insight into the requirements for an engaged learning redesign project.

Another method to gather data is to visit other campuses, either virtually or in person, that have created any type of collaborative commons within their library. Don't limit these visits only to medical campuses. Make notes on designs or concepts that you like or dislike, and bring these back to the table for discussion. If possible, involve student representatives and other faculty in offsite visits as their input gives a different perspective. Inform these nonlibrary participants of the project and its importance to the mission of the institution.

Using Lamb and Shraiky's framework for competency-based collaborative learning design (see figure 8.1), the library can begin testing the relationship "between physical design features and competency-based performance in teamwork and collaboration" (Lamb and Shraiky 2013). To begin planning for the new collaborative space, analyze the library's current available space using Lamb's four design themes: flexibility, visual transparency/proximity, technology, and environmental infrastructure. Address the facets separately, then work toward integrating these ideas into planning, and finally, reality. We will add other facets for consideration from Rowland's own experience.

Flexibility

Flexibility allows the students and other users to easily change or adapt the environment to their specific needs, to include group study, problem-solving, or presentations. Take a hard look around the existing library and square footage that is available for redesigned, engaged learning. Consider a variety of seating styles that are easily rearranged to meet the needs envisioned for a new IPE space and mentioned in student survey results. Vendors can bring in

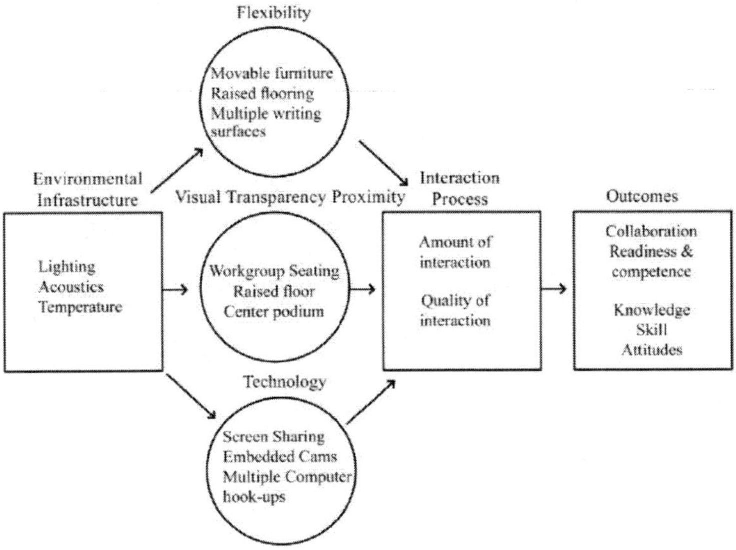

Figure 8.1. Collaborative Learning Environment Features and Collaboration-Readiness Model. Reprinted with permission from Taylor & Francis.

a variety of seating/table options that can be displayed, and students can vote on which style they consider most comfortable and conducive to learning. With planning, this activity could be incorporated into the overall student survey mentioned above. Other flexible equipment includes wiring (often a major challenge in older facilities), lighting, whiteboards (mounted or moveable), and access to power, presentation needs, and projection needs (Lamb and Shraiky 2013). Try to visualize this new flexible space encompassing various seating arrangements that will encourage collaborative learning. Involve all staff in the early stages of visualization. Many staff observe different behaviors at different times during service hours and can contribute their ideas to the planning.

Visual transparency/proximity

When in use by small or large groups, the space should provide clear sightlines for participants and instructors. Consider instructor-led sessions, ensuring that all students can see the activities without obstruction. Also, is the space visible from the rest of the library interior? Easy to find and access? Would there ever be a need for a podium? Should the space be totally open and flexible, or should some smaller rooms be available? Which would work better in your space for visibility: glass storefronts, or partial walls such as cubicles? See figure 8.2 for initial drawings for the Collaborative Learning Center (CLC) at Rowland Medical Library, which did not include the double glass storefront panels, which were incorporated later.

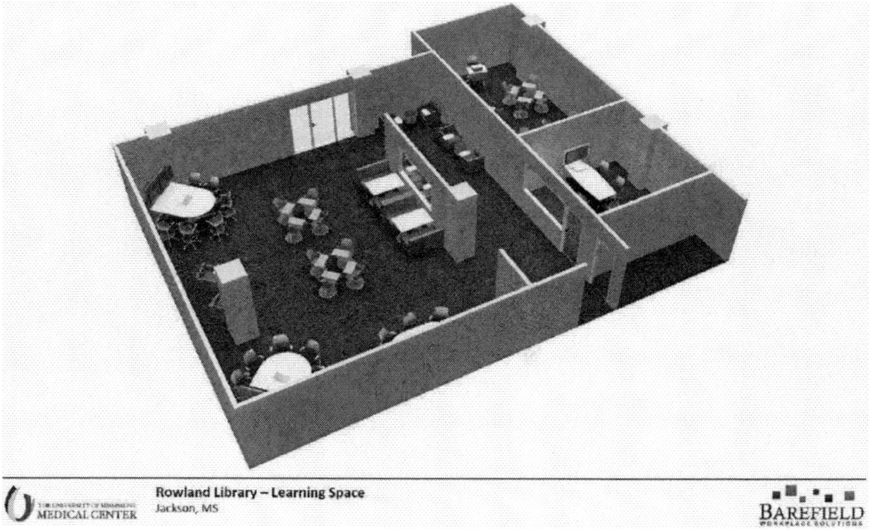

Figure 8.2. Anterior View, Barefield Drawing. Used with permission.

Technology

While it is difficult to envision the library housing a complete medical simulation center, this repurposed space can become the focal point for pre- and post-meetings for students and instructors to share their mutual interprofessional experiences. With the use of wired and wireless networks, software, distance learning, videoconferencing, projection systems, graphics, science software, and 3D visualization spaces, the opportunities for use are endless. Work with the campus IT division to see what is included in their future strategic plan for the campus and work together to replace the original equipment and remain on the cutting edge of educational needs (Sens 2010). Be part of the future; don't be left behind with empty, outdated space.

Environmental infrastructure

Though vendors and construction companies have a great deal of experience in this area, there is a need to learn what best serves the use of the space. Lighting itself comes in a vast variety of styles, but needs to work into the existing electrical infrastructure and flow with existing fixtures. Even the variety of lightbulbs may become an issue for the campus physical facilities unit.

Is this to be a quiet space in the library, or an area where more discussion is allowed? Should walls separate the space from outside areas to ebb this flow of sound? Should the HVAC have separate controls to adjust temperature in the area? Considering these minute details can play a pivotal role for students who will decide to either use, or not use, the new space. It may be too cold, too noisy, or not have enough electrical outlets. Try to conceptualize users' needs as the design becomes a reality.

Plans and drawings

Work with the construction or planning office of the campus to learn what campus standards need to be incorporated into the renovation. As a workable plan is visualized, begin to meet with vendors. Be open to their experience and perspective for the redesign, but be willing to express your specific needs without hesitation; be persistent (Yearwood 2015). Begin working with upper management to identify funding resources, emphasizing that this mission is not just for the library, but will be effective campus-wide for all students/patrons/staff. Any plans for redesign should align with the university's strategic plans. This show of support for institutional goals might assist with fundraising and planning efforts. Figure 8.3 gives an aerial view of Rowland's CLC, showing room for flexibility.

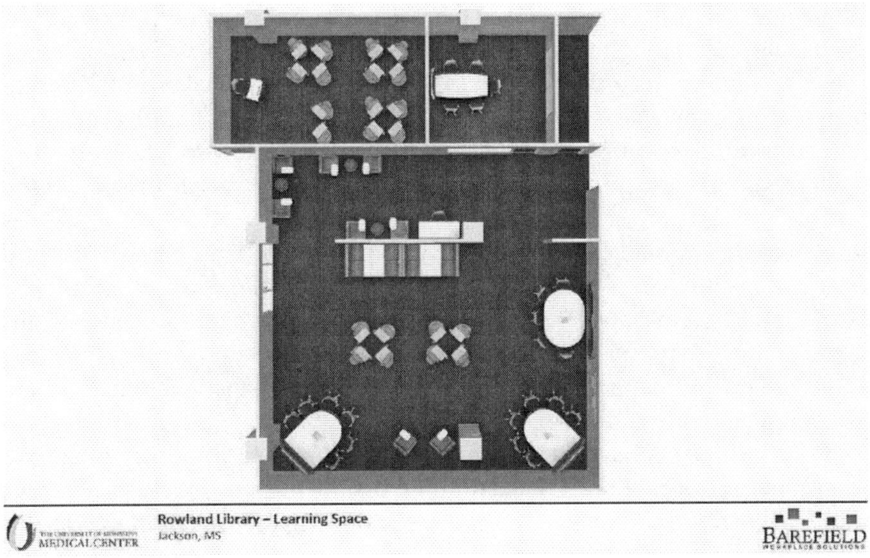

Figure 8.3. Aerial View, Barefield Floorplan. Used with permission.

Policy considerations

Start to visualize library policies that may need to be revised or newly written. Can the space be reserved? Will new services need to be offered? What will the food policies be? Should staff be assigned to the space to assist users? Our library gained a broad education on the use of dongles and had to devise a method for checking out these tiny links to the new Steelcase media:scapes. Training for staff on how to troubleshoot or assist users with connectivity must also be considered.

Publicity

Publicizing the newly redesigned space is a final step toward inviting use. Work with the IPE committee and host an event demonstrating the equipment and multiple purposes created by the redesign project. Emphasize the positives such as longer hours and neutrality to all schools. Seek publicity through campus news, reaching out to students and schools specifically. Ensure that this is not a competition for other spaces on campus with similar facilities, but a neutral space for all. Expectations for the use of the space will not be met unless patrons are aware that the space is available. Host an open house and demonstrate the equipment using library resources and databases, showing participants how to attach various devices to the Steelcase media:scape consoles.

Conclusion

Remember that the visualized purpose for the space may not be reflected in the actual outcome. Students tend to have their own ideas for space and seating, so be open to their needs. "Students use these spaces to take command of their own learning" (Bennett 2007). Start with a plan but expect numerous changes along the way. Initially, invite focus groups (figure 8.4) composed of students, faculty, and researchers to come, participate, and give feedback.

As academic medical libraries strive to redefine themselves and serve evolving institutional needs, there has been a major role reversal. Librarians now go outside the library and become embedded, while the students still come to the library, not to retrieve resources, but to enable them to thrive as engaged learners by participating in interprofessional experiences in this new environment designed for IPE.

Be proactive in choosing new partners to collaborate with to optimize the use of library space. Form connections across the campus from top administration, down to the faculty, researchers and students. Have a voice in the library's future.

Figure 8.4. Focus Group in Action in Rowland's New CLC. Photo by author.

SUPPORTING WITH RESOURCES

Providing access to resources is one of the primary functions of a library. This is equally true for medical libraries, which specialize in licensing niche, often very expensive, resources to meet the programmatic needs represented on campus. Resources can be viewed as falling into one of two categories: resources that are discipline-specific and support a small group of researchers and clinicians on campus; and resources that are cross-disciplinary in nature and of broader interest and relevance. This section presents a discussion of resources to meet both types of needs as it relates to interprofessional education.

Library Resources Supporting IPE

Discipline-specific resources

Good news for libraries making initial efforts to support IPE with resources is that they will already subscribe to numerous resources that will prove very useful to students. For accreditation purposes, the core journals for disciplines hosted on campus should already be available to students. Librarians have likely spent time training students and faculty on the use of these books, journals, and databases, so they will be confident moving around within their discipline's offerings. In an interprofessional setting, one would expect students to only be "expert" on the resources within their discipline. A meaningful exchange would find students contributing to the case study at hand employing evidence from their discipline's literature; their unique offering to the group. A sample list of journals that have included articles and special issues specifically addressing interprofessional education can be seen in appendix A of this chapter. The list, by no means exhaustive of all journals discussing IPE, represents the wide range of disciplines that are addressing IPE in their professional literature.

Multidisciplinary resources

Likewise, there is an increasing number of health sciences multidisciplinary journals that discuss interprofessional education, several of which are presented in appendix B of this chapter.

Interprofessional-specific resources

An extension of the discipline-specific resource discussion is to address the growth of interprofessional education as a discipline in its own right, with its own core journals. These journals provide valuable research on IPE as its own subject and address its integration into healthcare and education. Many have a target audience of the hospital and academic administrators working to negotiate the integration of IPE into their curricula in a meaningful way. Titles include, but are not limited to:

- *Health and Interprofessional Practice* (Pacific University Libraries);
- *International Journal of Integrated Care* (International Foundation for Integrated Care);
- *Journal of Interprofessional Care* (Informa Healthcare);
- *Journal of Research in Interprofessional Practice and Education* (*Journal of Research in Interprofessional Practice and Education*).

Libraries would be well-advised to consider nonperiodical resources in support of IPE, as well. For example, for students seeking evidence to support the case of their discipline, core books and textbooks with long-standing, discipline-specific protocols may be the first place students will turn when considering their unique approach to treatment within an interprofessional group. Databases with cross-discipline applications can serve as a thread of commonality and serve to unify students further in their discussions. Ensuring access to these types of resources will add depth to students' access to sources informing their disciplines' standards and protocols in diverse care situations.

Application of Library Resources

Interprofessional learning teams should be taught to utilize professional literature in order to develop evidence-based approaches for care. Learning exercises that successfully foster both information literacy and interprofessional development will find each team member researching their discipline's literature to bring their unique perspective to the group for consideration. Writing case studies that meaningfully engage all involved disciplines can be a challenge, particularly as the number of disciplines involved in the exercise grows. Case study development will often be accomplished by professors of the disciplines rather than librarians, but there are foreseeably circumstances in which it would be beneficial for librarians to provide case studies for learning teams. Interprofessional case studies have been made available online by a number of recognized authorities in the subject, to include:

- The University of Western Ontario's Office of Interprofessional Health Education and Research offers numerous, open-access case studies for interprofessional learning applications. Each case study is tagged with icons representing the disciplines represented in the exercise, making it easy to identify the best case study to utilize with a given group of students. Formats include video and text resources (http://www.ipe.uwo.ca/Administration/case.html).
- The Association for Prevention Teaching and Research (APTR), a public health and preventive medicine-geared association supporting education, has compiled an index of interprofessional case studies organized by emphasis (http://www.ipe.uwo.ca/Administration/case.html).
- The National Health Services of England (NHS) offers a collection of case studies for interprofessional learning, featuring a wide range of health issues (http://www.cmft.nhs.uk/education-and-training/ssp/interprofessional-learning-(ipl)/case-studies-for-interprofessional-learning).
- A search of the American Association of Medical College (AAMC) MedEdPORTAL for the term "interprofessional" brings a large number of results in a wide range of formats, to include research articles, case studies, evaluation tools and more (https://www.mededportal.org/ipe/).

A thorough web search will reveal numerous additional freely available interprofessional case studies authored by associations, organizations, and institutions of higher learning from around the globe (suggested search terms include "interprofessional case study," "IPE case studies," and "interprofessional practice case studies"). Librarians seeking to supply content as well as other forms of support for IPE exercises should consult these and other reliable sources of case studies.

Conclusion

Librarians can begin supporting IPE in their institutions now. Consider what might be the best approach for your library when considering the axis of space, resources and instruction. What does your library already have in place that it can maximize for this didactic approach?

Refer to the planning guide in Appendix C as a place to start mapping out where your campus is on the IPE timeline, where your library is, and how you can begin work now to support your academic programs in this initiative.

APPENDIX A: JOURNALS THAT HAVE PUBLISHED ARTICLES AND SPECIAL ISSUES SPECIFICALLY ADDRESSING INTERPROFESSIONAL EDUCATION

JOURNAL TITLE	COPYRIGHT HOLDER / PUBLISHER
Academic Emergency Medicine	Society for Academic Emergency Medicine / Wiley
Academic Radiology	Association of University Radiologists / Elsevier
American Journal of Pharmaceutical Education	American Association of Colleges of Pharmacy
American Journal of Public Health	American Public Health Association
Anatomical Sciences Education	American Association of Anatomists, published in cooperation with the American Association of Clinical Anatomists and the Human Anatomy and Physiology Society/ Wiley
Australasian Journal on Ageing	Wiley
BMC Medical Education	BioMed Central
Internal Medicine Journal	Royal Australasian College of Physicians / Wiley
JCN Journal of Clinical Nursing	Wiley
Journal of Allied Health	Association of Schools of Allied Health Professions / Ingenta

Journal of Dental Education	American Dental Education Association
Journal of Pain and Symptom Management	American Academy of Hospice and Palliative Medicine / Elsevier
Journal of the American Geriatric Society	The American Geriatrics Society/ Wiley
Medical Dosimetry	American Association of Medical Dosimetrists / Elsevier
Medical Teacher	Informa Healthcare
Nurse Education in Practice	Elsevier
Nurse Education Today	Elsevier
Surgical Clinics of North America	Elsevier
The Journal of Law, Medicine and Ethics	American Society of Law, Medicine and Ethics, Inc. / Wiley

APPENDIX B: HEALTH SCIENCES MULTI-DISCIPLINARY JOURNALS THAT DISCUSS INTERPROFESSIONAL EDUCATION

JOURNAL TITLE	COPYRIGHT HOLDER / PUBLISHER
Family Medicine	Society of Teachers of Family Medicine / American Academy of Family Physicians
The Journal of Continuing Education in the Health Professions	The Alliance for Continuing Education in the Health Professions, the Society for Academic Continuing Medical Education, and the Council on Continuing Medical Education, Association for Hospital Medical Education / Wiley
Clinical Teacher	Association for the Study of Medical Education / Wiley
Academic Medicine	Association of American Medical Colleges / Wolters Kluwer

APPENDIX C: SUPPORTING IPE @ THE LIBRARY PLANNING GUIDE

What instructional programs does the library currently offer?

Within these areas, where does IPE best fit?

Who are the IPE champions on campus?

Of these people, with whom do we already have a relationship?

Whom do we endeavor to form a relationship with in this effort?

How is IPE instruction being delivered on campus?

How can the library support these existing efforts?

Where are IPE activities being held on campus?

Does the library have space to support IPE activities?

Does the library have space that could be maximized with collaboration and IPE in mind?

What information resources does the library have to support IPE learning teams?

REFERENCES

Barr, Hugh. 2013. "Enigma Variations: Unraveling Interprofressional Education in Time and Place." *Journal of Interprofessional Care* 27, Supp. 2: 9–13.

Bennett, Scott. 2007. "First Questions for Designing Higher Education Learning Spaces." *Journal of Academic Librarianship* 33, no. 1 (January): 14–26.

Betz, Gail and Paula G. Raimondo. 2015. "Interprofessional Education (IPE): Limitless Opportunities for Libraries." Contributed poster presented at the Annual Meeting of the Medical Library Association, Austin, TX, May 19. Retrieved August 7, 2015, from http://www.eventscribe.com/2015/mla/assets/PosterAbstracts.pdf.

Brennan, Emily, Amy Chatfield, and Eileen Eandi. 2012. "Interleague Play: Campus Leadership through Interprofessional Education." Contributed paper presented at the Annual Meeting of the Medical Library Association, Seattle, WA, May 21. Retrieved August 3, 2015, from http://www.eventscribe.com/2012/mla/assets/pdf/17959.pdf.

Butera, Gisela, Alexandra W. Gomes, and Seema Kakar. 2014. "Expanding Our Roles: Embedded in Curriculum Design." *Medical Reference Services Quarterly* 33, no. 3: 292–301.

Cleveland, Benjamin and Thomas Kvan. 2015. "Designing Learning Spaces for Interprofessional Education in the Anatomical Sciences." *Anatomical Sciences Education* 8 (July/August): 371–80.

Cusack, Tara, and Grainne O'Donoghue. 2012. "The Introduction of an Interprofessional Education Module: Students' Perceptions." *Quality in Primary Care* 20, no. 3: 231–38.

Edwards, Mary E., Rae Jesano, Hannah F. Norton, and Nina C. Stoyan-Rosenzweig. 2015. "Breaking the Limits of Interprofessional Education: Library Faculty Integrating into Interprofessional Education (IPE)." Contributed paper presented at the Annual Meeting of the Medical Library Association, Austin, TX, May 18. Retrieved August 3, 2015, from http://www.eventscribe.com/2015/mla/assets/SectionPrograms.pdf.

Hinton, Elizabeth G., Mitzi R. Norris, and Lauren M. Young. 2015. "Collaborative Library Space and Resources: Focusing on Student Perceptions of Interprofessionalism in Medical Education." Contributed poster presented at the Annual Meeting of the American Library Association, San Francisco, CA, June 26. Retrieved August 3, 2015, from https://apply.ala.org/aia/docs/project/9856.

Interprofessional Education Collaborative. 2015. "About IPEC." Accessed August 3. https://ipecollaborative.org/About_IPEC.html.

Jordan, Elizabeth, and Tanya Ziebell. 2009. "Learning in the Spaces: A Comparative Study of the Use of Traditional and 'New Generation' Library Learning Spaces by Various Disciplinary Cohorts." Presented at the Next Generation Learning Spaces 2008 Colloquium, *Learning Spaces in Higher Education: Positive Outcomes by Design*, Proceedings of the Next Generation Learning Spaces 2008 Colloquium, University of Queensland, Case Studies, Chapter 5.7. Retrieved August 4, 2015, from http://www.uq.edu.au/nextgenerationlearningspace/proceedings.

Koffel, Jonathan, and Shannon Reidt. 2015. "An Interprofessional Train-the-Trainer Evidence-Based Practice Workshop: Design and Evaluation." *Journal of Interprofessional Care* 29, no. 4: 367–69.

Lamb, Gerri, and James Shraiky. 2013. "Designing for Competence: Spaces that Enhance Collaboration Readiness in Healthcare." *Journal of Interprofessional Care* 27, Suppl. 2: 14–23.

Latrobe Community Health Service and the Health and Socialcare Interprofessional Network (HSIN). 2009. "Readiness for Interprofessional Learning Scale (RIPLS) Questionnaire." August. http://www.ihi.org/education/ihiopenschool/Chapters/Documents/riplsquestionnaire 19.pdf.

Lewis, David W. 2007. "A Model for Academic Libraries, 2005 to 2025." Paper presented at Visions of Change, California State University, January 26. Retrieved August 3, 2015, from http://hdl.handle.net/1805/665.

Lorbeer, Elizabeth R., Emma O'Hagan, and Martha Knuth. 2015. "Developing an Interprofessional Education Event." Contributed paper presented at the Annual Meeting of the Medical

Library Association, Austin, TX, May 17. Retrieved August 3, 2015, from http://www.eventscribe.com/2015/mla/assets/SectionPrograms.pdf.

Ludwig, Logan, and Susan Starr. (2005). "Library as Place: Results of a Delphi Study." *Journal of the Medical Library Association* 93, no. 3 (July): 215–326.

Maggio, Lauren A., Nancy H. Tannery, H. Carrie Chen, Olle Ten Cate, and Bridget O'Brien. 2013. "Evidence-Based Medicine Training in Undergraduate Medical Education." *Academic Medicine* 88, no. 7: 1022–28.

McEwen, Heather, Susan P. Bruce, and John Sutton. 2010. "Librarian Participation in Interprofessional Health Professions Education." Contributed poster presented at the Annual Meeting of the Medical Library Association, Washington, DC, May 24. Retrieved August 3, 2015, from http://www.neomed.edu/library/library-posters-presentations-and-tutorials/LibrarianParticipationinInterprofessionaHealthProfessionsEducation.pdf.

Nolfi, David A., Marcia Rapchak, Lori J. Marra, Christine K. O'Neil, and Melanie T. Turk. 2015. "Interprofessional Information Literacy Education for Nursing, Allied Health, and Pharmacy Freshmen." Contributed paper presented at the Annual Meeting of the Medical Library Association, Austin, TX, May 18. Retrieved August 3, 2015, from http://www.eventscribe.com/2015/mla/assets/SectionPrograms.pdf.

Nordquist, Jonas, Simon Kitto, and Scott Reeves. 2013. "Living Museums": Is It Time to Reconsider the Learning Landscape for Professional and Interprofessional Education?" *Journal of Interprofessional Care* 27, Suppl. 2: 2–4.

Nova Southeastern University Libraries. 2015. "Center for Interprofessional Education and Practice: Interprofessional Education." July 13. Retrieved August 3, 2015, from http://nova.campusguides.com/CIPEP.

Olson, Rebecca, and Andrea Bialocerkowski. 2014. "Interprofessional Education in Allied Health: A Systematic Review." *Medical Education* 48, no. 3: 236–46.

Pritchard, Peggy A. 2010. "The Embedded Science Librarian: Partner in Curriculum Design and Delivery." *Journal of Library Administration* 50, no. 4: 373–96.

Sens, Thomas. 2010. "12 Major Trends in Library Design." DAHSL: Developing Academic Health Sciences Libraries: A Collaboration to Create the 21st Century Academic Health Sciences Library (January 4). Retrieved July 29, 2015, from https://newemergingmedicallibraries.wordpress.com/2010/01/04/12-major-trends-in-library-design/.

University of Massachusetts Medical School Lamar Soutter Library. 2015. "Interprofessional Education Regional Collaborative." July 16. Retrieved August 3, 2015, from http://libraryguides.umassmed.edu/interprofessional_education.

University of Nebraska Medical Center McGoogan Library of Medicine. N.d. "Interprofessional Education (IPE) Portal." Retrieved August 3, 2015, from http://unmc.libguides.com/ipe.

University of Nevada, Reno, University Libraries. 2015. "Health Literacy: Interprofessional Education." July 13. Retrieved August 3, 2015, from http://guides.library.unr.edu/healthliteracy/ipe.

University of Southern California Norris Medical Library. 2011. "Interprofessional Education (IPE)." Retrieved August 3, 2015, from http://usc-nml.v1.libguides.com/ipe.

Webster, Keith. 2010. "The Library Space as Learning Space." *EDUCAUSE Review Online* 45, no. 6 (November/December). Retrieved July 28, 2015, from http://www.educause.edu/ero/article/library-space-learning-space.

World Health Organization. 1988. *Learning Together to Work Together for Health*. Geneva: World Health Organization.

Yearwood, Simone L. 2015. "Catching Up with Time: Tips, Tricks and Best Practices for Library Renovations." *College and Research Library News* 76, no. 7 (July): 362–98.

Chapter Nine

Clinical Medical Librarians and Interprofessional Practice

Lisa Travis and Skye Bickett

To date, there is no agreed upon definition of or set of duties for clinical medical librarians (CML); however, some authors have created definitions and lists of duties for the purposes of their own research (Aldrich and Schulte 2014; Banks 2006; Davidoff and Florance 2000; Esparza et al. 2013; Plutchak 2002; Rankin, Grefsheim, and Canto 2008; Tan and Maggio 2013). Some literature suggests that a definition may limit the role of the CML and how it can change with patient care, technology, and other transformations that occur in interprofessional healthcare (Aldrich and Schulte 2014; Banks 2006; Plutchak 2002; Rankin, Grefsheim, and Canto 2008). Like a definition, the title of a CML may also vary. A person in this position may be called a clinical informationist, patient care librarian, hospital librarian, clinical medical librarian, librarian informationist, liaison librarian, or health sciences librarian, to name a few (Plutchak 2002; Rankin, Grefsheim, and Canto 2008; Tan and Maggio 2013). Even without a concise description, the justification for the need of a CML to support interprofessional healthcare teams in a variety of ways is clear (Urquhart et al. 2006). The incorporation of CMLs into interprofessional practice has the potential to improve patient care and safety, enhance the accuracy and timeliness of information used at the point-of-care, and stress the importance of using current, scholarly resources (Banks et al. 2007; Brandes 2007). For the sake of consistency and to avoid confusion with terminology, those who provide library services in the clinical setting will be termed clinical medical librarians (CMLs) throughout this chapter; this term will be used in place of other job titles and roles that are used in the literature, such as clinical informationist.

JUSTIFICATION OF CML

Literature suggests that CMLs are useful as part of interprofessional care teams for a variety of reasons. Changes in accreditation also support the need for CMLs in the clinical setting. Some accreditation standards include aspects of education for healthcare professionals and residents with which CMLs could assist. The information in these accreditation standards are for programs and institutions that work with physicians and residents. They include life-long learning programs, technology to enhance learning and practice, and education and improvement based on practice initiatives (Accreditation Council for Graduate Medical Education [ACGME] 2007). Perhaps the most important feature that points directly to the use of CMLs in interprofessional care is that the standards call for residents and physicians to be able to locate, evaluate, and synthesize literature to assist with patient care (Aldrich and Schulte 2014; Esparza et al. 2013).

This last feature highlights one of the most obvious and traditional roles of a librarian, which is to find and appraise literature for their users. CMLs are expert searchers and can use their skills to find and evaluate information pertaining to prognosis, drug interactions, and other aspects of patient care (Esparza et al. 2013; Jerome et al. 2001; Rankin, Grefsheim, and Canto 2008; Tan and Maggio 2013; Turman et al. 1997). This role is important to healthcare professionals and residents, because it allows them to focus on direct patient care instead of on finding information. In fact, physicians acknowledge the need to quickly locate literature to help care for their patients and recognize that CMLs can help with this task. Literature states that when CMLs help with this task, it not only assists with patient care but saves physicians time and helps increase physicians' knowledge of medical advances (Aldrich and Schulte 2014; Esparza et al. 2013). In some cases, CMLs have expanded their roles with regard to literature searching to benefit physicians. This role expansion involves reading the literature to decide what information is most pertinent to a patient case and summarizing the information for the physician (Jerome et al. 2001).

Another reason for the use of a CML in the clinical setting is to educate healthcare professionals and residents. The topics covered in educational sessions include accessing and using library resources, searching the literature for relevant information, and evaluating the literature (Algermissen 1974; Greco et al. 2009; Tan and Maggio 2013). This element of a CMLs role is almost as important as literature searching. These educational sessions can take place in small groups or one-to-one interactions (Tan and Maggio 2013). Instruction can assist in teaching healthcare professionals and residents how to answer questions surrounding patient care when the CML is not available and thus improve clinical practice (Jerome et al. 2001). Research has shown that the literature searching skills of those involved in educational sessions improve (Greco et al. 2009).

Evidence-based medicine support is an aspect of the CMLs role that can involve both literature searching and instruction, which have been shown to improve the use of evidence-based practice (Greco et al. 2009; Koonce, Giuse, and Todd 2004). Literature states that physicians rely on evidence to make a decision. Using a combination of knowledge, experience, and evidence assists physicians in making informed decisions about patient care. CMLs play an important role in the application and use of evidence in clinical decisions. They connect the evidence found in literature to the care of patients (Deshpande et al. 2003; Jerome et al. 2001; McKibbon 1998).

Perhaps the most justifiable reason for having a CML as part of an interprofessional team in the clinical setting is to assist busy physicians and residents find evidence to assist with patient care (Aldrich and Schulte 2014). Databases contain millions of abstracts and articles with more information added daily and new journals regularly beginning publication too. This inundation of information means that physicians and residents will never be able to peruse all of the available information. In general, physicians and residents will overlook some information and may not be aware of all of the resources available to them. This type of oversight impacts patient care and outcomes and, in some cases, means that evidence will not be found for some questions raised in the clinical setting (Davidoff and Florance 2000; Jerome et al. 2001). The use of a CML can alleviate the burden of information overload faced by physicians, residents, and other healthcare professionals. A CML, trained to find, appraise, and distill information, can help healthcare professionals and interprofessional healthcare teams obtain the evidence they need to answer clinical questions and assist in patient care (Esparza et al. 2013; Jerome et al. 2001; Urquhart et al. 2006).

CMLS AND THE HISTORY OF ROUNDING

The use of CMLs as part of interprofessional teams in the clinical setting first appeared in the literature in the 1970s in institutions around the United States (Algermissen 1974; Miller and Kaye 1985; Roach and Addington 1975; Turman et al. 1997; Vaughn 2009). According to these sources, the first CML position began in 1971 at the University of Missouri-Kansas City Medical Library. The person in this position worked mainly within the library to perform literature searches but still worked closely with rotating students, residents, and healthcare professionals. However, the CML soon began attending rounds, participating in discussions, and seeing patients. Two additional CMLs were added to this interprofessional team along with a secretary and library clerk to handle the increased workload (Algermissen 1974).

In 1973, the CML at the Cook County Hospital in Chicago began attending weekly rounds and supplying information to the interprofessional healthcare team based on these interactions. The CML also provided bibliographies for weekly seminars that were meant to orient students, residents, and healthcare professionals to the department and provided articles that reviewed previous evidence or included new information on specific topics. Collaboration and coordination between the CML and the department chair were very important to the success of this program (Roach and Addington 1975).

An experimental, part-time CML position started at the Florence A. Moore Library of Medicine in 1976 for the Department of Pediatrics. Due to the success of this position, another part-time position began for the Department of Surgery. By 1978, the library developed a full-time position at the Hospital of the Medical College of Pennsylvania for the Department of Medicine. In this position, the CML attended rounds and the morning report. Following these exchanges, the CML provided literature based upon information from the reports or cases, whether or not there was a specific request for information. Over time, the use of the CML increased and the number of questions almost doubled, with the majority of questions relating to patient cases. The CML provided educational sessions and literature searches and proved to be a timesaving, cost-effective service for the Department of Medicine (Miller and Kaye 1985).

The Tompkins-McCaw Library at the Medical College of Virginia Campus of Virginia Commonwealth University had a CML program from 1977 to 1983, when budget cuts forced the library to discontinue the program. During this time, the CML participated in rounds and was part of an interprofessional healthcare team. The CML provided literature searches and educated healthcare professionals about how to find information. In 1993, the library used information from this program to guide a program intended for third-year medical students. Instead of serving as an information provider, this program would focus on the CML as an educator. The CML provided education to the medical students on how to search for information in the clinical setting. Specifically, the CML introduced the medical students and their interprofessional healthcare team members to library resources and services, literature and drug information databases, and the document delivery service (Turman et al. 1997).

In the past five years, the acceptance of CML has grown, and more institutions have established the role. The CML is part of the interprofessional healthcare team and is involved in aspects of patient care. While some institutions, such as those in the previous examples, have had the CML position for decades, others have only recently employed this type of position. Instead of CMLs, some institutions have opted for a subject or liaison librarian, who may or may not be embedded in an interprofessional healthcare team (Aldrich and Schulte 2014). These examples demonstrate the need for and success of a CML since these types of service began.

The authors conducted a survey to gather information about librarians' experiences with rounding and serving as part of an interprofessional team. The survey was distributed via local, regional, and national listservs and individual e-mails in fall 2015. Forty-seven librarians responded to the survey, twenty-five of whom participate in rounding or are part of an interprofessional team at their institution. However, only eighteen respondents answered the remainder of the questions concerning rounding. The majority of these respondents (72 percent) began rounding between the years of 2011 and 2015. The next largest grouping of respondents (22 percent) began rounding between the years of 2001 and 2005. Finally, one respondent replied that the CML began rounding in 1950. This answer implies that, even though the literature does not mention CMLs participating in rounds until the 1970s, librarians may have been participating in rounds for years before that date.

For those that do not participate in rounds or participate in an interprofessional team, the survey asked why this was the case. Twenty-two respondents replied to a question that asked them to indicate all reasons that applied to their situation. Eight respondents answered that they did not have enough staff or that they rounded in the past, while seven respondents stated that they did not have enough time. Six respondents indicated that they were in the planning stages to begin a rounding program at their institution. Four respondents stated that they believed clinical personnel did not want them participating in rounds. Other comments indicated that respondents were not asked to participate in rounds, were new to the position and did not previously feel knowledgeable enough to participate in rounds, or have not looked into the possibility of rounding. Finally, it is interesting to note that no respondents answered that they had no desire to participate in rounds.

THE PROFESSIONALS AND DISCIPLINES COMPRISING THE INTERPROFESSIONAL TEAM

CMLs work with a variety of healthcare professionals and disciplines. One of the first CMLs worked with physicians, nurses, social workers, clerks, and administrators (Roach and Addington 1975). As interprofessional teams grew, so did the variety of professionals with which CMLs worked. One 1997 article reported that the CML mainly worked with third-year medical students, but also supported attending physicians, residents, interns, nurses, social workers, and pharmacists (Turman et al. 1997). Similar articles reported that CMLs rounded with more than one healthcare team, provided reference services, and conducted lectures. The interprofessional healthcare teams included medical students, residents, physicians, a pharmacist, and a social worker (Burdick 2004; Sladek, Pinnock, and Phillips 2004).

Other articles emphasized rounding with interprofessional teams. These interprofessional teams could include students, clinical clerks, nurses, physicians, pharmacist, nurse educators, case managers, dieticians, wound care specialists, and respiratory therapists. Depending on the situation, the team may also incorporate chaplains, palliative care professionals, speech therapists, physical therapists, and even family members. Some interprofessional teams are not as well-defined, meaning that healthcare team members are more broadly discussed as medical, nursing, or allied health professionals or students (Aitken et al. 2011; Aldrich and Schulte 2014; Brandes 2007; Esparza et al. 2013; Greco et al. 2009).

The authors' survey asked respondents to indicate all of the healthcare professionals with whom they rounded. Sixteen respondents rounded with physicians, fifteen with residents, twelve with medical students, and eleven with pharmacists. Seven respondents participated in rounds with RN nurses, four with a dietician, three with a surgeon, and three with a social worker. One respondent stated that they rounded with a physical therapist and one with a nursing student. Other respondents indicated that they rounded with interns and EPIC documentation specialists. One respondent gave a detailed list of their rounding team, stating that they rounded with physicians, residents, pharmacy students, physician assistants, and nurse practitioners.

As with the types of professionals the CML rounded with, the disciplines also varied. One of the most common disciplines that the CML has rounded with is the internal medicine department (Aitken et al., 2011; Aldrich and Schulte 2014; Burdick 2004; Esparza et al. 2013; Schwing and Coldsmith 2005; Turman et al. 1997). However, literature states that CMLs also round with general surgery, family medicine, obstetrics and gynecology, pulmonary medicine, intensive care unit, general medicine, ambulatory care, sleep disorder, and rheumatology departments (Brandes 2007; Greco et al. 2009; Roach and Addington 1975; Vaughn 2009).

The majority of those who responded to the authors' survey (seven each) indicated that they rounded with an internal medicine or critical/intensive care unit. Three respondents each stated that they rounded with a family medicine or pediatrics team, while two respondents rounded with the surgery department. Other respondents indicated that they participated in psychiatric, bariatric, chronic pain, endocrinology, cardiology, neonatal intensive-care unit, gynecology, cardiothoracic surgery, and neurology rounds.

DEFINITION AND DESCRIPTION OF ROUNDING

Rounding has a variety of meanings in clinical settings. This chapter will focus on bedside rounds in which healthcare providers go from patient room to patient room while discussing cases along the way. In addition to bedside rounds, there are other activities that are also called rounds, such as table-top rounds in which healthcare providers gather around a table to discuss a case (Lyons et al. 2015). Departments, committees, wards, and interprofessional teams may host a variety of rounds, such as ethics rounds (Svantesson et al. 2008) or turnover/shift change rounds (Lyons et al. 2015). Many hospitals host grand rounds that are lectures on topics of interest to a wide audience. One hospital calls its weekly morbidity and mortality conference "quality of care" rounds (Greco et al. 2009). CMLs may participate in a variety of rounds for the purpose of supporting interprofessional teams (Lyons et al. 2015) or patient education efforts (Lindner and Sabbagh 2004).

While rounding, CMLs work within an interprofessional team as they discuss cases and move from patient room to patient room. During rounds, CMLs may serve as patient advocates (Lyon et al. 2015), provide instruction, and respond to questions that arise from healthcare providers or are thought of by CMLs (Aitken et al. 2011); responses may be provided on the spot or within a short period of time after rounding ends (Esparza et al. 2013). Because of the nature of rounding, CMLs may only provide instruction in brief bursts, if at all. Figure 9.1 shows how the CML's presence affects how clinical problems are handled (Deshpande et al. 2003).

Examples of Questions Asked and Resources Used

Questions that arise during rounds may cover the full spectrum of patient care as well as institutional policies and procedures. Common question types include those that focus on diagnosis and therapy (Aldrich and Schulte 2014; Greco et al. 2009). Questions may be either background or foreground in nature, and review articles and guidelines are commonly requested items to meet interprofessional teams' needs (Aldrich and Schulte 2014).

> The range of questions to which the CML responds extends from the very general to the extremely specific. Often a faculty member or senior resident will request a "few good general articles" on a current patient problem, both as an update on present management and for teaching purposes. At the other end of the spectrum, there may arise the need to know something specific as "a list of diseases and/or drugs causing the urine to turn green," and questions can be as specific as: "Is the CPK elevated in Eaton-Lambert Syndrome?" (Miller and Kaye 1985)

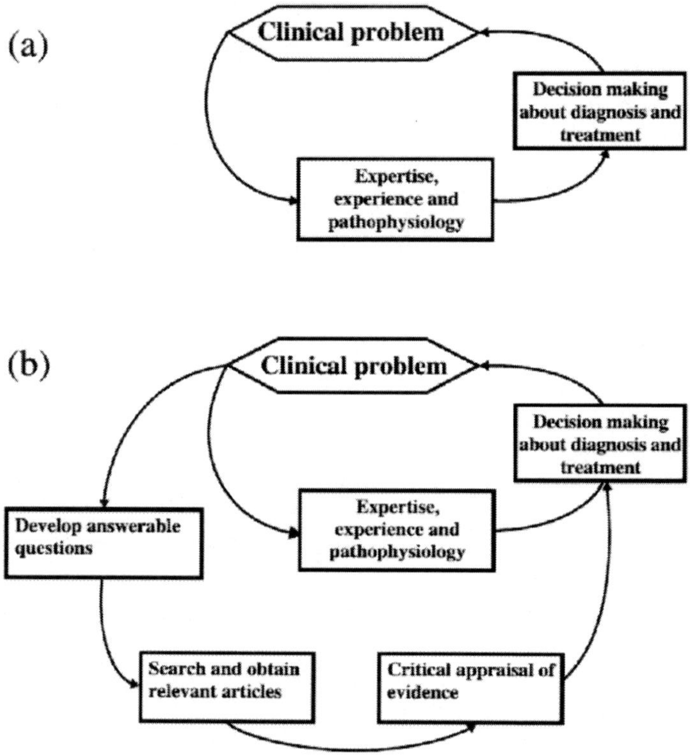

Figure 9.1. Comparison of Traditional (a) and Evidence-Supported Ward Rounds. Reprinted with permission from John Wiley and Sons.

As previously mentioned, questions may be answered quickly during rounds or require hours to answer after rounds. CMLs use a variety of resources to answer questions. Some questions may be answered quickly by using point-of-care tools, while other questions may require use of MEDLINE® (U.S. National Library of Medicine 2015) and other similar large databases. Occasionally CMLs must use nonmedical databases, such as business or legal databases, to answer questions.

CMLs and Use of Time

As previously stated with interprofessional CML rounding services, CMLs spend part of their time rounding and part of their time searching literature. Some CMLs participated in rounds once per week and held instructional sessions on other days (Burdick 2004; Deshpande et al. 2003; Turman et al. 1997). Other CMLs rounded two to three times per week or daily with each of their healthcare teams (Aldrich and Schulte 2014; Burdick 2004; Esparza et al. 2013). Depending on the institution and the CML, the time allotted to each of these activities varied. In some instances, the CML spent three to six hours per week rounding, while others spent ten to twelve hours per week rounding with healthcare teams (Aitken et al. 2011; Aldrich and Schulte 2014; Esparza et al. 2013; Schwing and Coldsmith 2005).

Eighteen respondents to the authors' survey answered the question regarding the frequency of rounds. Two respondents replied that they rounded every two weeks as part of an interprofessional team. Eight respondents stated that they rounded once per week with their teams, with one respondent specifying that they rounded as part of four to five different interprofessional teams and another stipulating that they participated in rounds one to two times per week. Six respondents indicated that they rounded twice per week, with one clarifying that they may round two to three times per week for each of their two teams. Three respondents said that they rounded four times per week.

When specifying the number of hours dedicated to rounding, respondents indicated a range of hours. Some respondents identified the number of hours per interprofessional team, while others simply identified their total number of weekly hours spent rounding. For the purposes of this study, answers were calculated per respondent. Two respondents rounded one hour per week, two more rounded one to two hours per week, one participated in rounds two hours per week, two other respondents rounded two to three hours per week, and one rounded three hours per week. Additionally, one respondent indicated that they rounded four to five hours per week, two joined in rounds seven hours per week, one rounded eight hours per week, and another rounded eight to nine hours per week. Other respondents answered with broader ranges for the number of hours they rounded per week. The ranges provided by these respondents were two to five, two to seven, six to nine, and twelve to fifteen hours per week. One respondent stated that they did not round weekly but that each round took two to three hours to complete.

When CMLs first began conducting literature searches in conjunction with rounds for interprofessional healthcare teams, it could take twenty-four hours to complete the request (Roach and Addington 1975). However, with the introduction of online databases, searches took less time. The literature indicates that a CML takes an average of two hours to answer simple questions and five hours to answer complicated questions, with one article stating that a CML spent over 636 hours over a seventeen-month period to answer literature searches (Esparza et al. 2013; Jerome et al. 2001). Other literature suggests that CMLs conduct nineteen to thirty searches per month for their healthcare teams (Aldrich and Schulte 2014; Vaughn 2009).

The survey also asked about the amount of time each week that it took to respond to literature searches and other tasks arising from rounds. One respondent spent less than an hour per week on searches and tasks resulting from rounds, two indicated that they spent an hour per week on these activities, three of the participants stated that they spent one to two hours per week on tasks, while three more devoted two to three hours per week on these responsibilities. Furthermore, one respondent said that they spent three hours on literature searches and other tasks, another stated that they spent three to four hours on these activities, two more respondents devoted four hours to these projects, and one spent ten hours per week on tasks associated with rounding. As with the number of hours spent rounding, some respondents provided a larger hourly range for the time spent on activities and questions that arose during rounds. Two respondents stated that they spent two to four hours on literature searching and other tasks, another spent four to six hours, and a final respondent said that they spent anywhere from eight to fifteen hours and up to twenty depending on the types of questions raised during rounds.

The authors' survey asked participants whether they considered rounding an effective use of their time. Seventeen of the respondents stated that they found participating in rounds an effective use of time, while one did not find rounding to be an effective use of time. Two of the respondents who answered "yes" added the caveat that rounding may not always be an effective use of time because they may not be always be consulted during rounds. Interestingly, the reason one respondent stated "no" was that they felt they were too old. Several themes emerged from the comments made by respondents. The main theme was that participating in rounds was an effective use of time because it increases the visibility and demonstrated the value of the library. The next two major themes that surfaced were building rapport with interprofessional healthcare teams and using evidence to support and improve patient care. The next theme that arose from respondent comments was that respondents found that they developed a greater understanding of patient care and the disciplines with which they worked. The final two themes emerging from survey answers were that respondents garnered additional opportunities and saved healthcare teams time so that they could focus more on their patients.

Devices Used When Rounding

When CMLs first began to round with healthcare teams, they used clipboards, paper and pen, MEDLINE®, and indices to perform their rounding, educational, reference, and literature searching duties (Algermissen 1974; Roach and Addington 1975; U.S. National Library of Medicine, 2015). As technology advanced, so did the systems and devices used and the availability of these resources to healthcare team members. The ACGME includes the use of technology to enhance resident learning as part of accreditation standards (ACGME 2007). The use of computers has increased, and portable computer terminals are seen throughout medical facilities. In addition to computers, tablets, cell phones, and other mobile devices are used by CMLs to answer questions during rounds (Aldrich and Schulte 2014; Brandes 2007; Burdick 2004). Fourteen of those who responded to the authors' survey stated that they carried devices with them during rounds to answer questions. Eleven used a tablet computer, six used a mobile phone, and one used a laptop.

PLANNING TO SET UP A ROUNDING SERVICE

Feasibility Studies

When planning to set up a rounding service as part of an interprofessional team for an existing clinical librarian or a new CML program for a hospital, one may want to conduct a feasibility study. Existing feasibility studies may serve as effective models for such a study. In one feasibility study, Sladek, Pinnock, and Phillips (2004) questioned medical doctors, including clinical unit heads and postgraduate trainees, about important issues related to a proposed service that included rounding by CMLs. Later Sladek, Pinnock, and Phillips (2004) conducted a prospective uncontrolled pilot study of fourteen physicians working in the selected units in which a CML attended ward rounds and clinical meetings. Lewis (1998) used a structured questionnaire to interview thirty clinicians at the Leicester General Hospital National Health Service (NHS) Trust about the feasibility of a CML service. After a six-month pilot of the service, a three-year project with a pre-planned evaluation was completed (Ward, Honeybourne, and Harrison 2001). After providing an introduction to a proposed evidence-supported delivery suite ward rounds service at Birmingham Women's Hospital, Deshpande and colleagues (2003) employed discussion groups and interviews to solicit opinions from fifteen clinicians as part of planning the service; they also conducted a pilot of the rounding service.

The feasibility study by Sladek, Pinnock, and Phillips (2004) examined "key issues in the development and delivery" of a CML service (termed informationist in the article). These issues included communication about the CML concept, perceptions of relevance and potential use of a CML, and "willingness to participate in a pilot, and identification of current barriers to searching for evidence or concerns about" a CML service. When asked if a CML would be useful, thirty-six of forty respondents (90 percent) indicated that a CML would be likely or very likely to be useful. When asked to identify a scenario in which a CML might be most useful, the most common responses were inpatient settings and ward rounds. With regard to the positive responses, the study acknowledged that social desirability bias may have played a role. Respondents also expressed concerns about the proposed service. Thirty-one of forty respondents (77.5 percent) were concerned that a CML service would likely have a high workload. Seven of forty doctors (17.5 percent) were concerned that a CML service could result in a worsening of clinician skills/responsibility (Sladek, Pinnock, and Phillips 2004).

Lewis concluded that clinicians were interested in the CML concept and were willing to be project participants. She decided to undertake a modified pilot project, with attending clinical meetings seen as more beneficial than joining ward rounds (Lewis 1998).

Deshpande and colleagues (2003) aimed to identify concerns about knowledge, skills, attitudes, and behaviors related to providing a CML rounding service and devising methods to effectively address barriers that were then employed in a pilot study. The study found that clinicians had little awareness of possible advantages to having a CML present during rounds. Clinicians were also unsure of their evidence-based practice skills. Clinicians were skeptical about the service, feared loss of autonomy, lacked motivation to change, and were resistant to change. A specific concern that arose was that a CML on rounds may "make the clinicians 'diverge from patient care.'" Deshpande and colleagues (2003) developed a variety of methods to address the barriers (see figure 9.2).

Integrating into the Interprofessional Team

In planning the integration of CMLs into an interprofessional team, it is important to get buy-in. If the library has champions in specialties in which the CML could round, approaching them with the idea would be a great place to start. Champions may be found in areas in which the library currently provides services, such as a journal club. At Birmingham Women's Hospital, time was used during journal club to solicit opinions on a proposed rounding service; once the rounding service was in place, questions and their related appraisals were presented at journal club, thus working to receive and increase buy-in (Deshpande et al. 2003). Rather than participating in rounds for several hours per week when initiating a rounding service, CMLs could ease into providing a rounding service (e.g., by attending one round per week) so as not to overwhelm themselves or the interprofessional healthcare providers and then gradually gain more buy-in for expanding the service.

For members of clinical teams with whom the CML is considering rounding, the CML could provide one or more relevant articles to introduce them to the concept of CML's participation in rounds. Deshpande and colleagues (2003) provided an article by Sackett and Straus (1998) to clinicians for this purpose as part of a feasibility study for a rounding service. CMLs could provide copies of the randomized trial by Marshall that showed that information-seeking behaviors by healthcare providers served by a rounding CML

Barrier	Methods to address the barrier
Knowledge	
Lack of familiarity	Presentation of approaches to evidence-based medicine (EBM) in journal clubs
Lack of awareness	Demonstration of question formulation and electronic searching in journal clubs
	Encouragement of participation in the process using small group methods
	Dissemination of critically appraised topics (CAT) in current awareness bulletins and journal clubs
Skills	Provision of training in critical appraisal and searching skills
	Provision of librarian support
Attitudes	
Fear	'Walk in and learn' sessions to overcome fear of computers and searching the Internet with the support of a clinical librarian
Resistance to change	Ensure support of lead clinician on delivery suite
Scepticism	Communicate with midwifery manager and staff
Poor motivation	Pilot implementation of the ward round
	Provide feedback about progress in journal clubs
	Seek organizational priority
	Link contribution in ward round to assessment and appraisal
	Actively disseminate successes of ward rounds at other forums
Behaviour	
External factors	Provision of computers on delivery suite connected to the Intranet and the Internet
Environmental factors	Link ward round activity to Clinical Governance and other national agendas
EBM factors	Ensure that all relevant databases and other sources are accessible on delivery suite (e.g. guidelines, CAT bank, electronic journals, Cochrane library, Best Evidence)

Figure 9.2. Some Strategies to Deal with Barriers to Evidence-Supported Ward Rounds. Reprinted with permission from John Wiley and Sons.

differed from others who did not receive the service (Marshall and Neufeld 1981). Other useful articles that could be used to promote the future service include studies by King (1987), Marshall (1992), and Klein and colleagues (1994) that all determined that services by CMLs affected patient care decisions and length of stay.

ACCREDITATION STANDARDS THAT ARE SUPPORTED BY ROUNDING SERVICES

Explaining that rounding with interprofessional teams is a service that supports accreditation standards may help a CML obtain buy-in for the service. Following are relevant standards for medical schools and graduate medical education that are supported by a CML's participation as part of the interprofessional team.

Relevant Accreditation Standards for Medical Schools

The accrediting body for allopathic medical schools, the Liaison Committee on Medical Education (LCME), developed the *Standards for Accreditation of Medical Education Programs Leading to the M.D. Degree*, which includes five relevant standards: Standards 3.2, 7.1, 7.4, 7.9, and 8. Standard 3.2 states, "A medical education program is conducted in an environment that fosters the intellectual challenge and spirit of inquiry appropriate to a community of scholars and provides sufficient opportunities, encouragement, and support for medical student participation in the research and other scholarly activities of its faculty." Standard 7.1 states, "The faculty of a medical school ensure that the medical curriculum includes content from the biomedical, behavioral, and socioeconomic sciences to support medical students' mastery of contemporary scientific knowledge and concepts and the methods fundamental to applying them to the health of individuals and populations." LCME's *Connections: A Detailed View of LCME Accreditation Standards and Elements for the 2015 Academic Year* includes a table of curriculum content in support of Standard 7.1 that includes evidence-based medicine and indicates for staff to check "whether the topic is taught separately as an independent required course and/or as part of a required integrated course" and in what year (first, second, or third or fourth) the topic is taught. LCME's Standard 7.4 states, "The faculty of a medical school ensure that the medical curriculum incorporates the fundamental principles of medicine, provides opportunities for medical students to acquire skills of critical judgment based on evidence and experience, and develops medical students' ability to use those principles and skills effectively in solving problems of health and disease." The detailed view document lists two skill sets in tables that staff use to compile information in support of meeting the standard: "skills of critical judgment based on evidence and experience" and "skills of medical problem solving." Entitled "Interprofessional Collaborative Skills," Standard 7.9 states, "The faculty of a medical school ensure that the core curriculum of the medical education program prepares medical students to function collaboratively on health care teams that include health professionals from other disciplines as they provide coordinated services to patients. These curricular experiences include practitioners and/or students from the other health professions." *Connections*'s guidance for standard 7.9 of the survey report states, "Provide three examples of required experiences where medical students are brought together with students or practitioners from other health professions to learn to function collaboratively on health care teams with the goal of providing coordinated services to patients" and lists five descriptive items to include in each example. Schools are also advised to "briefly summarize examples of learning experiences where medical students are brought together with students or practitioners from other health professions to learn to function collaboratively on health care teams with the goal of providing coordinated services to patients, including how medical students' attainment of the objectives of each experience is assessed." Standard 8 covers curricular management, evaluation, and enhancement; the detailed view document includes a table in which staff are to "provide and review school and national benchmark data from the AAMC Graduation Questionnaire (GQ) on the percent of respondents that *agree/strongly agree* (aggregated) that they are prepared in a variety of areas to begin a residency program" with one of the areas being "basic skills in clinical decision-making and application of evidence-based information" (LCME 2015).

For osteopathic medical schools, the accrediting body, the Commission on Osteopathic College Accreditation (COCA), has a document of standards entitled *Accreditation of Colleges of Osteopathic Medicine: COM (College of Medicine) Accreditation Standards and Procedures* that has four standards that are supported by CML interprofessional rounding services. Standard 6.1 states, "The COM must develop and implement a method of instruction and learning strategies designed to achieve its mission and objectives," and the guideline in support of it states, "The curriculum should at least include, but not be limited to, the following areas of biomedical sciences and disciplines related to osteopathic medicine: . . . basic knowledge of the components of research." Standard 6.4 states, "The COM must help to prepare students to function on health care teams that include professionals from other disciplines. The experiences should include practitioners and/or students from other health professions and encompass the principles of collaborative practices." COCA also states that "competencies for interprofessional collaborative practice may include the ability to: (1) Work with individuals of other professions in a climate of mutual respect, (2) Apply knowledge of the osteopathic physicians' and other professionals' training, knowledge, skills and competencies to address the health care needs of the patients and populations served, (3) Communicate with patients, families, communities, and other professionals in a manner that supports the team approach to the care of the patient, the maintenance of health and treatment of disease, (4) Apply principles of team dynamics to plan and deliver patient/population centered care that is safe, timely, efficient and effective" (AOA COCA 2015). Standard 6.5 states, "The COM must stipulate specific educational objectives to be learned in its educational program," and supporting Standard 6.5.1.3 states,

> At minimum, a graduate must be able to: demonstrate medical knowledge through one or more of the following: passing of course tests, standardized tests of the NBOME (National Board of Osteopathic Medical Examiners), post-core rotation tests, research activities, presentations, and participation in directed reading programs and/or journal clubs, and/or other evidence-based medical activities.

Standard 7.2 states, "The COM must show its commitment to research by having a strategic plan for research support, development, and productivity that is linked to faculty adequacy, facilities, outcome goals, and budget" with a guideline that states, "growth and development of research is closely linked to availability of human, financial, and physical resources required to support research efforts, as well as the education of osteopathic physicians to prepare them for conduct of research" (AOA COCA 2015).

Relevant Accreditation Standards for Graduate Medical Education

An agreement for a single accreditation system for graduate medical education programs in the United States has been reached by the American Osteopathic Association (AOA), the ACGME, and the American Association of Colleges of Osteopathic Medicine (AACOM). Accreditation will be overseen by ACGME, with training programs with AOA accreditation "transitioning to ACGME accreditation between July 1, 2015 and June 30, 2020" (AOA 2015). The accrediting body for many post-MD medical training programs and soon-to-be accreditor for programs currently accredited by the AOA, the ACGME, developed a competency for practice-based learning and improvement that is defined in *Competency Definitions and Recommended Practice Performance Tools* as "participation in the evaluation of one's personal practice utilizing scientific evidence, practice guidelines and standards as metrics, and self-assessment programs in order to optimize patient care through lifelong learning"; the document provides four practice performance measurements to use to indicate that the standard is met (ACGME 2007). Interprofessional practice falls under the competency for system-based practice, which states that trainees should "optimize coordination of patient care both within one's own practice and within the healthcare system. Consult with other healthcare professionals" (ACGME 2007).

When CMLs Are Most Effective during Patient Care

Another factor to consider when setting up CMLs as part of an interprofessional team is to consider when they will be most effective during patient care. According to one feasibility study, there are stages in patient care in which CML participation in rounds would be "most useful." These are "after admission and the initial diagnostic tests, usually within 24–48 hours of admission. . . . Analysis showed that suggested scenarios commonly related to questions about treatment and management decisions" by 51 percent (twenty out of thirty-nine) of respondents and "choice/interpretation of diagnostic tests for" 21 percent of respondents (eight out of thirty-nine) (Sladek, Pinnock, and Phillips 2004). In a study by Aitken and colleagues (2011), the CML participated in intake rounds related to new patient admissions.

Assessing the Rounding Service

CMLs should work with the department with which they will round as part of an interprofessional team to determine how and when a rounding service will be evaluated and whether the assessment data should be qualitative or quantitative in nature (Aldrich and Schulte 2014). To prove their worth to their institutions, CMLs should assess their services, including rounding with interprofessional teams. A variety of means can be used to assess a rounding service—statistics, other data, and surveys. Ambitious CMLs may even conduct a prospective uncontrolled study (Sladek, Pinnock, and Phillips 2004) or a randomized controlled trial (Marshall and Neufeld 1981; Mulvaney et al. 2008).

It is a good idea for CMLs to keep statistics and information on serving and rounding as part of an interprofessional team. At the bare minimum, the CML will want to keep statistics on number of questions answered during rounds and as follow-up to rounds. The number of questions answered may be used in a calculator for assigning value to library services, such as the "Valuing Library Services Calculator" available from the National Network of Libraries of Medicine (NN/LM) MidContinental Region (2013) online. A database of questions with notes about answers can help the CML prove the value of the service and save the CML time when a new question arises that is similar to one that has already been answered. Information about questions can be provided to healthcare providers to fuel further discussions in journal clubs and other settings (Deshpande et al. 2003). Supplemental information that the CML may want to keep includes type of question (diagnosis, therapy, etc.) (Aldrich and Schulte 2014) and whether the question came from healthcare providers or arose as the result of the CML being proactive and anticipating information that would be helpful to providers. In one project, each CML who participated in rounds drafted a weekly report with a narrative on the CML's activities. Reports included the time spent rounding with the team, the patient load of the rounding teams, opportunities for training by the CML, and issues with equipment. "In addition, the librarians recorded observations about team interactions, perceived effectiveness of instruction, and overall success of the program" (Turman et al. 1997).

The CML may also want to conduct one or more surveys to assess the effectiveness of the CML as part of an interprofessional rounding service. One could administer a survey focused solely on the rounding service or one may want to administer a survey that has been used by other researchers; examples include a comprehensive survey that assesses the value of all library and information services, the survey by Marshall and colleagues (2013), or a survey based on items from the aforementioned survey like Aldrich and Schulte (2014) administered. The survey could be aimed at determining satisfaction with the CML as part of the interprofessional rounding service or delve deeper and look for effects on clinical decision making (Vaughn 2009), length of stay, or readmission rates (Aldrich and Schulte 2014). Regarding clinical decision making, the survey could ask if the answer or evidence summary confirmed existing ideas or stimulated new ideas (Steele and Tiffin 2014), such as changes in diagnostic tests or therapies used. The survey could also ask questions related to how well the CML fit into the interprofessional healthcare team and whether the CML was seen as a necessary member of the team.

OUTCOMES OF ROUNDING

Outcomes for Librarians

In response to the survey question on the authors' survey that asked if they feel that rounding was an effective use of their time, seventeen out of eighteen respondents answered "yes." When asked why or why not rounding is an effective use of their time, one respondent replied, "Yes, many questions arise during rounds which the residents, students, and faculty may not have time to answer at that time and will forget and which I can answer for them." When asked if they feel that their participation in rounding was appreciated, seventeen of eighteen respondents answered "yes." When asked why or why not in regards to their responses to the two aforementioned questions and asked about benefits and drawbacks of rounding, one or more of the respondents' positive comments noted that the CML formed relationships with interprofessional team members, became aware of team members' information-seeking behaviors and time pressures, received positive feedback from rounding team members, contributed to improved patient care and safety without "being directly responsible/liable for patients," saw articles found by the CML used for discussion in journal club and quality of care committee meetings, experienced increased visibility for the library's staff and services (resulting in additional requests for assistance), were provided with additional service opportunities, used the CML's abilities and stretched them beyond the CML's comfort zone, and recognized that the CML became a valued team member. One respondent noted that the CML is "thanked for services almost every time they are used," and another said, "I have had physicians thank me for participating in rounds and filling in knowledge gaps that they may not have filled on their own." One respondent said that a director calls him or her "librarian extraordinaire." One respondent who conducted an annual survey said, "one of the questions is about the librarian's presence on rounds. It's a scale of one to five, and I've never gotten below a three from over 200 responses in three years." One respondent who began rounding in 2005 noted that "the longevity . . . speaks very positively to their value to the programs in question."

The survey also included some ambivalent and negative comments about CML rounding services. One respondent noted that CML services were not always needed (such as during table rounds), and the other noted that rounding takes "a lot of time (apart from the actual event)" and said, "I'm not totally convinced it's a good use of our resources." One respondent noted,

"There are some physicians and some residents that really do appreciate having a librarian present. I know this because they make statements to that effect. There are also some physicians and some residents who, frankly, don't care whether or not there's a librarian participating." One respondent to a question about benefits and drawbacks to participating in rounds stated, "Occasionally the . . . service is taken for granted. Seeing the same problem/issue/situation arise over and over can be very disappointing/disheartening (but have to keep in mind that the students/residents are often different every single year)."

There is no doubt that participating in rounds as part of an interprofessional team is stressful for the CML. There are a variety of sights, sounds, situations, and smells that may cause the CML stress in the clinical setting. The authors' survey results and a study reveal that difficulties with understanding the rounding discussion may leave the CML feeling lost (Lyons et al. 2015) and wondering whether to seek clarification during rounds or look up information in the library after rounds. The fact that not all questions have clear-cut answers can be stressful and disheartening. One respondent in the authors' survey noted, "physicians have seemed disappointed when the evidence for a certain topic is vague or conflicting, and I wonder if that causes them to question my searching skills." Another respondent summed up their experience with stress well by saying, "you do need to have physical and emotional stamina. Physically, one must consider that you'll be standing for several hours each day. While I am able to handle this, I do know that it is not for everyone. Emotionally, one must consider that you will be seeing sick patients and their families and working aside potentially stressed out clinicians. Massages and meditation are key!"

Outcomes for Healthcare Providers

The effectiveness of the CML in interprofessional rounds and with the provision of literature searches is evident in the literature. As early as 1975, CMLs proved effective interprofessional team members by improving patient care. The CML also saved healthcare professionals time by conducting literature searches on specific topics. Additionally, members of the interprofessional healthcare team stated that CMLs would be useful in other areas and that information provided by the CML could be used by other professionals and departments (Roach and Addington 1975). CMLs may be most useful to healthcare teams who provide care for patients with difficult or multifaceted medical issues. Comparing the effectiveness of CMLs can prove challenging due to the practice setting, physician knowledge, how information is used, and the specific patient (Esparza et al. 2013).

Healthcare providers within interprofessional teams benefit in a variety of ways from having a CML participate in interprofessional rounds. Studies show that CML services save healthcare providers' time (Barbour and Young 1986; Davidoff and Florance 2000; Demas and Ludwig 1991), provide them with literature to aid in clinical care (especially diagnosis and treatment) (Barbour and Young 1986; Veenstra and Gluck 1992), help them discover helpful new tools and sources (Barbour and Young, 1986; Scura and Davidoff 1981), and save them money (Grose and Hannigan 1982; Scura and Davidoff 1981). Another benefit of CML services for physicians is summed up well by this statement from a randomized trial, "Several physicians noted that the service made them aware of many patient care questions which were discussed at rounds but not followed up" (Marshall and Neufeld 1981). One study of healthcare providers showed that information provided by the library was seen as being more important than diagnostic images, lab tests, and discussions with colleagues (Marshall 1992). The Rochester study showed that information provided by CMLs helped providers avoid adverse effects (see figure 9.3) (Marshall 1992).

Outcomes for Patients

The information that CMLs provide to healthcare providers sometimes results in changes in patient care. One example of this is a CML-identified guideline that "indicated that a patient with suspected placenta praevia could safely be examined with a transvaginal ultrasound scan" (Deshpande et al. 2003). In another institution, the CML's information made a positive difference in the management of pregnant women over the age of forty (Vaughn 2009). When a medical librarian rounded with a multidisciplinary team in Colorado; a new intensive care unit (ICU) order set, a change in a total parenteral nutrition protocol, a new oral care protocol, and other changes in patient care resulted (Brandes 2007). The Rochester study provided data on changes in patient care as the result of information provided by CMLs (Mar-

Avoidance of adverse events reported by physicians (percentage)*

Adverse event avoided	Urban physicians (n = 113)	Residents (n = 52)	Rural physicians (n = 43)	All (n = 208)	X^2	df	*P*
Hospital admission	12.4	7.7	14.0	11.5	1.08	2	.58
Patient mortality	16.8	28.8	14.0	19.2	4.29	2	.12
Hospital-acquired infection	5.3	15.4	7.0	8.2	4.92	2	.09
Surgery	18.6	30.8	16.3	21.2	3.94	2	.14
Additional tests or procedures	45.1	67.3	37.2	49.0	10.04	2	.00†
Additional outpatient visits	28.3	25.0	23.3	26.4	.48	2	.78

* The percentage represents the proportion of physicians who answered "yes" to the items. All "no," "not applicable," and missing values were coded as "no."
† Result statistically significant at the 0.05 level or better.

Figure 9.3. Avoidance of Adverse Events Reported by Physicians (Percentage). Reprinted by permission of the *Journal of the Medical Library Association (JMLA)*.

shall 1992). Marshall (1992), King (1987), Klein and colleagues (1994), and Banks and colleagues (2007) all concluded that CML services affect patient care decisions and length of stay. In one study that compared outcomes of patient cases for which CMLs supplied information to providers with patient cases that did not receive such information, "no statistically significant differences between the intervention and control groups were found for median difference in the total number of diagnostic codes, length of stay, or hospital cost" (Esparza et al. 2013). See figure 9.4 for a summary of changes in patient care reported by physicians (percentage) in the Rochester study by Marshall (1992).

CONCLUSION

Clearly CMLs provide benefits to interprofessional healthcare teams and their patients by participating in interprofessional rounds. To ensure that interprofessional rounding services continue and, perhaps, are even expanded, CMLs must be sure that interprofessional team members and hospital administrators are aware of data that indicates that the CML rounding service benefits the interprofessional team members and their patients. One method for distributing data to support the rounding service is to publish results in newsletters for the various professions represented on the interprofessional rounding team. Successful CMLs offer services that are appreciated by interprofessional healthcare teams (such as rounding), market current and future services effectively, look for new ways to serve interprofessional healthcare teams, and provide assessment data to support the services that they offer.

Changes in patient care reported by physicians (percentage)*

Changes reported	Urban physicians (n = 113)	Residents (n = 52)	Rural physicians (n = 43)	All (n = 208)	X^2	df	*P*
Handled situation differently	71.7	88.5	86.0	80.4	7.70	2	.02†
Diagnosis	31.0	38.5	14.0	29.3	7.14	2	.02†
Choice of tests	44.2	59.6	55.8	50.5	3.98	2	.14
Choice of drugs	45.1	42.3	48.8	45.2	.40	2	.82
Choice of other treatment	54.0	65.4	67.4	59.6	3.30	2	.19
Length of stay (reduce)	16.8	25.0	18.6	19.2	1.55	2	.46
Posthospital care or treatment	42.5	38.5	27.9	38.5	2.79	2	.25
Changed advice given to patient	73.5	73.1	65.1	71.6	1.13	2	.57

* The percentage represents the proportion of physicians who answered "yes" to the items. All "no," "not applicable," and missing values were coded as "no."
† Results statistically significant at the 0.05 level or better.

Figure 9.4. Changes in Patient Care Reported by Physicians (Percentage). Reprinted by permission of the *Journal of the Medical Library Association (JMLA)*.

REFERENCES

Accreditation Council for Graduate Medical Education (ACGME). 2007. *Competency Definitions and Recommended Practice Performance Tools*. October 18. https://www.acgme.org/acgmeweb/Portals/0/PFAssets/ProgramResources/430_CompetencyDefinitions_RO_ED_10182007.pdf.

Aitken, Elizabeth M., Susan E. Powelson, Renee D. Reaume, and William A. Ghali. 2011. "Involving Clinical Librarians at the Point of Care: Results of a Controlled Intervention." *Academic Medicine* 86, no. 12 (December): 1508–12.

Aldrich, Alison M., and Stephanie J. Schulte. 2014. "Establishing a New Clinical Informationist Role in an Academic Health Sciences Center." *Medical Reference Services Quarterly* 33, no. 2: 136–46.

Algermissen, Virginia. 1974. "Biomedical Librarians in a Patient Care Setting at the University of Missouri-Kansas City School of Medicine." *Bulletin of the Medical Library Association* 62, no. 4 (October): 354–58.

American Osteopathic Association (AOA). 2015. *Postdoctoral Training Approval*. Accessed November 23, 2015. http://www.osteopathic.org/inside-aoa/accreditation/postdoctoral-training-approval/Pages/default.aspx.

American Osteopathic Association (AOA) Commission on Osteopathic College Accreditation (COCA). 2015. *Accreditation of Colleges of Osteopathic Medicine: COM Accreditation Standards and Procedures*. July 1. http://www.osteopathic.org/inside-aoa/accreditation/predoctoral%20accreditation/Documents/COM-accreditation-standards-current.pdf.

Banks, Daniel E., Runhua Shi, Donna F. Timm, Kerri Ann Christopher, David Charles Duggar, Marianne Comegys, and Jerry McLarty. 2007. "Decreased Hospital Length of Stay Associated with Presentation of Cases at Morning Report with Librarian Support." *Journal of the Medical Library Association* 95, no. 4 (October): 381–877.

Banks, Marcus A. 2006. "Defining the Informationist: A Case Study from the Frederick L. Ehrman Medical Library." *Journal of the Medical Library Association* 94, no. 1 (January): 5–7.

Barbour, Galen L., and Matilda N. Young. 1986. "Morning Report: Role of the Clinical Librarian." *Journal of the American Medical Association* 255, no. 14 (April): 1921–22.

Brandes, Susan. 2007. "Experience and Outcomes of Medical Librarian Rounding." *Medical Reference Services Quarterly* 26, no. 4 (Winter): 85–92.

Burdick, Amrita. 2004. "Informationist? Internal Medicine Rounds with a Clinical Medical Librarian." *Journal of Hospital Librarianship* 4, no. 1 (March): 17–27.

Davidoff, Frank, and Valerie Florance. 2000. "The Informationist: A New Health Profession?" *Annals of Internal Medicine* 132, no. 12 (June): 996–98.

Demas, Jean M., and Logan T. Ludwig. 1991. "Clinical Medical Librarian: The Last Unicorn?" *Bulletin of the Medical Library Association* 79, no. 1 (January): 17–27.

Deshpande, Neelima, Mary Publicover, Harry Gee, and Khalid S. Khan. 2003. "Incorporating the Views of Obstetric Clinicians in Implementing Evidence-supported Labour and Delivery Suite Ward Rounds: A Case Study." *Health Information and Libraries Journal* 20, no. 2 (June): 86–94.

Esparza, Julia M., Runhua Shi, Jerry McLarty, Marianne Comegys, and Daniel E. Banks. 2013. "The Effect of a Clinical Medical Librarian on In-patient Care Outcomes." *Journal of the Medical Library Association* 101, no. 3 (July): 185–91.

Greco, Elisa, Marina Englesakis, Amy Faulkner, Boguslawa Trojan, Lorne E. Rotstein, and David R. Urbach. 2009. "Clinical Librarian Attendance at General Surgery Quality of Care Rounds (Morbidity and Mortality Conference)." *Surgical Innovation* 16, no. 3 (August): 266–69.

Grose, Nellie P., and Gale G. Hannigan. 1982. "A Clinical Librarian Program in a Family Medicine Residency." *Journal of Family Practice* 15, no. 5 (November): 994, 998.

Jerome, Rebecca N., Nunzia B. Giuse, Kimbra Wilder Gish, Nila A. Sathe, and Mary S. Dietrich. 2001. "Information Needs of Clinical Teams: Analysis of Questions Received by the Clinical Informatics Consult Service." *Bulletin of the Medical Library Association* 89, no. 2 (April): 177–84.

King, David N. 1987. "The Contribution of Hospital Library Information Services to Clinical Care: A Study in Eight Hospitals." *Bulletin of the Medical Library Association* 75, no. 4 (October): 291–301.

Klein, Michele S., Faith V. Ross, Deborah L. Adams, and Carole M. Gilbert. 1994. "Effect of Online Literature Searching on Length of Stay and Patient Care Costs." *Academic Medicine* 69, no. 6 (June): 489–95.

Koonce, Taneya Y., Nunzia Bettinsoli Giuse, and Pauline Todd. 2004. "Evidence-based Databases versus Primary Medical Literature: An In-house Investigation on their Optimal Use." *Journal of the Medical Library Association* 92, no. 4 (October): 407–11.

Lewis, S. 1998. "An Investigation into the Viability of Implementing the Clinical Librarian Concept at Leicester General Hospital NHS Trust" (master's diss., Loughborough University).

Liaison Committee on Medical Education (LCME). 2015. *Functions and Structure of a Medical School.* April. http://www.lcme.org/publications.htm.

Lindner, Katherine L., Lia Sabbagh. 2004. "In a New Element: Medical Librarians Making Patient Education Rounds." *Journal of the Medical Library Association* 92, no. 1 (January): 94–97.

Lusher, Anne. 1998. "Getting Evidence to the Bedside: The Role of the Clinical Librarian." In *Libraries Without Walls: Changing Needs-Changing Roles, Proceedings of the 6th European Conference of Medical and Health Libraries*, edited by S. Bakker, 66–70. Dordrecht: Kluwer Academic Publisher.

Lyons, Jennifer A., Gretchen M. Kuntz, Mary E. Edwards, Linda C. Butson, and Beth Auten. 2015. "The Lived Experience and Training Needs of Librarians Serving at the Clinical Point-of-Care." *Medical Reference Services Quarterly* 34, no. 3 (July–September): 311–33.

Marshall, Joanne Gard. 1992. "The Impact of the Hospital Library on Clinical Decision Making: The Rochester Study." *Bulletin of the Medical Library Association* 80, no. 2 (April): 169–78.

Marshall, Joanne Gard, and Victor R. Neufeld. 1981. "A Randomized Trial of Librarian Educational Participation in Clinical Settings." *Journal of Medical Education* 56, no. 5 (May): 409–16.

Marshall, Joanne Gard, Julia Sollenberger, Sharon Easterby-Gannett et al. 2013. "The Value of Library and Information Services in Patient Care: Results of a Multisite Study." *Journal of the Medical Library Association* 101, no. 1 (January): 38–46.

McKibbon, K. Ann. 1998. "Evidence-based Practice." *Bulletin of the Medical Library Association* 86, no. 3 (July): 396–401.

Miller, Naomi, and Donald Kaye. 1985. "The Experience of a Department of Medicine with a Clinical Medical Library Service." *Journal of Medical Education* 60, no. 5 (May): 367–73.

Mulvaney, Shelagh A., Leonard Bickman, Nunzia B. Giuse, Warren Lambert, Nila A. Sathe, and Rebecca N. Jerome. 2008. "A Randomized Effectiveness Trial of a Clinical Informatics Consult Service: Impact on Evidence-based Decision-making and Knowledge Implementation." *Journal of the American Medical Informatics Association* 15, no. 2 (March–April): 203–11.

National Network of Libraries of Medicine (NN/LM) Midcontinental Region. 2013. Retail Value Calculator. October 4.

Plutchak, T. Scott. 2002. "The Informationist—Two Years Later." *Journal of the Medical Library Association* 90, no. 4 (October): 367–69.

Rankin, Jocelyn A., Suzanne F. Grefsheim, and Candance C. Canto. 2008. "The Emerging Informationist Specialty: A Systematic Review of the Literature." *Journal of the Medical Library Association* 96, no. 3 (July): 194–206.

Roach, Agnes A., and Whitney W. Addington. 1975. "The Effects of an Information Specialist on Patient Care and Medical Education." *Journal of Medical Education* 50, no. 2 (February): 176–80.

Sackett, D. L., and SE Straus. 1998. "Finding and Applying Evidence During Clinical Rounds: The 'Evidence Cart.'" *Journal of the American Medical Association* 280, no. 15: 1336–38.

Schwing, Laurie J., and Elizabeth E. Coldsmith. 2005. "Librarians as Hidden Gems in a Clinical Team." *Medical Reference Services Quarterly* 24, no. 1 (February): 29–39.

Scura, Georgia, and Frank Davidoff. 1981. "Case-related Use of the Medical Literature. Clinical Librarian Services for Improving Patient Care." *Journal of the American Medical Association* 245, no. 1 (January): 50–52.

Sladek, Ruth M., Carole Pinnock, and Paddy A. Phillips. 2004. "The Informationist: A Prospective Uncontrolled Study." *International Journal for Quality in Health Care* 16, no. 6: 509–15.

Steele, Rachel, and Paul A. Tiffin. 2014. "'Personalised Evidence' for Personalised Healthcare: Integration of a Clinical Librarian into Mental Health Services—A Feasibility Study." *Psychiatric Bulletin* 38, no. 1 (February): 29–35.

Svantesson, Mia, Agneta Anderzén-Carlsson, Håkan, Thorsén, Kjell Kallenberg, and Gerd Ahlström. 2008. "Interprofessional Ethics Rounds Concerning Dialysis Patients: Staff's Ethical Reflections Before and After Rounds." *Journal of Medical Ethics* 34, no. 5 (May): 407–13.

Tan, Maria C., and Lauren M. Maggio. 2013. "Expert Searcher, Teacher, Content Manager, and Patient Advocate: An Exploratory Study of Clinical Librarian Roles." *Journal of the Medical Library Association* 101, no. 1 (January): 63–72.

Turman, Lynn U., Jodi L. Koste, Andrea S. Horne, and Claire E. Hoffman. 1997. "A New Role for the Clinical Librarian as Educator." *Medical Reference Services Quarterly* 16, no. 1: 15–23.

Urquhart, Christine, Janet Turner, Jane Durbin, and Jean Ryan. 2006. "Evaluating the Contribution of the Clinical Librarian to a Multidisciplinary Team." *Library & Information Research* 34, no. 94 (Spring): 30–43.

U.S. National Library of Medicine. 2015. May 11. *Fact Sheet: MEDLINE ®*. https://www.nlm.nih.gov/pubs/factsheets/medline.html.

Vaughn, Cynthia J. 2009. "Evaluation of a New Clinical Librarian Service." *Medical Reference Services Quarterly* 28, no. 2 (February): 143–53.

Veenstra, Robert J., and Eric H. Gluck. 1992. "A Clinical Librarian Program in the Intensive Care Unit." *Critical Care Medicine* 20, no. 7 (July): 1038–42.

Ward, Linda M., Claire J. Honeybourne, and Janet Harrison. 2001. "A Clinical Librarian can Support Clinical Governance." *British Journal of Clinical Governance* 6, no. 4 (November): 248–51.

Chapter Ten

Assessing Interprofessional Education

Erin Blakeney and Brenda Zierler

There are many factors to consider when developing interprofessional education (IPE) content, but the most important thing to consider is how the learners will be assessed and how the activity or program will be evaluated to determine its effectiveness in meeting the learning goals and objectives of the IPE intervention. The assessment plan should be developed when the IPE activity/curricula is being developed or iteratively throughout the implementation process as is done in developmental evaluation (Patton 2011). Ideally, those engaged in developing IPE would also participate in the evaluation of IPE.

There has been a lot of national and international attention on the return of investment (ROI) of IPE—in other words:

1. Does IPE make a difference?
2. Should we be investing resources to promote IPE?

The answers to these questions are relevant to this chapter on assessing IPE and the following discussion should help the reader (a key stakeholder) understand the contributions they can make by being better informed on the current state of IPE assessment.

IPEC COMPETENCIES

As a starting point, it is important for developers and evaluators of IPE to be familiar with the four core IPE competency domains—teamwork, team communication, roles and responsibility, and values and ethics. These competency domains were defined by the Interprofessional Education Collaborative (IPEC 2011) to clearly articulate core competencies for interprofessional collaborative practice. In other words the purpose for creating IPE activities/ curriculum is to graduate health professionals who can work together collaboratively to provide safe and high-quality care to patients/populations (IPEC 2011). The national concern about ROI is directly related to the quality of evaluation data and existing research on the impact of IPE to promote collaborative practice. Every faculty member developing activities/curricula should ask themselves how an IPE learning activity will contribute to improving interprofessional collaborative practice. In order to begin to answer the ROI question, a Consensus Committee on Measuring the Impact of IPE on Collaborative Practice and Patient Outcomes, sponsored by the Institute of Medicine (IOM) published a report that included three conclusions and two recommendations (IOM 2015). The report is available online at: http://www.aacn.nche.edu/education-resources/ipecreport.pdf.

INSTITUTE OF MEDICINE REPORT ON THE IMPACT OF IPE

Prior to discussing the impact of IPE on collaborative practice and patient outcomes, the Consensus Committee drew three conclusions from the available evidence and testimonials and all three are relevant to this chapter on evaluation: (1) closely aligning the education and healthcare delivery systems; (2) developing a conceptual framework for measuring the impact of IPE; and (3) strengthening the evidence base for IPE through more purposeful, well-designed and thoughtfully reported studies. The committee also made two data-related recommendations directed to IPE stakeholders, funders, and policymakers that will be described below and threaded throughout this chapter.

> Recommendation 1: Interprofessional stakeholders, funders and policy makers should commit resources to a coordinated series of well-designed studies of the association between interprofessional education and collaborative behavior, including teamwork and performance in practice. These studies should be focused on developing broad consensus on how to measure interprofessional collaboration effectively across a range of learning environments, patient populations, and practice settings. (IOM 2015, 43)

> Recommendation 2: Health professions educators and academic and health systems leaders should adopt mixed-methods study design for evaluating the impact of IPE on health and system outcomes. When possible, such studies should include an economic analysis and be carried out by teams of experts that include educational evaluators, health services researchers, and economists, along with educators and other engaged in IPE. (IOM 2015, 52)

In order to demonstrate the association between IPE and collaborative behavior, the first data-related recommendation highlighted the need for resources to conduct a coordinated series of well-designed studies. Otherwise, there will continue to be one-off reports of isolated, nongeneralizable, descriptive studies if dedicated resources to conduct robust evaluations or research are not committed. The second data-related recommendation called attention to the most robust methodological approach needed (e.g., mixed-methods approach) for evaluating the impact of IPE on health and systems outcomes. The Consensus Committee also suggested that economic analyses be carried out by teams of experts to answer the ROI question. Without clearly defining the ROI, including both quality and cost outcomes, there will be little incentive for key stakeholders like health system leaders, funders, or policymakers to support interprofessional collaborative practice.

KIRKPATRICK EVALUATION FRAMEWORK AND THE INTERPROFESSIONAL LEARNING CONTINUUM MODEL

To encompass the education-to-practice continuum, the Consensus Committee proposed a conceptual model, called the "Interprofessional Learning Continuum Model" (see figure 10.1). The Interprofessional Learning Continuum Model utilizes a modified Kirkpatrick Evaluation Framework (IOM 2015) to describe a broad array of learning, health, and system outcomes. The model was designed intentionally to align specific interprofessional competencies with the professional's developmental stage (from prelicensure to continuing professional development) (IOM 2105). Having a comprehensive conceptual model provides a taxonomy and framework linking IPE interventions to specific outcomes (e.g., learning, health, and system outcomes). Without such a framework, evaluating the impact of IPE on health and systems outcomes is difficult, if not impossible. The IOM Consensus Committee developed this model as a framework and recommended that it be tested.

When IPE is assessed, key stakeholders should pay attention to the outcomes they are most likely targeting based on the intervention (e.g., learning [intermediate] outcomes versus health [final] outcomes). If the goal of the IPE intervention is to increase attitudes or perceptions of other professions, then the outcome would be a learning or intermediate outcome. If the IPE intervention was developing an interprofessional collaborative approach to managing heart failure then the outcome of the intervention would more likely be a health or systems outcome. Faculty leading IPE activities (courses, curricula, activities) should be able to map their interventions to the outcomes presented in the model to get a sense of the outcomes they are targeting with the IPE interventions. If the outcomes of the IPE activities are always learning outcomes and not targeted to health or systems outcomes, then they are creating IPE activities for IPE sake, and not IPE for collabora-

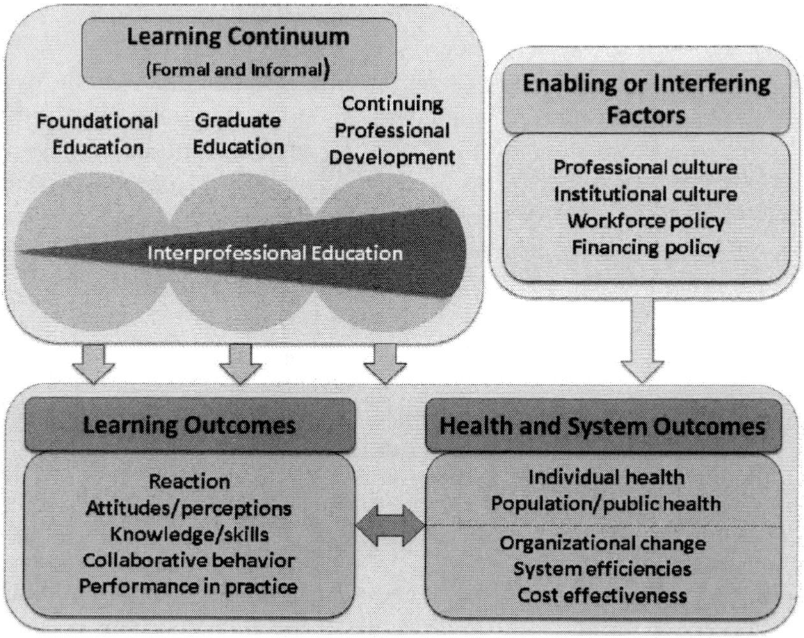

Figure 10.1. Interprofessional Learning Continuum Model. IOM 2015.

tive practice as was defined by the IPEC in 2011. The model helps distinguish the level and timing of outcomes based on the purposeful integration of IPE across the learning continuum.

PLANNING FOR IPE ASSESSMENT AND EVALUATION

Assessment and evaluation are two different but complementary activities. Assessment occurs when you are "making a judgement about a learners and groups of learners" and is distinct from "evaluation" where you are making a "determination of the value of the IPE program" (Blue et al. 2015). In this chapter we will use the term assessment to describe tools and materials used to assess learners and the term evaluation to describe the process of determining the value of the overall IPE program. This section describes important elements of evaluation design.

To start, the purpose for the evaluation needs to be clearly understood among those who developed the IPE activities, because the purpose and questions that need to be answered will influence the design of the evaluation. An evaluation design will help determine whether and, possibly, what parts of a project are working as intended and what parts need to be changed.

There are many potential evaluation designs for IPE—just as there are for all types of evaluations in both education and research. Evaluation can be formative or summative or both. A formative evaluation is similar to process improvement and focuses on ways to improve the IPE activity, whereas, a summative evaluation focuses on the outcome or impact of the activity or program in nature (Reeves et al. 2015). Reeves and colleagues (2015) described several qualitative and quantitative evaluation designs for IPE and similar to the recommendations made from the IOM Consensus Committee on Measuring the Impact of IPE (IOM 2015) a mixed-methods approach (using both quantitative and qualitative designs) is recommended. See table 10.1 for examples of the types of evaluation designs and their associated strengths and weaknesses from the Reeves and colleagues (2015) primer on evaluating IPE.

Careful construction of the evaluation questions by an interprofessional team representing multiple perspectives should be the first step in determining the direction and the nature of an evaluation. From there it is key to gather as much information about how others have approached similar types of questions (e.g., with a comprehensive literature review) as well as to assess the type of information that it will be possible gather during the IPE project to be evaluated (e.g., observations, pre/post surveys, interviews, simulations, etc.). With this information it is possible to start outlining an evaluation design. It is much easier to describe an evaluation plan and results to others by clearly articulating the research design and approach.

Table 10.1. Types of Study Designs Used in IPE Evaluation.

Design type	*Description*	*Strengths*	*Limitations*	*Selected IPE evaluation examples*
		Qualitative		
Ethnography	A design that investigates the nature of social interactions, behaviors, and perceptions that occur within teams, organizations, networks, and communities. The central aim of ethnography is to provide rich, holistic insights into people's views and actions, as well as the nature of the location they inhabit, through the collection of detailed observations and interviews.	Generates detailed accounts of *actual* interactive processes from observational work	Time consuming and expensive	Freeth, Reeves, Parker, Haynes, and Pearson (2001) Reeves (2008)
Grounded theory	This is an approach that is used to explore social processes that present within human interactions. Grounded theory differs from other approaches in that its primary purpose is to develop a theory about dominant social processes rather than to describe particular phenomena. Through application of the process researchers develop explanations of key social phenomena that are grounded or derived in the data.	Provides rich data; can generate new theoretical insight	Development of "micro" theories with limited generalizability	Christofilos, DeMatteo, and Penciner (2014) Murray-Davis, Marshall, and Gordon (2014)
Phenomenology	This form of inquiry brings individuals' perceptions of human experience with all types of phenomena. Phenomenology is both an approach that allows for the exploration and description of phenomena important to the developers or participants of an IPE activity. The goal of phenomenology is to describe lived experience. Phenomenology is therefore the study of "essences."	Provides rich and detailed descriptions of human-lived experience	Focus on very small number of individuals can generate concerns about limited transferability of findings	Price, McGillis-Hall, Angus, and Peter (2013) Veerapen and Purkis (2014)
Action research	This approach is known by various names, including cooperative learning, participatory action research, and collaborative research.	Empowers research participants to	Difficult and time consuming; typically smaller	Seif et al. (2014) Hall, Brajtman, Weaver, Grassau,

	Action research is a form of inquiry, which involves stakeholders in a process of evaluation and change based on professional, organizational, or community action. It adopts a more collaborative approach than other evaluation designs, as a key role for the evaluator is to work with participants in processes of planning, implementing, and evaluating change.	make changes in practice	scale methods	and Varpio (2014)
		Quantitative		
Randomized control trials	This type of design randomly selects participants for inclusion in either the intervention or control groups. Randomized control trials (RCTs) can provide a rigorous understanding of the nature of change associated with an IPE activity.	The randomization of individuals reduces bias related to selection or recruitment	Difficult to generalize to those who don't meet the selection criteria (individuals do not always represent larger populations)	Barcelo et al. (2010) Campbell et al. (2001)
Controlled before and after studies	This design adopts a similar approach to a RCT design, but does not randomize who receives the intervention (i.e., an IPE activity).	Can robustly measure change and controls for differences between study and comparison groups	Less rigorous than RCTs due to the lack of randomization. Also, one cannot evaluate whether any reported change is sustained over time	Janson et al. (2009) Rask et al. (2007)
Interrupted time series studies	This is a nonrandomized design that uses multiple measurements before and after an IPE intervention to determine if it has an effect that is greater than the underlying trend. This design requires obtaining data at multiple time points before the IPE to identify any underlying trends or any cyclical phenomena, and at multiple points afterwards to see if there is any	Allows for statistical investigations of potential biases in the estimate of the effect of an IPE intervention; strengthens	Does not control for outside influences on outcomes. These types of studies are also difficult to undertake in settings where	Hanbury, Wallace, and Clark (2009) Taylor, Hepworth, Buerhaus, Dittus, and Speroff (2007)

	change in the trend measured previously.	before and after designs as measurement occurs at multiple time periods	routine outcome data are not collected	
Before-and-after study	This is a nonrandomised design where the evaluator collects data before and after an IPE activity	Relative ease of employing this design in comparison to other quantitative evaluation designs data can help generate more insightful findings	Difficult to detect accurately whether any change was attributable to the intervention or another confounding influence design is methodolog-ically challenging	Brock et al. (2013) Cameron et al. (2009)
Mixed methods	These designs aim to gather different types of quantitative and qualitative data (e.g., surveys, interviews, documents observations) to provide a more detailed understanding of IPE processes and outcomes. There are two main types: sequential (where data are gathered and analyzed in different stages) and convergent (where data are combined together).	Comparison between quantitative and qualitative data can help generate more insightful findings	Combining different data sets when using a convergent design is methodologically challenging	Gould, Lee, Berkowitz, and Bronstein (2014) Lachman, Fossum, Johansson, Karlgren, and Ponzer (2014)

At the University of Washington, we almost always carry out mixed-methods IPE evaluations to help us triangulate answers to a number of questions, including whether: (1) intended learning occurred, (2) behavior changed among program participants, and (3) the approach/process was effective and how it could be improved. We have established interprofessional curricular teams and evaluation teams for various programs—e.g., interprofessional faculty development training program (Hall and Zierler 2015), advanced practice IPE activities (Willgerodt et al. 2015), interprofessional collaborative practice with advanced heart failure population, and simulation-based IPE training (Brock et al. 2013). There is overlap of faculty and staff on both teams with expertise in evaluation, health services research, and "lean processes" (e.g., Evaluation Team) and instructional design, curriculum development, conceptual models and adult learning theories, and evidenced-base practice (e.g., Curricula Committee). This infrastructure supports purposeful development and evaluation of IPE for a variety of learning contexts (classroom, simulation laboratory, and practice and community settings) and has created a community of IPE scholars. Early in the development of an IPE activity, the two teams collaborate to determine purpose of training, identify conceptual frameworks for design and evaluation of the IPE activities, create learning and program objectives, establish level of learners most appropriate for the case, map the learning objectives to the IPE competencies (IPEC 2011), and then determine timing in program across the interprofessional learning continuum—foundational, graduate, or continuing professional development (IOM 2015). Together the evaluation questions are written to match the goals and impact of the training (formative, summative, or both).

A formative evaluation can be used when piloting new content, trialing new facilitators, or practicing innovative approaches to training that can lead to improvement in content, processes, and evaluation questions prior to rolling out a program and initiating a summative evaluation. For example, a national Interprofessional Faculty Development Program (Hall and Zierler 2015) was piloted for one year in 2012 with faculty from eight universities and then evaluated using formative and summative evaluations (Blakeney et al. 2015). Even though the program was well received and impact at local universities was noted (Blakeney et al. 2015), improvements were made to the content, length of training, approaches to teaching, faculty skill development, and evaluation methods. The evaluation contributed to improvements in processes and outcomes and subsequently, a four-year Interprofessional Train-the-Trainer (T3) Faculty Development Program was funded by the Josiah Macy, Jr., Foundation and a new curriculum is being implemented and evaluated at three national sites in the United States (Blakeney et al. 2015; Hall and Zierler 2015)

The IOM Consensus Committee (IOM 2015) identified the need to use more robust evaluation designs and methods when evaluating IPE projects—

to determine whether IPE really does change learning outcomes and behavior across the learning continuum (foundational, graduate, continuing professional development). The first conclusion of the report (2015) was to more closely align the education and healthcare delivery systems. Bringing together educators and clinicians to cocreate and evaluate IPE activities helps link IPE with collaborative practice. The lack of alignment has also been described as a "gap" between the health professions education and healthcare delivery systems. At the same time, most IPE projects are not funded at the local level to examine these types of questions. Therefore, it is important to use existing resources (e.g., National Center for Interprofessional Practice and Education https://nexusipe.org/; MedEdPORTAL https://www.mededportal.org/) as much as possible to capitalize on lessons learned by others in developing and implementing IPE.

TIMING OF IPE ASSESSMENT AND EVALUATION

Timing is a major factor to consider in IPE from both the perspective of when you should start developing an evaluation plan, as well as when to actually carry out assessment and evaluation activities. In order to be successful in both of these areas, it is recommended to "begin with the end in mind" and start developing an evaluation plan while developing your curriculum or educational intervention (Blue et al. 2015; Kahaleh et al. 2015; Reeves et al. 2015; Willgerodt, et al. 2015). For example, if the goal of the IPE activity is to improve or increase knowledge, attitude, skills, or other learning outcomes then obtaining measures at baseline (pre-activity) and following the training (post-activity) may help in determining effectiveness of the intervention (training). It is much easier to plan for a pre/post evaluation with assessment of learning or to obtain necessary human subject approvals (which can take weeks to months depending on your project and institution) in time to evaluate a project if you start at the beginning by thinking about: (1) what you are trying to change (starting with your end in mind), (2) how to evaluate whether your desired outcomes were achieved, (3) when are you going to carry out those evaluations, and (4) how assessment data will be used by your project team. If, however, an evaluation was not initially planned—it is still advisable to start as soon as is feasible or even to plan an evaluation in retrospect. While not ideal, it is better to attempt some evaluation of an IPE activity than to not evaluate at all.

Starting early when planning an IPE project can also facilitate an evaluation of the process of developing the curriculum, help a working group track lessons learned in their project, and build in time for reflection (Kahaleh et al. 2015; Willgerodt et al. 2015). Evaluation planning from the beginning also allows the group time to develop thoughtful, relevant, evidence-based evaluations that build off of existing research. It takes time to develop new evaluation tools as well as to review existing tools to determine whether they will be appropriate to your project—especially when a new team has formed or when multiple institutions are working together to implement assessment and evaluation activities (Blakeney et al. 2015; Hall and Zierler 2015). Time is needed to work with team members to review and pilot assessment tools and plan evaluation approaches, because input from team members is essential to gaining consensus prior to implementing IPE activities. Librarians can be of particular help in this area by advising developers of IPE projects about resources for identifying assessment tools and planning evaluations—for example the National Center for IPE, existing IPE evaluations in PubMed (Blue et al. 2015).

Creating assessment tools and an evaluation plan while developing curriculum can also help to improve IPE content by helping to identify places where the curriculum could be tightened or revised to better meet its goals. For example, in a recent project at the University of Washington, the content of a training for an interprofessional team of healthcare professionals was framed more explicitly after initial drafts of assessment questions, aimed at assessing learning, were reviewed by a curriculum team with the realization that the overall learning goals might not be as explicit to learners as we had hoped. As a result, both the curriculum and assessment tools were revised to be better aligned with overall project goals.

Timing also influences when and how you can carry out assessment and evaluation activities. It is essential to plan time in the curriculum for participants to complete assessment materials as well as to convey to participants and other stakeholders how the program will be evaluated and what will be requested of them (if anything) in terms of completion of assessment materials, requests for interviews, and such. Academic calendars and other competing demands (e.g., accreditation requirements) should also be taken into consideration when planning evaluations.

EVALUATORS: EXTERNAL OR INTERNAL?

Who will carry out assessments and evaluations is important to establish early on in an IPE project. As described earlier an evaluation approach needs to be determined and assessment tools to support that approach have to be selected (and possibly developed or adapted). The identity and the role of the person or team that leads this aspect of the project will influence how the project is carried out and what type of evaluation questions and approach needs to be pursued. Rossi and colleagues (2004) identified four main approaches utilized by the person or team carrying an evaluation: (1) participatory, (2) objective, (3) advocacy, and (4) coaching. A description of each of these approach types can be found in table 10.2. There are benefits and drawbacks of each approach, and it is important for evaluators/evaluation teams to have a plan for how they will mitigate disadvantages and benefit from advantages of the evaluation role-type they choose to pursue (Grembowski 2016; Reeves et al. 2015). Librarians can provide valuable guidance for faculty as they determine what type of evaluator role would best meet their project needs and guide them toward resources (Blue et al. 2015).

At the University of Washington, we typically take a participatory or coaching evaluation team approach. As described earlier, we have found this type of approach beneficial as a diverse evaluation team contributes multiple perspectives, requires that a common language be established, and models an interprofessional approach to coproducing and coevaluating IPE activities (Kahaleh et al. 2015; Reeves et al. 2015; Willgerodt et al. 2015). Our evaluation teams include students or family members, educators, researchers, and clinicians (as relevant to the topic) so that we can iteratively develop, evaluate, and improve IPE activities and projects (Willgerodt et al. 2015). This approach is also consistent with the tenets of developmental evaluation (Patton 2011) and fosters coproduction relationships among key stakeholders and end-users (patients, families, students, and healthcare teams) (Bovaird 2007).

Involving students or families in evaluation can also help with real-time feedback on faculty skills in facilitating IPE as well as with integration of learning. For example, we have found that having students observe interprofessional clinical simulations can be very informative for those observing—particularly when they are provided with evaluation rubrics to reference during observations. Insights of student observers during debriefs of clinical simulations have proved effective as a way to share feedback and learning among all of the students.

DISSEMINATING EVALUATION RESULTS

As referenced above it is very important to disseminate and share lessons learned from evaluations so that others can learn from your successes and challenges as well as to promote replication within the field to improve efficiency and spread of effective programs (without other sites needing to reinvent the wheel). There are many journals that accept short reports, primers, or works in progress—for example the *Journal of Interprofessional Care*—in addition to the traditional research manuscripts and librarians can assist in identifying these opportunities (Blue et al. 2015). There are also a number of domestic and international conferences that focus specifically on interprofessional education and collaborative practice, including: Collaborating Across Borders (every other year; odd years), All Together Better Health (every other year; even years), and an annual conference held in the United

Table 10.2. Evaluator Roles Summary.

Role	*Role Description*	*Benefits*	*Drawbacks*
Participatory	Evaluator works closely with program developers and decision makers throughout development and implementation process	Increased likelihood evaluation will produce answers that will be useful to decision makers	Scope or focus of evaluation may be co-opted or biased toward positive findings; this process may be conscious or unconscious
Objective	External/outside neutral evaluator who uses research methods to produce an objective evaluation or a program/ project	Useful when decision makers need objective, unbiased information about a program to be able to address competing demands from different groups	Unclear if can ever be truly unbiased (even if external). External evaluator may not be familiar and may miss qualitative information that would provide important insights about the program/ project
Advocacy	Evaluators act as advocates for spreading findings of an evaluation. Based on the idea that it is difficult, if not impossible, for evaluators to be truly neutral so instead should evaluate whether a program meets defined values	Increases the likelihood that an evaluation will be implemented	Risk that evaluators will no longer be impartial when framing questions, collecting evidence, and in fairly evaluating program worth
Coaching	Evaluator offers help, advice, and guidance as project members lead planning, implementation, and evaluation of their own programs. Often used in community settings	Increases the likelihood that the evaluation will address interests of project members	May lead to inaccurate or incomplete findings if project members lack knowledge and experience to conduct evaluation even with help from the coach

States (starting in 2016) cohosted by the National Center for Interprofessional Practice and Education (NCIPE) and the American Interprofessional Healthcare Collaborative (AIHC).

Dissemination to a variety of stakeholders—in addition to the IPE research and education literature—should be considered. Potential stakeholders include student participants, patients and families, developers of IPE materials, administrators, grantors, and the broader community (Blue et al. 2015; Reeves et al. 2015). These different audiences are likely to be most interested/benefit from a variety of different modes of communication including, blog posts, articles in newsletters, summary evaluation letters for facilitators, and such. Health systems leaders and managers are also included as a target audience to receive data and an executive summary related to the interprofessional team-based training that is implemented and evaluated within their health system.

Different audiences also may be interested in different types of information—with participants and facilitators often primarily interested in formative feedback and the larger IPE research community most focused on new knowledge or summative findings (Reeves et al. 2015). For example, we have found that faculty participating in our programs have appreciated hearing how their sessions went from an evaluation perspective as well as receiving thank-you letters cc'ing their department chairs to keep in their files for promotion and tenure. Students and other IPE learners and facilitators also appreciate hearing how evaluation data are used to revise or improve the education program and sharing information with them helps them to become important partners in dissemination of findings (Reeve et al. 2015).

Assessment and Evaluation as a Scholarly Activity for IPE Faculty

Establishing an IPE committee, center, or organizing group that focuses on dissemination of IPE activities helps to build a learning community that creates opportunities for scholarly activities. At the University of Washington, we hold at least two IPE writing retreats (one to two days) per year to bring together those interested in developing scholarship around IPE and collaborative practice. Graduate students and family members who participated in the development of IPE activities also contribute to the writing and dissemination of the IPE activities and are invited to the writing retreats. Goals for the IPE writing retreat are prioritized based on timing (responding to an external grant opportunity, completing an IPE book chapter, writing a manuscript related to an IPE activity, submitting an IPE curriculum to MedEdPORTAL, creating a poster for a meeting, etc.). In addition to considering external funding opportunities or national meetings that might influence the prioritization of the writing retreat goals, the needs of individual faculty who need scholarly writings for promotion are considered.

The topic of promotion and scholarly activities related to IPE should be considered early in the formation of the team developing and evaluating IPE activities. Criteria for promotion and tenure vary based on profession, school criteria, and specific appointment. A discussion early in the development of the IPE curriculum/evaluation team is essential for planning subsequent scholarly activities. For example, if a member is in a clinician educator's track, then developing curriculum and receiving feedback from learners would contribute to their scholarly activities, whereas a member who is in a traditional research track might be more involved with the scholarly writing related to the evaluation and assessment. IPE requires a team approach and one of the core principles of IPE is that it is cocreated by multiple professions, patients, and students, so a paper related to an IPE activity should include multiple professions.

Establishing team-writing principles early in the process is necessary, especially when multiple institutions are collaborating. Other key factors to support team writing include: identify the order of authors early in the process (based on contribution and journal requirements); identify key journals with librarians; establish writing deadlines with consequences for missing the deadlines; develop strategies for recognizing those who facilitated or supported the IPE activities but did not contribute to the development or evaluation of the content; and provide opportunities for graduate students and junior faculty (literature reviews to inform an IPE activity).

FUTURE DIRECTIONS FOR IPE EVALUATION

The number of high quality IPE studies will be increased when evaluation models are consistently employed and when more robust evaluation designs (e.g., mixed-methods approach) are utilized by a team of educators, clinicians, and researchers. One-off studies of small-scale IPE activities will not contribute new knowledge to the literature, therefore establishing and disseminating best practices in the design of IPE studies will help to increase the evidence. As more IPE activities and studies move to practice or community settings (IPE for collaborative practice), the opportunity to evaluate the effects of IPE on health and system outcomes increases.

REFERENCE

Barcelo, A., E. Cafiero, M. deBoer, A. E. Mesa, M. G. Lopez, and R. A. Jimenez. 2010. "Using Collaborative Learning to Improve Diabetes Care and Outcomes: The VIDA Project." *Primary Care Diabetes* 4: 145–53.

Blakeney, E. A.-R., Pfeifle, A., Jones, M., Hall, L. W., and B. Zierler. 2015. "Findings from a Mixed Methods Study of an Interprofessional Faculty Development Program." *Journal of Interprofessional Care*, 1–7. http://doi.org/10.3109/13561820.2015.1051615.

Blue, A. V., B. J. Chesluk, L. N. Conforti, and E. S. Holmboe. 2015. "Assessment and Evaluation in Interprofessional Education: Exploring the Field." *Journal of Allied Health* 44, no. 2: 73–82.

Bovaird, R. 2007. "Beyond Engagement and Participation: User and Community Coproduction of Public Services." *Public Administration Review* (Sept/Oct): 846–60.

Brock, D., E. Abu-Rish, C. R. Chiu, D. Hammer, S. Wilson, L. Vorvick, . . . B. Zierler. 2013. "Interprofessional Education in Team Communication: Working Together to Improve Patient Safety." *BMJ Quality and Safety* 22: 414–23.

Cameron, A., M. Ignjatovic, S. Langlois, S. Dematteo, L. DiProspero, S. Wagner, and S. Reeves. 2009. "An Introduction to Interprofessional Education for First-Year Health Science Students: Perspectives of Pharmacy Students and Faculty." *American Journal of Pharmacy Education* 73: S1–S7.

Campbell, J. D., J. H. Coben, E. McLoughlin, S. Dearwater, G. Nah, and N. Glass. 2001. "An Evaluation of a System-Change Training Model to Improve Emergency Department Response to Battered Women." *Academic Emergency Medicine* 8: 131–38.

Christofilos, V., D. DeMatteo, and R. Penciner. 2014. "Outcomes of Commitment to Change Statements after an Interprofessional Faculty Development Program." *Journal of Interprofessional Care*, Early Online.

Freeth, D., G. C. Reeves, P. Parker, S. A. Haynes, and S. Pearson. 2001. "'Real Life' Clinical Learning on an Interprofessional Training Ward." *Nurse Education Today* 21: 366–72.

Gould, P. R., Y. Lee, S. Berkowitz, and L. Bronstein. 2014. "Impact of a Collaborative Interprofessional Learning Experience Upon Medical and Social Work Students in Geriatric Health Care." *Journal of Interprofessional Care*, Early Online.

Grembowski, David. 2016. *The Practice of Health Program Evaluation*, second edition. Los Angeles: SAGE Publications, Inc.

Hall, L. W., and B. K. Zierler. 2015. "Interprofessional Education And Practice Guide No. 1: Developing Faculty To Effectively Facilitate Interprofessional Education." *Journal of Interprofessional Care* 29, no. 1: 3–7. http://doi.org/10.3109/13561820.2014.937483.

Hall, P., S. Brajtman, L. Weaver, P. A. Grassau, and L. Varpio. 2014. "Learning Collaborative Teamwork: An Argument for Incorporating the Humanities." *Journal of Interprofessional Care* 28: 519–25.

Hanbury, A., L. Wallace, and M. Clark. 2009. "Use of a Time Series Design to Test Effectiveness of a Theory-Based Intervention Targeting Adherence of Health Professionals to a Clinical Guideline." *British Journal of Health Psychology* 14: 505–18.

Institute of Medicine. Measuring the Impact of Interprofessional Education on Collaborative Practice and Patient Outcomes. Washington, DC: The National Academies Press, 2015. Doi: 10.17226/21726.

Interprofessional Education Collaborative Expert Panel. 2011. *Core Competencies for Interprofessional Collaborative Practice: Report of an Expert Panel*. Washington, DC: Interprofessional Education Collaborative.

Janson, S., M. Cooke, K. W. McGrath, L. A. Kroon, S. Robinson, and R. Baron. 2009. "Improving Chronic Care of Type 2 Diabetes Using Teams of Interprofessional Learners." *Academic Medicine* 84: 1540–48.

Kahaleh, A. A., J. Danielson, K. L, Franson, W. A. Nuffer, and E. M. Umland. 2015. "An Interprofessional Education Panel on Development, Implementation, and Assessment Strategies." *American Journal of Pharmaceutical Education* 79, no.6: 78. http://doi.org/10.5688/ajpe79678.

Lachman, H., B. Fossum, U. B. Johansson, K. Karlgren, and S. Ponzer. 2014. "Promoting Reflection by Using Contextual Activity Sampling: A Study on Students' Interprofessional Learning." *Journal of Interprofessional Care* 28: 400–406.

Murray-Davis, B., M. Marshall, and F. Gordon. 2014. "Becoming an Interprofessional Practitioner: Factors Promoting the Application of Pre-Qualification Learning to Professional Practice in Maternity Care." *Journal of Interprofessional Care* 28: 8–14.

National Center for Interprofessional Practice and Education: https://nexusipe.org/.

MedEdPORTAL: https://www.mededportal.org/.

Patton, M. Q. (2011). *Developmental Evaluation: Applying Complexity Concepts to Enhance Innovation and Use*. New York: Guilford Press.

Price, S., L. McGillis-Hall, J. Angus, and E. Peter. 2013. "The Social Context of Career Choice among Millennial Nurses: Implications for Interprofessional Practice." *Journal of Interprofessional Care* 27: 509–14.

Rask, K., P. A. Parmelee, J. A. Taylor, D. Green, H. Brown, and J. Hawley. 2007. "Implementation and Evaluation of a Nursing Home Fall Management Program." *Journal of the American Geriatrics Society* 55: 342–49.

Reeves, S. 2008. "Planning and Implementing a Collaborative Clinical Placement for Medical, Nursing and Allied Health Students: A Qualitative Study." *Medical Teacher* 30: 699–704.

Reeves, S., S. Boet, B. K. Zierler, and S. Kitto. 2015. "Interprofessional Education and Practice Guide No. 3: Evaluating Interprofessional Education." *Journal of Interprofessional Care* 29, no. 4: 305–12. http://doi.org/10.3109/13561820.2014.1003637.

Rossi, P. H., M. W. Lipsey, and H. E. Freeman. 2004. *Evaluation: A Systematic Approach*, 7th ed. Thousand Oaks, CA: Sage Publications.

Seif, G., P. Coker-Bolt, S. Kraft, W. Gonsalves, K. Simpson, and E. Johnson. 2014. "The Development of Clinical Reasoning and Interprofessional Behaviors: Service-Learning at a Student-Run Free Clinic." *Journal of Interprofessional Care* 28: 559–64.

Taylor, C. R., J. T. Hepworth, P. I. Buerhaus, R. Dittus, and T. Speroff. 2007. "Effect of Crew Resource Management on Diabetes Care and Patient Outcomes in an Inner-City Primary Care Clinic." *Quality and Safety in Health Care* 16: 244–47.

Veerapen, K., and M. E. Purkis. 2014. "Implications of Early Workplace Experiences on Continuing Interprofessional Education for Physicians and Nurses." *Journal of Interprofessional Care* 28: 218–25.

Willgerodt, M. A., E. Abu-Rish Blakeney, D. M. Brock, D. Liner, N. Murphy, and B. K. Zierler. 2015. "Interprofessional Education and Practice Guide No. 4: Developing and Sustaining Interprofessional Education at an Academic Health Center." *Journal of Interprofessional Care* 29, no. 5: 421–25. http://doi.org/10.3109/13561820.2015.1039117.

Index

About the Editor and Contributors

Mary E. Edwards is the reference and liaison librarian at the University of Florida Health Science Center Libraries, where she has worked since 2004. Dr. Edwards holds a MLIS degree from the University of South Florida and in 2011 she earned a doctorate (EdD) in Educational Technology from the University of Florida. In addition to supporting distance education, she liaises to a number of clinical and research departments in the Colleges of Medicine and Public Health and Health Professions. As part of her liaison duties Dr. Edwards collaborates on instruction and research with faculty from her departments and is currently teaching in the course "Putting Families First," which is the cornerstone of the university's interprofessional education (IPE) program. In addition to her numerous library-specific publications (journal articles and book chapters), she has coauthored scholarly works related to medical education. These include a systematic review (on using video feedback in medical education) and a book chapter (on assessing the learning needs of medical students) coauthored with faculty from the Department of Anesthesiology. Dr. Edwards's research interests include medical education topics (how health science students employ self-directed learning strategies), instructional design in libraries, online teaching and learning, and new literacies including media, digital, and information.

* * *

James Ballard is executive director of the Indiana Area Health Education Center (AHEC) and associate professor in the Department of Family Medicine at the Indiana University (IU) School of Medicine. Before joining the faculty at IU, he held the position of associate director of the University of Kentucky (UK) Center for Interprofessional Health Education. During his tenure at the center he was instrumental in designing and implementing a required core interprofessional curriculum for all entering students in the five health professions colleges in addition to a number of voluntary curricular and cocurricular interprofessional opportunities for students. Additionally, he served as an educationist in the UK Department of Family and Community Medicine. Prior to this he held positions as the associate director of the UK Area Health Education Center (AHEC), manager of the Community Faculty Program, and director of the Medical Professions Placement Service. Nationally, he has served as a steering committee member of the Generalists in Medical Education, cochair of the National Area Health Education Center (NAO) Education Committee, and member of the Research in Medical Education (RIME) committee within the AAMC Southern Group on Educational Affairs (SGEA). He is a graduate in psychology from the University of Notre Dame and received a masters of educational psychology at UK and a doctorate in educational leadership at Northern Kentucky University.

Skye Bickett is the assistant director for the Georgia campus of the Philadelphia College of Osteopathic Medicine. She was a hospital librarian from 2008 to 2011 and joined the Philadelphia College of Osteopathic Medicine in 2011. She provides support to faculty, staff, and students by assisting with research activities, offering education on research and the use of library resources, creating online material to supplement course work, and serving on campus committees. Ms. Bickett is an active member of the Medical Library Association (MLA), Southern Chapter of MLA (SC/MLA), American Association of Colleges of Pharmacy (AACP), Georgia Health Sciences Library Association (GHSLA), and the Atlanta Health Science Libraries Consortium (AHSLC). She has served, and continues to serve, on several committees and in leadership roles. Ms. Bickett's hobbies include hanging out with her husband and kids, playing video games, photography, and cooking.

Erik W. Black is an assistant professor of pediatrics and educational technology and serves as the associate director of the Office of Interprofessional Education at the University of Florida (UF) Health Science Center. He earned a PhD in curriculum and instruction with focuses in educational technology and research and evaluation methodology from the University of Florida, a masters of arts from the College of New Jersey, and a bachelor of science from Virginia Tech. In addition to roles in medical student and resident physician education, Dr. Black is responsible for facilitating interprofessional learning involving more than two thousand learners, 150 faculty, and two hundred volunteer families across the six UF Health Science Colleges and three geographically diverse campuses annually. Dr. Black maintains an active research agenda focused on the development of professional identity and the evaluation and assessment of learning and media environments across a broad range of ages and life stages. Dr. Black was the first assistant professor to be inducted into the University of Florida College of Medicine's Society of Teaching Scholars, a society for faculty who excel as instructors and educational researchers. The author of more than sixty journal articles, book chapters, and monographs and one book, *Social Media in Medicine*, his research has been funded by the United States Department of Education, the National Institutes of Health, United States Health Resources and Service Administration and the Josiah H. Macy Foundation.

Erin Abu-Rish Blakeney is a nurse with a background in community health, public/social policy and interprofessional education. She completed her PhD at the University of Washington (UW) School of Nursing with a concentration in social science statistics and has over 10 years of experience in interprofessional education research—with a particular focus on evaluation. Starting in 2006, while working as a research scientist and master's student at New York University, she helped integrate graduate nursing students into international service learning projects with dental students in Honduras and Nicaragua. During her doctoral work at the UW (2009-2014), Erin worked as a graduate research assistant on interprofessional education grants with the UW Center for Health Sciences Interprofessional Education, Research and Practice (CHSIE). In her role as a graduate research assistant, she was the lead author on a review paper on the state of IPE and developed a structured reporting tool for describing IPE interventions for replication that won the 2012 Baldwin Award (awarded for "research that adds significantly to the evidence base informing interprofessional care and education worldwide") (Journal of Interprofessional Care, 2012) and was also invited to speak about IPE at the Institute of Medicine and an international conference plenary session (Collaborating Across Borders IV). She also helped to establish UW Health Science Students IHI Open School Chapter. Currently, Erin is on faculty at the UW School of Nursing and where she leads the evaluation teams on three interprofessional education and collaborative practice grants including a Macy Foundation faculty development grant and two federal HRSA-funded grants that focus on improving team function and patient outcomes among advanced heart failure patients at the University of Washington Medical Center and throughout the WWAMI (Washington, Wyoming, Alaska, Montana, Idaho) region.

Amy V. Blue is the associate vice president for interprofessional education, health sciences and the associate dean for educational affairs in the College of Public Health and Health Professions at the University of Florida. She holds a doctorate in medical anthropology from Case Western Reserve University and completed a National Institute of Mental Health (NIMH) postdoctoral fellowship in behavioral science at the University of Kentucky. Dr. Blue has been engaged in medical and health professions education for over twenty years. In 2007, she became the founding director of the interprofessional education program at the Medical University of South Carolina and served there as the assistant provost for education until her move to the University of Florida in 2013. Dr. Blue has authored numerous publications regarding medical and interprofessional education and her research has been funded by the National Board of Medical Examiners, the United States Health Resources and Services Administration, the Robert Wood Johnson Foundation, and the Josiah H. Macy Foundation. Dr. Blue was a founding member of the American Interprofessional Health Collaborative (AIHC) and served as a member of the Interprofessional Education Collaborative Expert Panel that wrote the *Core Competencies for Interprofessional Collaborative Practice Report* in 2011.

Sue Chase-Cantarini has been a clinical faculty member at the University of Utah College of Nursing since 1998. She has taught multiple courses in the baccalaureate program and has helped develop many innovative programs. Her interests range from cultural diversity, health literacy, health promotion, clinical teaching, online learning, simulation in the undergraduate program, and now interprofessional education. Her work has been widely presented at several national and international conferences. She has been involved in interprofessional collaborations for the past decade. This has included the development, implementation, and evaluation of the Health Sciences Leap Program, Health Professions Academy, Cultural Competence and Mutual Respect Modules, Health Literacy Tutorial, and now interprofessional simulation. For three years, she represented the College of Nursing on the Interprofessional Oversight Committee and chaired the IPE Scenario Development Committee. She currently cochairs the Interprofessional Advisory Committee and immerses herself in future program development opportunities.

Susan B. Clark serves as director of the Rowland Medical Library and chair of Academic Information Services at the University of Mississippi Medical Center (UMMC). She oversees the integration of information seeking and life-long learning skills into the curriculum of all six schools housed at UMMC. She is particularly invested in positioning the library as an active partner in the educational, research, and clinical missions. Her previous roles at UMMC include head of reference and instruction. She received the master of librarianship degree from Emory University. She holds memberships in various library associations statewide, regionally, and nationally. Throughout her career in librarianship, she has worked in academic, school, special, and medical libraries.

John Cyrus is an assistant professor at the Tompkins-McCaw Library for the Health Sciences at Virginia Commonwealth University (VCU). As research and education librarian, he serves as liaison to the VCU School of Medicine and the VCU Health System. Mr. Cyrus works closely with students, residents, and faculty to support research and incorporate information resources and best practices into their curricula.

Robyn Dickie is an experienced registered nurse and health professional educator within the university and hosptial settings. Ms. Dickie currently works as the interprofessional education coordinator at Mater Health Services, Brisbane, Australia. In this role, Ms. Dickie coordinates the development, implementation, and evaluation of simulation-based educational opportunities for medical, nursing, and allied health graduates and students. Over the past five years, Ms. Dickie has been led a number of interprofessional projects focusing on the introduction of interprofessional student placements, simulation-based interprofessional education to replace clinical placement hours, and the develeopment of an interprofessional health science student cirriculum. Ms. Dickie has a keen interest in simulation-based training to enhance health professional teamwork and collaboration to improve patient outcomes. During this time, she has commenced doctoral studies to evaluate postgraduate experiences of interprofessional education.

Alan Dow is the director of the Center for Interprofessional Education and Collaborative Care and the Ruth and Seymour Perlin Professor of Medicine and Health Administration at Virginia Commonwealth University. Under his leadership, the center develops, implements, and studies programs related to interprofessional education and practice. He has been funded in this work by the Josiah H. Macy Foundation, the Donald W. Reynolds Foundation, the Health Resources and Services Administration, and the Center for Medicare and Medicaid Services. Dr. Dow is a practicing internist and serves on the editorial board of the *Journal of Interprofessional Care* and the *Journal of Interprofessional Education and Practice*.

Paulette Hahn is a physician in the University of Florida Department of Medicine and Division of Rheumatology. Her experience as a nurse prior to entering medicine nurtured her interest in interprofessional healthcare collaboration, and she continues to meld the practice of nursing and medicine. Her current leadership roles include associate vice chair of education in the Department of Medicine and course director for the second year medical student Dermatology/Musculoskeletal Module. She has taught courses in biomedical ethics, evidence-based medicine, Interdisciplinary Family Health, and Introduction to Clinical Medicine with a focus on communication and patient-centered interviewing. Dr. Hahn's other educational involvement includes her work as portfolio advisor for the Medicine Clerkship, which incorporates reflection as a key pedagogical method. She has designed an elective for medical students, The Art and Scholarship of Physical Diagnosis and Clinical Reasoning, with a capstone educational experience in visualization and observation at the Harn Museum of Art. Her longstanding interest in medical humanities enhances her understanding of the patient and family life experience. She was inducted into the Chapman Chapter of the Gold Humanism Honor Society, and received the American College of Rheumatology Clinician Scholar Educator three-year Grant Award.

Elizabeth G. Hinton is reference librarian at the University of Mississippi Medical Center's Rowland Medical Library. After receiving her MSIS from the University of Tennessee, Knoxville, she completed a postgraduate internship at the University of Tennessee Medical Center. In her current position, she serves as library liaison to the School of Nursing and the School of Pharmacy. Her professional interests include systematic literature reviews, library and educational assessment, and interprofessional education.

Tanya Huff is a clinical assistant professor at Virginia Commonwealth University's School of Nursing. She has over thirty years of critical care experience as a clinician and nurse educator. She has worked with communication and team training exercises throughout her career with a focus on simulation for the last fifteen years. She is the nursing lead faculty for the Interprofessional Critical Care Simulation Course where senior nursing students and fourth-year medical students use simulation to practice rapid response and code scenarios. A current DNP student, she is studying how learning in simulation transfers into practice and translates into patient outcomes.

Colleen Lynch is assistant director for quality improvement education at the Center for Interprofessional Education and Collaborative Care at Virginia Commonwealth University. Colleen has extensive background in quality improvement, risk management, and patient safety in a variety of healthcare settings to include academic medical centers, primary care physician practices, federally qualified health centers, the Centers for Medicare and Medicaid Services Quality Improvement Organization (QIO) program, and the medical malpractice industry. She has served as project director for multiple health outcomes-focused grants from HRSA and CMS focused on organizational culture change, IT systems improvement, care process redesign, and clinical performance measurement and improvement. At VCU, she is the course director for the Interprofessional Quality Improvement and Patient Safety course, as well as the Interprofessional Quality Improvement Capstone experience.

Connie K. Machado, associate professor, is the head of technical services/ associate director at Rowland Medical Library. She has worked in the areas of cataloging and library automation, special libraries, and private industry libraries. In over twenty years at Rowland Medical Library, she has assisted with multiple systems changes as electronic resources have become the norm instead of the exception. She earned her MLS from Louisiana State University, and is a distinguished member of the Academy of Health Information Professionals. She is an active member of the Southern Chapter/Medical Library Association, and is chair elect for 2018 and a member of the state library association. She serves on the Madison County (MS) Library Board.

Karen McDonough is an associate professor in the Division of General Medicine at the University of Washington School of Medicine, and co-directs clinical skills education for preclinical medical students. She received her bachelor of science degree in biochemistry and later her MD from the University of Washington. Dr. McDonough has coordinated classroom-based IPE for early students, and works on the inpatient medical service at the university hospital.

Mitzi R. Norris is the executive director for academic effectiveness at the University of Mississippi Medical Center where she oversees academic accreditation, assessment, new program development, and continuing medical education. She also is an associate professor in the School of Health Related Professions where she teaches leadership. Dr. Norris earned both her BS and MS in microbiology from Mississippi University for Women. Her PhD in educational leadership is from the University of Mississippi.

Andrea Pfeifle is assistant dean and director of the Indiana University Interprofessional Health Education and Practice Center and associate professor of family medicine. Dr. Pfeifle graduated from the University of Kentucky with a BHS in physical therapy. She holds a master of science in instructional systems design and a doctor of education degree in educational administration and curriculum and instruction also from the University of Kentucky. Prior to coming to academics, she was the owner and president of Physical Therapy Services, a contract rehabilitation business managing and staffing multiple ambulatory care, outpatient, home health, nursing home, and hospital-based rehabilitation services in Kentucky. She leads the implementation of Indiana University's Foundational Interprofessional Curriculum, TEACH (Team Education Advancing Collaboration in Health Care) across the health science education programs and academic health centers. Through TEACH, Indiana University intends to prepare all of its health sciences students to work together to improve individual and population health.

Jean P. Shipman is director, Spencer S. Eccles Health Sciences Library, the MidContinental Region and National Training Center of the National Network of Libraries of Medicine at the University of Utah and director for information transfer, Center for Medical Innovation. She served as president of the Medical Library Association from 2006 to 2007 and promoted health literacy as her primary presidential initiative. Ms. Shipman graduated from Case Western Reserve University and Gettysburg College. She has worked in academic health sciences libraries (Johns Hopkins University, University of Washington, VCU), a hospital library (Greater Baltimore Medical Center) and with the Southeastern/Atlantic NN/LM, University of Maryland, Baltimore. Professional interests: health literacy, scholarly communications, innovation, and LEAN principles.

Nina Stoyan-Rosenzweig is on the faculty of the University of Florida Health Science Center Libraries, where she serves as archivist and historian. She also teaches in the College of Medicine, serves on the advisory council of the Center for African Studies and has held courtesy appointments in the Department of History and the Center for the Arts in Healthcare Research and Education. She works developing medical humanities programming in the College of Medicine and at UF and teaches both undergraduates and medical students. Undergraduate courses include Culture, Health and the Arts in Sub-Saharan African and the United States, Medical Humanities and Clinical Practice, a variety of courses in the honors program focused on single books, including *The Island of Dr. Moreau*; *Animal, Vegetable, Miracle*; *Molokai, Cutting for Stone*; and *The Man Who Mistook his Wife for a Hat*. Courses in the College of Medicine include an elective for first and second year students, leading small group discussions in biomedical ethics, and a number of fourth-year electives including teaching in the elective HEART IM, a month-long course organized and run by fourth-year students with faculty input. She also teaches in the interprofessional course Interdisciplinary Family Health. She has been deeply involved with the Arnold P. Gold Foundation's efforts to promote humanism in medicine, for whom she has served as reader for the essay contest, on the Gold Humanism Honor Society advisory council and membership committee, and she has served as advisor and coadvisor for UF's Chapman Chapter of the Gold Humanism Honor Society. She also has presented widely on her work with medical humanities and developed and co-developed exhibits on aspects of the history of medicine.

Nichole Stetten is a PhD student in public health with a concentration in social behavioral sciences at the University of Florida and serves as a graduate assistant for the Office of Interprofessional Education. She earned a MPH at the University of Florida and bachelor of arts at Berea College. At Berea College, Ms. Stetten was actively involved in running service-learning programs in the local community for four years. In addition to interprofessional health service-learning research, Ms. Stetten is actively involved in research involving public health and technology use, and obesity among people with disabilities.

Lisa Travis worked in a variety of positions during college and for a few years post-graduation prior to becoming a librarian. While studying criminal justice at Texas Christian University, she worked as a legal secretary and spent two semesters, a fall and a summer, working at Walt Disney World as part of its College Program. While completing her information sciences studies, she worked as a bookseller and library specialist. In her first professional position, she spent four of the five years of her tenure as a branch manager for a library that served nursing and allied health students. She then spent the next six-and-a-half years choosing databases and library resources, negotiating license agreements, providing reference assistance, and earning an educational specialist degree as a medical librarian for a newly opened osteopathic medical school. Currently she is a clinical informationist for Emory University. In her free time, she enjoys swimming, volunteering, reading, and playing Scrabble and other board games.

Alice I. Weber worked at Spencer S. Eccles Library beginning in 2001, and retired as of July, 2015. She is now emeritus faculty. Ms. Weber worked as collection development librarian, research librarian, coordinator of educational technologies, a research coordinator, and interprofessional education librarian. She was active in professional organizations such as Utah Library Association (ULA), Medical Library Association (MLA), Midcontinental Chapter of the Medical Library Association (MCMLA), Utah Academic Library Consortium (UALC), and Utah Health Sciences Libraries Consortium (UHSLC).

Rebecca D. Wilson is an assistant professor in the College of Nursing at the University of Utah, with director responsibilities for the nursing education specialty track. In her previous position, Dr. Wilson was the director of Interprofessional Education in Health Sciences, which included providing direction and oversight for the interprofessional education program for health professions students from five health science colleges/schools at the University of Utah. She has coordinated a variety of simulation-based interprofessional education, been involved in faculty development, and is cochair of the IPE curriculum subcommittee.

Lauren M. Young is instruction coordinator/reference and research services librarian at Samford University Library. Her library career has seen equal time spent in academic technical services and public services roles, and she specializes in serving the information needs of health sciences programs and patrons. Ms. Young earned her MLIS from the University of Southern Mississippi and her MA in English from the University of Mississippi. She is an active member in state, regional, and national associations and is a senior member of the Medical Library Association's Academy of Health Information Professionals.

Brenda Zierler's research explores the relationships between the delivery of healthcare and outcomes—at both the patient and system level. Her primary appointment is in the School of Nursing at the University of Washington (UW), but she holds three adjunct appointments—two in the School of Medicine and one in the School of Public Health. Currently, Dr. Zierler is Co-PI on a Josiah Macy funded grant with Dr. Les Hall, to develop a national train-the-trainer (T3) faculty development program for interprofessional education and collaborative practice. She also leads three HRSA training grants—one focused on technology enhanced interprofessional education for advanced practice students, the second focused on interprofessional collaborative practice for advanced heart failure patients, and the third training grant focused on an education-practice partnership to improve advanced heart failure training and outcomes for rural and underserved populations in an accountable care organization. Dr. Zierler is the co-director for the UW Center for Health Sciences Interprofessional Education, Practice and Research and director of Faculty Development for the UW Institute for Simulation and Interprofessional Studies in the School of Medicine. Dr. Zierler is a board member and past chair of the American Interprofessional Health Collaborative, and a member of the Institute of Medicine's Global Forum on Innovation in Health Professions Education.